Reconciliation as a Controversial Symbol

An Analysis of a Theological Discourse in South Africa

Demaine J. Solomons

ACADEMIC

© 2024 Demaine J. Solomons

Published 2024 by Langham Academic
An imprint of Langham Publishing
www.langhampublishing.org

Langham Publishing and its imprints are a ministry of Langham Partnership

Langham Partnership
PO Box 296, Carlisle, Cumbria, CA3 9WZ, UK
www.langham.org

ISBNs:
978-1-83973-874-6 Print
978-1-78641-047-4 ePub
978-1-78641-048-1 PDF

Demaine Solomons has asserted his right under the Copyright, Designs and Patents Act, 1988 to be identified as the Author of this work.

All rights reserved. No part of this publication may be reproduced, stored in a retrieval system or transmitted, in any form or by any means, electronic, mechanical, photocopying, recording or otherwise, without the prior written permission of the publisher or the Copyright Licensing Agency.

Requests to reuse content from Langham Publishing are processed through PLSclear. Please visit www.plsclear.com to complete your request.

Scriptures taken from the Holy Bible, New International Version®, NIV®. Copyright © 1973, 1978, 1984, 2011 by Biblica, Inc.™ Used by permission of Zondervan.

British Library Cataloguing-in-Publication Data
A catalogue record for this book is available from the British Library

ISBN: 978-1-83973-874-6

Cover & Book Design: projectluz.com

Langham Partnership actively supports theological dialogue and an author's right to publish but does not necessarily endorse the views and opinions set forth here or in works referenced within this publication, nor can we guarantee technical and grammatical correctness. Langham Partnership does not accept any responsibility or liability to persons or property as a consequence of the reading, use or interpretation of its published content.

Reconciliation is a central word in the Christian narrative, but questions of what it means, what its conditions are, and in which contexts it can be used have been the topic of a continuing debate within the evolving Christian tradition. Christians in South Africa discussed this during the apartheid era again and again, and produced statements at various occasions. One statement, the *Kairos Document*, finally summarized the different positions in three categories, and it would most convincingly plea for a third so-called prophetic position on reconciliation: before reconciliation, apartheid must end and justice should reign. If you want to understand the political reconciliation after the end of apartheid, then first read this important study on the discussions among Christians, and how they prepared the way for the political debate that followed. A must-read for the Christian understanding of reconciliation and for making sense of the history of South Africa over the last fifty years.

Eddy Van der Borght, PhD
Emeritus Professor and Desmond Tutu Chair,
Faculty of Religion and Theology, Vrije Universiteit Amsterdam, Netherlands

Despite the critical work of the Truth and Reconciliation Commission (TRC) in addressing the atrocities of apartheid, many would argue that South Africa's reconciliation process has failed. Solomons makes a vital contribution in a country where reconciliation has become politicized and its theological applicability is often ignored. Solomons emphasizes the radical theological nature of reconciliation with a creative and exciting methodology that joins the fundamental theological concepts of justice through Jesus Christ and reconstruction with reconciliation. This book assists in taking stock of the brand of reconciliation almost thirty years into the "new" South Africa, where the "least among us" are yet to experience the "new" in their everyday lives. It is a timely publication as the legacies of colonialism and apartheid, coupled with neo-liberalist economic policies and globalization, obstruct the reconstruction process. It is a necessity for both students of, and those working towards, reconstruction through justice and biblical reconciliation.

Eugene Fortein, PhD
Senior Lecturer, Historical and Constructive Theology,
University of the Free State, South Africa

Processes of fostering reconciliation that are coupled with justice are central to the Christian faith. However, some notions of reconciliation are socially naive, politically inadequate, and theologically misguided. As a result, they deepen the divides between persons rather than healing them. This book offers a comprehensive and powerful reconsideration of the symbol of reconciliation, drawing on South Africa as a case. It is a must-read for anyone who longs to work for reconciliation with justice.

Dion A. Forster, PhD
Professor of Public Theology, Vrije Universiteit Amsterdam, Netherlands
Beyers Naudé Centre for Public Theology, Stellenbosch University, South Africa

Contents

Acknowledgements ix

Abbreviations xi

Chapter 1 1
Introduction
    1.1 Introduction 1
    1.2 Context of the Study 1
    1.3 Relevance of the Study 4
    1.4 Reconciliation in the Christian Context 5
    1.5 Research Question 8
    1.6 Methodological Clarification 12
    1.7 Book Outline 13

Chapter 2 15
The Symbol of Reconciliation in Christian Theology
    2.1 Introduction 15
    2.2 Reconciliation in the Christian Tradition 16
        2.2.1 The Old Testament 16
        2.2.2 The New Testament 18
        2.2.3 The Early Church Fathers 22
        2.2.4 The Medieval Period 25
        2.2.5 The Reformation Period 27
        2.2.6 The Post-Reformation Period 29
    2.3 The Three Main Views of Atonement: An Overview of
        Aulén's *Christus Victor* 30
        2.3.1 Background 31
        2.3.2 The Ransom View (*Christus Victor* or Classic Theory) 31
        2.3.3 The Latin View (Anselmian or Penal Substitutionary
            Theory) 36
        2.3.4 The Subjective View (Moral Influence
            Theory) 38
    2.4 Responses to the Atonement Models as Outlined in
        Christus Victor 42
        2.4.1 Responses to the Ransom View (*Christus Victor* or
            Classic Theory) 42
        2.4.2 Responses to the Latin View (Anselmian or Penal
            Substitutionary Theory) 49

    2.4.3 Responses to the Subjective View (Moral Influence Theory) 56
  2.5 Closing Reflections 59

Chapter 3 61
Justice through Reconciliation in Jesus Christ
  3.1 Introduction 61
  3.2 The Message to the People of South Africa (1968) 62
    3.2.1 Cottesloe 62
    3.2.2 Cottesloe in Perspective 67
    3.2.3 *The Message to the People of South Africa*: An Overview 71
    3.2.4 *The Message* in Perspective 75
  3.3 The Belhar Confession (1982/1986) 77
    3.3.1 *Ras, Volk en Nasie en volkeverhoudinge in die lig van die Skrif* 77
    3.3.2 *Ras, Volk en Nasie* in Perspective 80
    3.3.3 The *Belhar Confession*: An Overview 87
    3.3.4 The *Belhar Confession* in Perspective 91
  3.4 The *National Initiative for Reconciliation* (1985) 94
    3.4.1 The Rise of Neo-Pentecostalism 94
    3.4.2 The Theological "Third Way" 97
    3.4.3 The NIR, Statement of Affirmation: An Overview 100
    3.4.4 The NIR in Perspective 102
  3.5 Closing Reflections 106

Chapter 4 109
Justice and Reconciliation after Liberation
  4.1 Introduction 109
  4.2 Historical Background to the *Kairos Document* 110
    4.2.1 The Study Project on Christianity in an Apartheid Society 110
    4.2.2 The World Council of Churches Programme to Combat Racism 114
    4.2.3 The SACC National Conference at Hammanskraal 117
    4.2.4 The Emergence of the Black Consciousness Movement ... 120
    4.2.5 The Emergence of a Black Theology of Liberation 124
    4.2.6 Prologue to Kairos 129
  4.3 The *Kairos Document* 135
    4.3.1 An Overview of the *Kairos Document* 135
    4.3.2 The *Kairos Document* in Perspective 143
  4.4 Closing Reflections 149

Chapter 5 151
   Reconstruction Requires National Reconciliation
      5.1 Introduction 151
      5.2 Towards the Truth and Reconciliation of South Africa 151
          5.2.1 The Transitional Period 152
          5.2.2 Rustenburg: Redefining the Role of the Churches 155
          5.2.3 Rustenburg in Perspective 159
          5.2.4 The Proposal for a Theology of Reconstruction 163
      5.3. The Truth and Reconciliation Commission of South Africa.....167
          5.3.1 Reconciliation as a National Initiative 167
          5.3.2 The Mandate of the TRC 171
          5.3.3 Religious Symbolism and the TRC 174
          5.3.4 The Framing of Reconciliation at the TRC 177
          5.3.5 Narrative and the TRC...179
          5.3.6 Forgiveness and Repentance at the TRC 180
          5.3.7 The Notion of Guilt at the TRC 180
          5.3.8 The Churches and Their Involvement at the TRC 182
          5.3.9 The TRC in Perspective 184
      5.4 Closing Reflections...188

Chapter 6 191
   Conclusion
      6.1 Recapitulation 191
      6.2 Reconciliation in Christian Soteriology...195
      6.3 Integrating the Three Approaches to Reconciliation? 203
      6.4 The Quest for Reconciliation Deferred?..206
      6.5 The Quest for Reconciliation as a Shared Dispute........................208
      6.6 Navigating the Discourse on Reconciliation in South Africa.....212
      6.7 Towards an Agenda for Further Theological Reflection on
          Reconciliation 216

Bibliography...219

Acknowledgements

This book is the result of the academic and personal support of several organizations and individuals whom I wish to thank. This includes the National Research Foundation of South Africa (NRF), the Faculty of Religion and Theology at the Vrije Universiteit Amsterdam, South Africa-VU-Strategic Alliances (SAVUSA), the Erasmus Mundus EM2SA, and the Ryoichi Sasakawa Young Leaders Fellowship Fund (Sylff). Their financial support allowed not just for the completion of this project but also for a formative period in Amsterdam.

My heartfelt gratitude goes to my doctoral advisor, Prof Eddy Van der Borght. His encyclopedic knowledge of the intellectual history of the South African churches during and after apartheid and his critical eye to the rendering of this history has been invaluable. Above all, I am most grateful for his availability and goodwill on a personal level, not forgetting the Earl Grey tea and Belgian chocolates that we often enjoyed together. It is a privilege to study under the guidance of an individual of such intellectual and personal qualities. Many of the theological and personal discussions we had in Amsterdam and Cape Town will remain with me for the rest of my life. The same holds with regard to my doctoral advisor, Prof Ernst Conradie, a great international scholar and an exceptional person whose encouraging approach served as a constant source of inspiration and support. His incalculable thematic and methodological suggestions and advice were of great importance – you do not often meet a scholar who is as excited about the wonders and mysteries of the theological project. Together with my former supervisors and lecturers, Profs Hans Engdahl, Christo Lombard, Douglas Lawrie, Wollie Cloete, Charles Amjad-Ali and Miranda Pillay, they have contributed to my academic formation, for which I remain truly grateful. To my colleagues in the Department of Religion and Theology at the University of the Western Cape, especially Prof John Klaasen, thank you for your constant encouragement and support.

My parents, Willem and Julia Solomons, made the best of a difficult situation and often emphasized the importance of education. They have been a constant source of love and support. My wife and partner, Sam, was there through good and bad times. Her commitment is a crucial ingredient in making this come to fruition, the inspiration behind my aspiring to be a better scholar, moreover, husband and father. To my kids, Aaron, Anika, and Ailsa, I hope this book will help build the South Africa you can be proud of. Love her, care for her, and never take her people for granted.

Praise be to God, who made all of this possible!

Abbreviations

AACC	All Africa Conference of Churches
AFM	Apostolic Faith Mission Church
ANC	African National Congress
BCP	Black Community Programme
BPC	Black People's Convention
Christian Council	Christian Council of South Africa
Christian Institute	Christian Institute of South Africa
CODESA	Convention for a Democratic South Africa
ICT	Institute for Contextual Theology
IFP	Inkatha Freedom Party
NG Sendingskerk	Nederduitse Gereformeerde Sendingskerk
NGK	Nederduitse Gereformeerde Kerk
NHK	Nederduitsch Hervormde Kerk
NIR	National Initiative for Reconciliation
PAC	Pan-Africanist Congress of Azania
PCR	Programme to Combat Racism
PSC	Programme for Social Change
RDP	Reconstruction and Development Programme
SACC	South African Council of Churches
SASO	South African Student's Organisation
SPRO-CAS	Study-Project on Christianity in Apartheid South Africa
The Message	Message to the People of South Africa
TRC	Truth and Reconciliation Commission of South Africa
UCM	University Christian Movement
UDF	United Democratic Front

WARC	World Alliance of Reformed Churches
WCC	World Council of Churches
WCP	White Community Programme

CHAPTER 1

Introduction

1.1 Introduction

This book entails a conceptual analysis of "reconciliation" as one of the guiding concepts in Christian discourse in the South African context. It is abundantly clear from the literature that reconciliation is understood in very different ways. This is observed in publications beginning in the 1960s. Since then, it is often used to offer theological reflection on social conflict in the country.[1] In this book, I propose a framework in which one can identify, describe and assess at least three distinct ways the concept of reconciliation is understood in theological literature emanating from South Africa. I describe them as a) Justice through reconciliation in Jesus Christ, b) Justice and reconciliation after liberation, and c) Reconstruction requiring national reconciliation. This contribution aims to aid continued theological reflection on the basis of a conceptual analysis of creative ways in which the term may be used in a Christian context. I conclude this study with an attempt to offer a constructive reinterpretation of reconciliation in contemporary South Africa.

1.2 Context of the Study

Violent forms of conflict have continued to erupt in different locations all over the world since the end of World War II. Such conflict may be addressed

---

1. For a detailed account on how the term was used in the South African context in the 20th century, see De Gruchy, *Reconciliation: Restoring Justice*, 30–43.

at various levels, including dealing with the personal trauma associated with such conflict. Politically, the gross violations of human rights associated with such conflict are typically addressed in terms of criminal law and international law. The (in)famous Nuremberg trials may serve as an apt example. More recently, various forms of a Truth and Reconciliation Commission (TRC) have been introduced to facilitate the transition from such social conflict to a new dispensation.[2] The introduction and subsequent proceedings of the TRC in South Africa since 1994 are widely regarded as an outstanding example of such an approach. Frequently held up as the focal point of reconciliation, the TRC has enjoyed premier status in accounts of the South African transition.

While the proceedings of the TRC have elicited much interest outside South Africa, it led to much controversy inside the country. Indeed, the need for and the very symbol of national reconciliation was highly contested. This controversy has to be understood in terms of the years of struggle against apartheid. In the mid-1980s, the question was whether political liberation for the poor and oppressed black majority or reconciliation between blacks and whites should have precedence. In the famous *Kairos Document* (1985), the emphasis on reconciliation was severely criticized as a form of "church theology." During the transition to democracy (1990–1994), the need for a negotiated settlement became widely accepted. As part of such a settlement, the need to come to terms with the history and legacy of apartheid became evident. Both the experiences of the victims of apartheid and the gross violations of human rights by the perpetrators simply had to be addressed. The decision to establish the TRC followed these developments in 1994. This was soon supported by calls for "national reconciliation," "nation building," the "healing of memories," the rediscovery of humanity (ubuntu) and a celebration of the so-called "rainbow people of God," as popularized by Desmond Tutu.[3] Nevertheless, as the proceedings of the TRC unfolded, many criticisms were raised regarding such an emphasis on reconciliation.[4] These criticisms related to various aspects of the process: the very possibility of amnesty, the need for criminal justice, the objectivity of the commission,

---

2. Hayner, Same Species Different Animal.

3. Tutu, *No Future without Forgiveness*.

4. See for instance Mamdani, A Diminished Truth, In: James and Van de Vijver, *After the TRC: Reflections on Truth*, 60; Mamdani, Reconciliation without Justice, 22–25; Soyinka, *Burden of Memory*; Jeffery, *Truth about the Truth*, 157.

the understanding of "truth," the emphasis on reconciliation, the leadership role of Archbishop Tutu, the associations with Christian symbolism, the need for compensation for the victims and so forth.[5]

The proceedings of the TRC were concluded in 1998, followed by a set of extensive reports. The legal aspects of the proceedings about amnesty and reparation need not be addressed here. Reflection on the legacy and significance of the TRC has continued unabated since 1998. In this sense, the TRC cannot be reduced to a set of legal proceedings. It allowed ordinary South Africans (who were neither perpetrators nor victims of gross human rights violations) to reflect on their past and future through the publicity around the TRC. Its significance, therefore, has to be understood in terms of calls for national reconciliation and the implications of that in various spheres of society. More than fifteen years after the conclusion of the TRC's work, it is all too obvious that reconciliation between individuals and groups in South Africa remains a high priority. The South African Reconciliation Barometer of the Institute for Justice and Reconciliation clearly indicates how South African citizens remain deeply divided in terms of race, class, ethnicity and culture.[6]

Such South African discourse over the symbol of national reconciliation cannot be separated from the influence of Christianity in South Africa. This has to be understood in terms of the allegiance to Christianity in South Africa, the use of the term "reconciliation" in Christian soteriology and the significance of what is aptly described as the *church* struggle against apartheid. The influence of Christianity is also evident with respect to the TRC. The pivotal role played by Archbishop Tutu, the charismatic chairperson of the TRC, needs no elaboration here. One may also mention the leadership roles of several other church leaders (such as Alex Boraine, the deputy chairperson) and theologians (including Charles Villa-Vicencio and Piet Meiring).

---

5. For a detailed account on the role of religion (and Christianity in particular) in the TRC, see Shore, *Religion and Conflict Resolution*.

6. Institute for Justice and Reconciliation, "Confronting Exclusion: Time for Radical Reconciliation."

1.3 Relevance of the Study

The term "reconciliation" was indeed at the heart of the church struggle against apartheid.[7] This is evident at least since the publication of the famous *Message to the People of South Africa* (1968). In the 1980s, the term was further used in conflicting ways in the *Belhar Confession* (1982/1986), the *Kairos Document* (1985) and the *National Initiative for Reconciliation* (launched in 1985). The term elicited much controversy, especially in the *Kairos Document*.[8] In the context of local congregations, the theme of reconciliation prompted many further debates, including the criteria for church membership, ordinations, expressions of and structures for church unity and the need for a ministry of reconciliation across the divides of culture, race, and class.

It is, therefore, not surprising that the term reconciliation came under scrutiny in Christian theological reflection in South Africa at least since 1968. One may suggest that such theological controversies had to do with the search for appropriate theological models and root metaphors. The symbol of "reconciliation" offered one such concept, but "ecclesial unity," "liberation," "justice," "nation-building," "human dignity" (ubuntu), "reconstruction," and "development" offered alternatives. At the very least, the question had to be addressed on how these concepts are related to each other. How, for example, is reconciliation related to liberation theologically and methodologically? Should justice and liberation follow upon reconciliation or vice versa? How is reconciliation between different social groups related to the reconciliation in Jesus Christ? In other words, what connotations are attached to the symbol of "reconciliation?" While there may well be a general understanding in theological publications on what "reconciliation" entails, the controversies over the symbol of reconciliation suggest diverging interpretations of its significance for theological reflection in South Africa.[9] Thus, reconciliation appears to lack a fixed or singular meaning, lending credence to the idea that it is best conceived as an essentially contested concept.[10]

---

7. De Gruchy, *Reconciliation*, 33–38.

8. Conradie, "Reconciliation as One," 13.

9. De Gruchy suggests the difficulties are heightened as reconciliation comes loaded with the weight of Christianity and the problem of how to differentiate between a transformative form of love that may well have useful lessons for secular life and a piety that presupposes the facticity of a divine gift. See De Gruchy, 25–26.

10. Doxtader, *With Faith in the Works*, 12.

While it is easy for academics to overstate the importance of their work, ranging from arguments that an idea has never been studied before to the significance of the work on a broader scale, this study focuses on the controversial nature of reconciliation as one of the guiding concepts in South Africa. From a South African perspective, the theology of reconciliation is undoubtedly not a new idea. However, because of the lack of conceptual clarity, most would agree that continued work in this area is necessary. In this context, I think a theology of reconciliation, on a social level, has not been explored extensively enough. Thus, this study aims to aid the continued theological reflection based on a conceptual analysis of the different ways the term is used in a Christian context. This also requires reflection on the distinct ways the term is used in everyday life, in South African society and discourses in mediation and conflict resolution. As a concept, reconciliation has not always been a useful means of bringing people together in conflict situations. Mostly, this is related to differing understandings of the concept and the resulting practical application of these considerations. With conceptual clarity comes legitimacy. In this sense, the discourse on reconciliation in South Africa is more nuanced than the way it has been represented in the past. This study aims to interpret the discourse on reconciliation through the eyes of the different stakeholders. This will offer a more complete version of how the country's reconciliation "narrative" is understood. In theory, this may also provide general insights into how this theological concept might be understood in other social contexts.

1.4 Reconciliation in the Christian Context

The problem underlying conceptual clarification is that "reconciliation" is used quite differently. Ernst Conradie's reference to "reconciliation as one guiding vision for South Africa?" on the various uses of the term is quite useful here.[11] In his view, "reconciliation" may refer to personal relationships that may have become distorted in marriage, personal life, between neighbours or colleagues and so on. Here reconciliation is required to avoid unwanted animosity and to allow the relationship to flourish again.

---

11. Conradie, 17–21.

In the social and political context, the term may be used to describe individuals' and groups' perceptions, attitudes, and behaviour towards other social groups. These groups are typically defined through markers such as race, class, culture and sexual orientation, among others. The term "reconciliation" is thus used as a barometer for social cohesion, as a means to establish how members of different social groups respect, cooperate and tolerate to avoid open conflict.

In addition to this, the Christian discourse on reconciliation presents at least three additional layers of meaning:

1. Reconciliation with God following alienation as a result of sin; this is understood in the light of a broken relationship with God.
2. Reconciliation through being one with Christ in the Body of Christ (the church).
3. The ministry of reconciliation through the Holy Spirit in church and society.

These additional layers raise questions on how the use of the term "reconciliation" inside the church is related to the use outside of the Christian context. Furthermore, one may also reflect on how the relatedness of these theological, ecclesial and social layers of meaning are understood. Given the history of division in South Africa, one may well ask what the relationship is between the politics of national reconciliation and the Christian doctrine of reconciliation? For obvious reasons, the compartmentalization of the three layers would be problematic. However, it would be equally problematic to fuse them together and thus confuse the genres.[12] The issue is the subject of much debate because it raises classic theological questions on the relationship between God and the world, text and context, church and society, faith and science. Moreover, these three layers of meaning bring into play all three articles of the Christian confession in relation to each other.

Conradie suggests that some employ a "deductive" logic, moving from reconciliation with God to the ministry of reconciliation in society. According to this logic, the fruits of reconciliation are dependent upon reconciliation with God. This approach assumes that no lasting solution to social conflict can be found without addressing the deep roots of such social conflict. In this case,

---

12. This is the point raised by De Gruchy as quoted in Conradie, 18.

social conflict is linked directly to our alienation from God. However, this can be overcome through God's gracious forgiveness of sins. From a classic Reformed perspective, such forgiveness is appropriated through justification, sanctification and the vocation of believers. Furthermore, such reconciliation in Christ enables and requires reconciliation with one's brothers and sisters, regardless of the social markers that may separate them ("We are all one in Christ"). In this way, the church constitutes what David Bosch describes as an "alternative community."[13] The social significance of such ecclesial forms of reconciliation is most evident in the *Belhar Confession* (1982/1986).

According to this "deductive" logic, the ministry of reconciliation in church and society is only possible based on reconciliation in Christ. In this sense, the ministry goes beyond the requirements for social cohesion, and its primary focus remains firmly rooted in reconciliation with God. It is only through reconciliation in Christ that social conflict can be addressed adequately. Without this, reconciliation remains superficial, if not misplaced, thus opening itself to renewed conflict. In other words, reconciliation in society springs from the celebration of the Holy Communion. God's reconciliation in Jesus Christ thus becomes the basis for Christians to reject any social system that assumes the fundamental irreconcilability of people.

By contrast, some employ what may be described as "inductive" logic. According to this approach, the "deductive" logic does not account for the process behind the conclusion reached, namely that the deepest root of social conflict is rooted in human alienation from God. This conclusion can only be reached through contextual and pastoral reflection on such conflict. It is the result of preliminary analysis, namely recognising that sin constitutes the deepest roots of the human predicament. In this context, theological perspectives may help deepen the common understanding of what may be at stake. These views aid reflection by situating personal and social relationships within a more expansive, cosmic frame of reference. However, it may be limited because it would not necessarily apply to those outside of the Christian faith.

According to this "inductive" logic, the need for a broader frame of reference follows the argument that any breach in a relationship has broader implications than only for the two parties concerned. If such a breach has almost cosmic ramifications, the final resolution of such conflict must consider

---

13. Bosch, "Church as an Alternative," 3–11.

the problem's widest possible scope. In this context, reconciliation between two individuals is only possible if the whole of that society is reconciled with itself. Ultimately, reconciliation between two people is possible only through reconciliation with God. In turn, this invites reflection on the cosmic scope of God's work of reconciliation. This would include not only human beings and human societies but the whole created order. In other words, everything is included in God's work of reconciliation in Christ. Therefore, reconciliation should be understood in the context of both God's work of creation and salvation. What is at stake is the tension between the Creator and the creature that has emerged because of captivity to the principalities and powers of this world (Col 1:18–23). "God's cosmic reconciling activity precedes and provides the framework within which God's reconciliation of humanity occurs."[14] This "inductive" logic is most evident in the approach of the *Kairos Document* (1985).

Embedded in the "deductive" approach is the danger of using abstract theological language. Here more focus is placed on the church than on social needs. In other words, theological legitimacy is considered more important than social relevance. On the other hand, the "inductive" approach is confronted with the danger of self-secularization, of reducing the Christian confession to nothing more than an example of religious affiliation that may be tolerated as long as its particular claims are not foregrounded. The apparent danger is being socially relevant without having anything distinct to offer in response to the challenge one may face.

1.5 Research Question

Against this background, this study investigates theological discourses in South Africa on the symbol of reconciliation published in the period from 1968 to 2010. It is abundantly clear from the available literature that "reconciliation" is understood in very different ways. I will identify, describe and assess the diverging ways this symbol was understood in the literature (ecclesial and academic publications) from this period.

On this basis, the problem that will be investigated may be formulated as follows:

---

14. De Gruchy, 53.

How has the symbol of reconciliation been understood in Christian theological literature emanating from the South African context between 1968 and 2010?

The formulation of the research problem calls for further clarification on a number of aspects:

The English word "atonement" initially meant "at-one-ment," i.e. being "at one" or in harmony with someone else. In the Christian context, the word is used with reference to the saving work that God did through Christ, enabling reconciliation between God and creation. In De Gruchy's words:

> Scripture and the Christian tradition employ a range of metaphors, symbols and words to express God's saving activity in the world. These reflect the rich and multifaceted character of redemption as experienced and understood by Jewish and Christian believers in a variety of changing historical contexts. "Reconciliation" is one of the words used in English to describe this experience, though the word "atonement" has often functioned as its equivalent in theological textbooks. But "at-one-ment" is a peculiarly English construction coined to describe the reuniting of God and humanity through the sacrifice of Christ on the cross. As such, atonement expresses but does not exhaust, the meaning of reconciliation. In Christian doctrine, the word "reconciliation" carries a range of meaning and is used in two fundamental or primary ways. First of all to express the sum total of what Christians believe about God's saving work in Jesus Christ. As such it is the equivalent of the more comprehensive German *Versöhnung*, and is interchangeable with "salvation," "redemption," or "atonement," each of which has been used to describe the doctrine. Partly for this reason we will sometimes use these metaphors in an interchangeable way to describe the doctrine as a whole. Yet each word gives the doctrine a particular emphasis and character, drawing on different biblical traditions and metaphors. This brings us to the second way in which the

word is used, namely as the term derived chiefly from the letters of Paul to explicate the meaning of the doctrine.[15]

In this context, the term "reconciliation" may be used both as a theological term (the "reconciliation in Jesus Christ") and as a social term (the need for "national reconciliation"). This study will focus on literature where these are used in association with each other, thus excluding theological literature on theories of atonement without such associations and literature with a sociopolitical orientation with no overt reference to the religious interpretation of this symbol.

"Reconciliation" is not merely a concept or metaphor but also a symbol with significant connotations. Like other religious symbols in South Africa, "reconciliation" plays a decisive role in the social construction of reality, including the social transformation of reality. However, as Dirkie Smit observed in 1986, the symbol of reconciliation is deeply tied up with ideological conflict in South Africa, so there is little agreement on the meaning of the symbol of reconciliation itself. Also, consider Smit's doubts over the potential of the symbol of reconciliation to transform society since the term needs clarification, and the moment an idea needs to be clarified, it has already lost its power as a symbol. A symbol is precisely something that needs no explanation but is self-evident and immediately grips the imagination.[16] Because of this, people frequently find it necessary to speak of "true," "real," or "authentic" reconciliation, thereby implying that they reject some other kind of reconciliation, which may be considered "cheap" or "false." This study will focus on literature aimed at the South African context where these different, sometimes conflicting notions of "reconciliation" are discussed.

This project will entail a historical survey based on the relevant literature. Such literature would include publications of an explicitly theological nature in English or Afrikaans. It would not necessarily include Christian discourse on reconciliation in the form of popular literature, ecclesial magazines, sermons, speeches, newspaper articles or letters to the press. An investigation of the attitudes towards reconciliation among "lay" Christians in South Africa

---

15. De Gruchy, 44–45.

16. Smit, "Symbol of Reconciliation," in: Vorster, *Reconciliation and Construction*, 88; Doxtader makes a similar point in highlighting the contestability of reconciliation as a concept. See Doxtader, 2–4.

may be highly fascinating but will require empirical research beyond this study's scope. It will also not survey contributions in African traditional religion or on theological reflections in the context of other religious traditions, such as Islam, Judaism, and Hinduism.

This study will focus on literature published in South Africa or on publications which were authored with a specific focus on South Africa. There is, of course, considerable interest in the South African discourse on reconciliation (and on the TRC) from outside the country. Literature from this perspective will be considered if this is situated in explicit conversation with South African authors.

In this project, I will explore how reconciliation has been understood since the publication of the *Message to the People of South Africa* (1968). While this is somewhat arbitrary, it provides one of the most explicit early markers of ecclesial discourse on reconciliation and therefore helps to demarcate the study. Of course, the *Message to the People of South Africa* cannot be understood apart from the events leading to that – which will be addressed in summary form.

In the aftermath of the proceedings of the TRC and the publication of its final reports, theological reflection on the relationship between reconciliation, justice, and restitution has continued unabated. Such theological literature typically seeks to come to terms with the legacy of the TRC. This study forms part of such theological discourse. In order to identify a suitable demarcation date, the year in which this study was first envisaged (2010) is used as an again somewhat arbitrary terminus.

In this study, I will identify, describe, contrast and analyse the different ways the symbol of reconciliation has been understood in the available theological literature. This study may, therefore, be understood as a form of contemporary history, in this case, the history of the interpretation of a controversial theological symbol. The study aims to clarify what was at stake in such controversies in South Africa. Such a study would also be of ecumenical significance beyond the South African context. It may also facilitate dialogue with notions of reconciliation in other religious traditions.

1.6 Methodological Clarification

How has the symbol of reconciliation been understood in Christian theological literature emanating from the South African context between 1968 and 2010? The hypothesis investigated in this study is that one may identify at least three distinct discourses in response to this question. Firstly, there is an approach which may be described as "Justice through reconciliation in Jesus Christ." This approach assumes that the significance of reconciliation with God in Jesus Christ may be explored through a ministry of reconciliation in a divided social context. Such reconciliation will have far-reaching implications for social justice and, therefore, for restitution. This approach is evident especially in the Message to the People of South Africa, the Belhar Confession, the National Initiative for Reconciliation, and the current discourse on the legacy of the Belhar Confession. Rhetorically, this approach was aimed at apartheid theology and its assumptions about the fundamental irreconcilability of people.

Secondly, one may identify an approach which may be labelled "Justice and reconciliation after liberation." In this approach, the need for political, economic and cultural liberation is emphasized. It is assumed that social justice can only follow upon such liberation and that reconciliation is only possible on the basis of (following) justice. This approach is evident especially in the *Kairos Document*, in comments on reconciliation in the context of Black Theology and in critical engagements with the proceedings of the TRC from within the same discourse. It is still found in current forms of prophetic theology. Rhetorically, this approach was aimed mainly against what the *Kairos Document* described as "church theology."

Thirdly, one may identify an approach where it is maintained that "Reconstruction requires national reconciliation." This approach became evident after the negotiated settlement reached between 1990 and 1994 in South Africa. This prompted the recognition of the need for a reconstruction of society and social development. However, this required coming to terms with the apartheid past (including amnesty) for national reconciliation and nation-building. This was expressed (and legitimized) theologically in diverse ways, including the emergence of a theology of reconstruction, but primarily through engagements with the proceedings of the TRC. Rhetorically, this approach is aimed at calling for social and moral responsibility and against the privatization of religion after the advent of democracy.

This research hypothesis will be tested and developed through a survey and critical analysis of the available literature. It will, therefore, entail a literature-based study.

1.7 Book Outline

On the basis of this research problem and the research hypothesis stated above, the following phases and corresponding chapters of the rest of this thesis are envisaged.

Chapter 2: The Symbol of Reconciliation in Christian Theology: An Overview

The symbol of reconciliation (or atonement) is a central tenet of the Christian faith. Its social significance has also been widely recognized. This chapter will aim to offer a cursory survey of the ways in which reconciliation (in Christ) has been understood in the history of Christian theology. This provides the background for South African discourse on reconciliation.

Given the enormous scope of the literature available in this regard, the aim cannot be to offer a comprehensive overview. Instead, the famous typology on atonement provided by Gustaf Aulén will be used as a point of departure to provide a history of the interpretation of "reconciliation" up to 1930 (when *Christus Victor* was published).[17] This will be supplemented by a general reception of Aulén's typology. In order to offer a survey of further historical developments on the symbol of reconciliation outside the South African context, several South African contributions offering such a historical survey will be used. Although this may well lead to a one-sided survey, this approach will at least demonstrate how the historical background is perceived in the relevant literature.

Chapter 3: Justice through Reconciliation in Jesus Christ

This chapter will aim to describe and analyse a particular way in which the symbol of reconciliation has been understood in South African discourse, namely based on an Anselmian, Lutheran and Calvinist notion that the reconciliation of humanity with God in Jesus Christ implies a ministry of

---

17. Aulén, *Christus Victor*.

reconciliation in a context divided by race, class, and culture and that this necessitates a concern for distributive and restorative justice.

This description and analysis will be done mainly on the basis of literature regarding the *Message to the People of South Africa* (1968), the *Belhar Confession* (1982/1986) and the *National Initiative for Reconciliation* (1985).

Chapter 4: Justice and Reconciliation after Liberation

The aim of this chapter is similar, namely, to describe and analyse the way in which the symbol of reconciliation is understood in the context of liberation theology, in particular, Black Theology in South Africa. One may suggest that the question addressed here is how reconciliation between people relates to the victory established by Christ over the forces of death, destruction, and oppression. This also leads to a different notion of the relationship between justice and reconciliation.

This description and analysis will be done mainly on the basis of literature emerging from and responding to the *Kairos Document* (1985).

Chapter 5: Reconstruction Requires National Reconciliation

This chapter will follow a similar pattern, namely to describe and analyse how the symbol of reconciliation has been understood amongst proponents of a theology of reconstruction and development, by those emphasising the need for national reconciliation and nation-building, by those recognising that the reconciliation is a requirement for processes of social transformation and moral regeneration.

This description and analysis will be done primarily based on literature during the period of the transition to democracy (1990–1994) and in the ongoing theological discourse on nation-building, development, social transformation and moral regeneration reflected in the work of the TRC.

Chapter 6: Conclusion

The aim of this chapter will be twofold. Firstly, the results of the previous three chapters will be compared to contrast the three interpretations of the symbol of reconciliation identified above. Secondly, the significance of such findings will be explored concerning the social context in South Africa, the history of Christian discourse on reconciliation, the broader ecumenical context, and dialogue between various stakeholders in South Africa.

CHAPTER 2

The Symbol of Reconciliation in Christian Theology

2.1 Introduction

The symbol of reconciliation (or atonement) is a central tenet of the Christian faith. This view is critical because, essentially, the Christian Gospel is about overcoming alienation and estrangement between God and humanity. In light of this observation, the Christian tradition portrays Jesus Christ as the mediator of the broken covenant between God and humanity. Christian reflection on the work of Christ is traditionally discussed with reference to a theology of reconciliation. However, unlike the "person of Christ," in which the ecumenical councils formally stated their position, the question regarding Christ's work on reconciliation does not have a central ecumenical reference point. This makes it difficult to single out any one view as the traditional (Nicene) Orthodox position.[1] In this light, Christ's work of reconciliation has been understood in very different ways throughout the history of Christianity.

Given the enormous scope of the literature available, the aim cannot be to offer a comprehensive overview. Instead, the famous typology developed by Gustaf Aulén will be used as a point of reference to provide a history of the interpretation of reconciliation up to 1930 (the date Aulén's *Christus Victor*

---

1. See for instance Kelly, *Early Christian Doctrines*, 163–164, 375; Weber, *Foundations of Dogmatics*, vol. 2, 177–191.

was published).² In *Christus Victor*, Aulén describes the three main "types" of Christ's work of reconciliation (or atonement). In Christologies developed during the twentieth century, Aulén's analysis of the three main views has become highly influential, although the details of his argument have often been criticized.

In reviewing Aulén's analysis, I do not intend to engage in a thorough critique or comparison of the three theories he identified. Instead, the review is primarily intended as a soteriological map to engage with at least three different ways in which Christ's work of atonement may be understood and its implications for the discourse on reconciliation in South Africa. So, while the review of Aulén's work is directly related to reconciliation in Christ, I appropriate these discussions to make them more fruitful for reconciliation within a pneumatological framework. In other words, this applies less to reconciliation in Christ and more to the implications of Christ's atoning work for the ministry of reconciliation in South Africa. I will also briefly sketch the history of this Christian doctrine as a background to the three main views that Aulén analysed.

2.2 Reconciliation in the Christian Tradition

This section entails a brief survey of a theology of reconciliation from the Old Testament to the post-Reformation period. I will briefly describe the views of some key theologians on reconciliation in Christ. This is done to outline the history of this Christian doctrine as a background to the three main views described in *Christus Victor*.

2.2.1 The Old Testament

Offering some insight into the idea of reconciliation in the Old Testament, Carmel McCarthy remarks:

> There is, in fact no single specific term in Hebrew or Aramaic to express the concept of reconciliation in the Old Testament,

---

2. The original Swedish title, *Den Kristna Försoningstanken* (The Christian Idea of the Atonement) was published in 1930 in the wake of his series of lectures that were delivered at Uppsala University that same year. The English translation appeared in 1931: Aulén, *Christus Victor*.

even though the underlying reality itself is caught in a variety of shades through terms such as "shalom," "atonement" and renewal of "covenant." Through many and varied images one of the connecting threads permeating very different Old Testament narratives, stories, psalms and laments is that the human condition is one of limitation and misunderstanding, alienation and estrangement. Not only is this the situation on the horizontal level in interpersonal relations of every kind, but the Bible makes it very clear that this situation is but symptomatic of a more fundamental disorder and estrangement between human beings and God.[3]

The term "covenant," as used in the Old Testament, refers to the relationship between God and the people of Israel. The five significant examples where the term is used include, Noah and his family (Gen 9:8–17), Abraham and his descendants (Gen 12:1–3; 17:1–14; 22:16–18), Moses and the Israelites (Exod 19:5–6; 3:4–10; 6:7), David and the Kingdom of Israel (2 Sam 7:8–19), and the promise of the new covenant (Jer 32:36–41).[4] Although the word reconciliation is not used explicitly in these instances, McCarthy explains that its attributes are intrinsically present in covenantal discourses.[5]

Karl Barth goes as far as to say: "The covenant is the presupposition of reconciliation . . . The fellowship which originally existed between God and man, which was then disturbed and jeopardised, the purpose of which is now fulfilled in Jesus Christ and in the work of reconciliation." Barth explains that the exact meaning of the word covenant is unknown but that it could have practical origins, such as in circumcision and meal ceremonies. "It denotes an element in a legal ritual in which two partners together accept a mutual obligation."[6]

De Gruchy makes a similar point in highlighting the connection between the covenant in the Old Testament and the theology of reconciliation. Because humanity was created in the image of God, he explains, the whole of humankind shares an intimate link while simultaneously existing under the

---

3. McCarthy, "Response [to Bible and Reconciliation]," 43.
4. Robinson, "Influence of Social Context," 21.
5. McCarthy, "Response [to Bible and Reconciliation]," 43.
6. Barth, *Doctrine of Reconciliation*, 24.

umbrella of God's cosmic intention. This link is often solidified through the use of the term "covenant" in the Old Testament. De Gruchy sees the theology of reconciliation as contingent on this understanding of creation because it explains the actual need, not just the desire, for humanity to be restored to God and one another when they have been separated. This provides the interpretative framework for the Christian understanding of the mission and fate of Christ as God's anointed mediator of redemption, in and through whose life, death and resurrection, the power of evil, sin and death were overcome. "For those who shared in the renewal of the covenant in Christ through faith and baptism, reconciliation with God and life in the Spirit became a reality."[7]

2.2.2 The New Testament

In the New Testament, the Greek word "reconciliation" or "reconcile" appear fifteen times, almost exclusively in the Pauline writings.[8] Paul uses the phrase in different forms throughout his texts: the noun καταλλαγγη, reconciliation (Rom 5:11, 11:15; 2 Cor 5:18, 19); the verb ἀποκαταλασσω, to reconcile (Eph 2:16; Col 1:20, 22); καταλασσω (Rom 5:10; 1 Cor 7:11; 2 Cor 5:18, 19, 20); συναλασσω (Acts 7:26); on occasion the word εἰρηνη is translated reconciliation (Acts 12:20).[9] The translation of these words is a compound of the Greek αφαλλαω, meaning "to exchange" and deriving from the word αλλοζ, meaning "the other." The words carry with them the sense of exchanging places with "the other" and therefore being in solidarity rather than being opposed to "the other."[10] Christoph Schwöbel observes that the classical Greek writers used this phrase as a metaphor for "exchanging enmity, wrath and war with friendship, love and peace."[11] This detailed understanding of reconciliation offers some insights into how the Greek writers may have understood the passages in which Paul refers to such an exchange with the other. This applies to both the relationship with God and between individuals. Furthermore, in De Gruchy's words:

---

7. De Gruchy, 48–49.
8. DeYoung, "Reconciliation in the Empire," 11–12.
9. De Gruchy, *Reconciliation*, 218.
10. De Gruchy, 51.
11. Schwöbel, "Reconciliation: From Biblical," 16.

Reconciliation literally has to do with the way in which God relates to us, the human "other," and in turn with our relationship to "the other," whether understood as an individual person or a group of people. It has to do with the process of overcoming alienation through identification and in solidarity with "the other," thus making peace and restoring relationships. Reconciliation has to do, if we may put it colloquially, with God making us friends.[12]

This understanding of restored relationships is expanded upon those New Testament texts in which the terms reconciliation is found outside the Pauline Letters, the Sermon on the Mount in Matthew 5:23–24: "Therefore, if you are offering your gift at the altar and there remember that your brother has something against you, leave your gift there in front of the altar. First go and be reconciled [διαλλασομαι] to your brother; then come and offer your gift."[13]

The Matthew text and Paul's own teaching highlight the importance of reconciliation as it relates to personal relationships. The main difference, however, is found in Paul extending the semantic range of the term. According to Paul, reconciliation includes not only personal relationships but also connotes God being the subject or agent of reconciliation. In speaking about God in this way, Paul became the first Greek author to portray the person offended as the one who initiates the act or process of reconciliation. This approach differed significantly from other Hellenistic sources, cultures, and languages, where reconciliation typically had to be initiated by the person responsible for the alienation and hostility.[14]

In general terms, Paul's teaching offers significant insight into how reconciliation is used in the New Testament. Ralph Martin has gone as far as to suggest that reconciliation is the overall theme of Paul's theology.[15] This is motivated not by the number of times Paul uses the term but by how it represents the whole of his missionary work. In Martin's words: "Reconciliation provides a suitable umbrella under which the main features of Paul's *kerygma*

---

12. De Gruchy, 51.
13. Matthew 5:23–24, New International Version.
14. De Gruchy, 52.
15. Martin, "Center of Paul's Theology", 94.

and its practical outworking may be set."[16] The varied ways in which Paul's understanding of reconciliation develops are observed in how he uses the term to address different issues and needs in varied contexts.

In 2 Corinthians, for example, Paul links the gospel of reconciliation to the new creation in Christ, the righteousness of God and the mission of the Church.[17] The background of the text revolves around Paul's rejection by the Christian community in Corinth, who questioned his authority and motives in writing to them. In responding to this situation, Paul uses language intended to bring about reconciliation. The words of reconciliation, Erik Doxtader adds, "afford Paul the vocabulary needed to invite his audience to enter the Word of reconciliation."[18] In doing so, De Gruchy adds, Paul extends the semantic range of the term by connecting the divine act of reconciliation in Christ with the human appropriation of the act.[19]

The use of reconciliation in Colossians is somewhat different from that in 2 Corinthians. Here the background revolves around Paul's acute sense of disorder in which the world is portrayed as being held captive by "principalities and the powers of this world." Whatever these cosmic powers may be, these powers are brought under God's control to the extent that there is no more hostility and alienation between the Creator and creation. Thus:

> The world is not at the mercy of fate, a world in cosmic free-fall, but one that has been reconciled to God through Christ. As a result, Christians have no need to engage in vain speculation, but rather to live a life that matches up to their reconciliation in Christ. Not only humanity, but the whole created cosmos is included in God's act of reconciliation in Christ, thereby linking redemption and creation.[20]

God's cosmic reconciling activity thus provides the framework within which God's reconciliation of humanity occurs.

In Paul's letter to the Romans, reconciliation is derived from Christ's work of expiation, through which humanity is justified by faith. De Gruchy

---

16. Martin, 94.
17. Martin, *Reconciliation: A Study*, 81.
18. Doxtader, "Reconciliation in a State," 57.
19. De Gruchy, 53.
20. De Gruchy, 53.

mentions that justification is a key metaphor in Paul's theology and that much has been done to determine the relationship between justification and reconciliation. He explains that:

> One way of doing so is to argue that whereas justification is interpreted "in terms of the legal character of the Old Testament covenant of God (Rom 3:2–6)" reconciliation is understood "in terms of the Old Testament covenant of God as electing love (cf. Rom 9, 11, 13; Col 3:12)." Justification is about the expiation of sin; the justification by grace through faith of the sinner before God . . . reconciliation is God's overcoming estrangement and establishing a new relationship not just with individuals who come to faith, but also with the world in all its complex relationships.[21]

Martin suggests that Paul's use of reconciliation in Romans shifts the focus of Christ's redeeming work from a forensic-cultic idiom of individual guilt, justification, and acquittal to a universal, personal and inclusive understanding.[22] Reconciliation thus becomes more than just a theological term for God restoring men and women to himself. Moreover, it refers to a way of life in which Christians are called into the world, sharing in God's work of reconciliation. Thus:

> Just as Paul anchored reconciliation in the historical events of Jesus' passion, so he tied it to the ethical transformation of historical and material conditions. Reconciliation has to do with the breaking down of the walls of enmity that separate Jews and Gentiles, men and women, masters and slaves, thereby creating the conditions on which harmonious relations can be established.[23]

In summary, Paul's reconciliation is grounded in the life, death, and resurrection of Jesus Christ and the life and mission of the Church. That is, to proclaim the gospel of reconciliation (2 Cor 5:11–20) and the eschatological hope of God's restoration and renewal of the whole creation. This includes

---

21. De Gruchy, 54.
22. Martin, *Reconciliation*, 154.
23. De Gruchy, 55.

the ethical responsibility of the Church in the world. The question of how the doctrine of reconciliation has been conceived and constructed in the course of Christian history thus becomes essential.

2.2.3 The Early Church Fathers

Irenaeus (130–202 CE) postulates that human history is entirely subject to the powers of evil. The powers of darkness enslave humanity, and that redemption implies freedom from these evil powers. Furthermore, humanity cannot compete with these evil powers and is therefore left wholly dependent on God. Irenaeus develops this idea further by introducing the notion of Christ's total identification with humankind through his life, death, and resurrection. This is done through asking: "For what purpose did Christ come down from heaven?"[24] Irenaeus begins with the sin of Adam and Satan's continued power over humanity and ends with Christ's deliverance of humankind from sin and reclaiming God's rightful place as ruler of the earth.[25] In other words, what humanity lost in Adam, namely, being in the image and likeness of God, is regained in and through Christ.[26] Velli-Matti Kärkkäinen further suggests that the parallels between Adam and Christ are crucial for Irenaeus. "Whereas the former was the beginning of disobedient humanity, the latter brings about redeemed and renewed humanity, thus helping to perfect the image of God."[27] Irenaeus thus anticipates the ransom theory of atonement.

For Clement (150–215 CE), if Christ laid down his life for the sake of humanity, a life worth no less than the universe, then Christ demands of humanity, in return, that they offer their lives on behalf of each other.[28] Clement, it may be said, pre-empted the later "moral influence" theory of Abelard.

For Tertullian (160–220 CE), it was seemingly illogical that humanity should have forgiveness of sins without any payment in exchange.[29] Later, Cyprian (200–258 CE) seized upon this idea and developed the understanding of God's wrath as satisfied through the "overplus of merit earned by Christ."[30]

---

24. Irenaeus, *Against Heresies*, Book II, 14.7.
25. Irenaeus, *Against Heresies*, Book II, 18.7.
26. Kelly, *Early Christian doctrines*, 375–376.
27. Kärkkäinen, *Christ and Reconciliation*, 300.
28. Mozley, *The Doctrine of the Atonement*, 95.
29. Tertullian, *Concerning the Resurrection*, 20–23.
30. Lochman, *Reconciliation and Liberation*, 88–89.

Along with the idea of heavenly salvation, the notion of atonement through "satisfaction" is continued on the earthly stage, highlighting Cyprian in the way of "works of righteousness" through the Church.[31] At a later stage, the term "satisfaction" became a keyword in characterising what became the Anselmian position of the atonement.

The views of Tertullian and Cyprian paved the way for later developments of the Latin theory, as seen in Gregory the Great (540–604 CE) and Augustine (324–430 CE). Gregory rejected the idea that a ransom was paid to Satan or God. According to Gregory, the Devil did not have the authority to demand a ransom consisting of Godself. He also found it inconceivable that God would find satisfaction in the blood of his only Son. The truth is, God accepted the ransom not because God demanded it or even needed it, "but because in the economy of redemption, it was fitting that sanctification should be restored to human nature through the humanity which [Christ] had assumed."[32] Gregory later details this substitution by highlighting human sin as needing an equal human sacrifice to receive God's forgiveness.[33] The notion of "sacrifice" went on to play a significant role in Gregory's view of the atonement.[34]

For Augustine, God justly committed humanity to the power of the Devil when Adam sinned. He contends, however, that the Devil overextended his reach when he accepted Christ's innocent blood as a ransom for the sinfulness of humanity. As a penalty for abusing his power, the Devil is required to deliver up humanity who, because of their sinfulness, was in bondage to him. For example, Augustine speaks of Christ's blood as the price paid for humanity, which the Devil accepted, only to find himself enchained, and again of Christ's body as bait by which Satan was caught like a mouse in a trap.[35] Augustine's view can be summarized as follows: (i) Satan owned no rights, in the strict sense, over humankind; what happened was that, when

---

31. Cyprian of Carthage, *Treatises*, 8.5.
32. Kelly, *Early Christian doctrines*, 383–384.
33. Gregory the Great, Morals on the Book
34. It was Gregory who used the (in)famous image of God paying the ransom through deceiving the Devil with the trickery of a fish hook. Hidden under human nature was Christ's deity, which the Devil devoured as a bait and thus helped destroy his own power. Well aware of the potential objections such rhetoric, Gregory defended the divine deception by reminding his readers that it was just recompense because of the Devil's own deceitful nature. See Kärkkäinen, 302.
35. Kelly, 391.

humans sinned, they passed inevitably into his power, and God permitted rather than enjoined this; (ii) No ransom as such was therefore due to the Devil, but on the contrary, when Christ's sacrifice procured the remission of sins, God's favour was restored, and humanity might well have been freed; (iii) God preferred, however, as a course more consonant with his justice, that the Devil should not be deprived of his dominion by force, but as the penalty for abusing his position; (iv) Hence Christ's passion, the primary object of which was of course quite different, placed the Son of God in Satan's hands, and when the latter overreached himself seizing the divine prey, with the arrogance and greed which were characteristic of the Devil, he was justly constrained, as a penalty, to deliver up humankind.[36] Thus, Augustine represents the release of humanity from the power of the Devil as consequent upon and presupposing their reconciliation with God. The Devil is conquered precisely because God has received satisfaction and has bestowed pardon. For Augustine, the emancipation from the Devil is regarded as a consequence of, and thus subordinate to, the reconciliation itself. The essence of redemption lies in an expiatory sacrifice offered for humanity by Christ in His passion.[37]

Augustine also stressed the importance of the exemplary aspect of Christ's work. He argues that Christ, the mediator, demonstrated God's wisdom and love in His person and what He had done. The spectacle of such love should have the effect of inducing humanity to love Him in return. More particularly, it should inspire humanity to adore God's humility, which, as revealed in the incarnation, breaks human pride. So, for Augustine, the humility of the Word revealed in His unique self-abasement forms a vital part of Christ's saving work.[38] In this way, Augustine anticipated both the "ransom" and the "moral influence" theory of the atonement.

Hilary of Poitiers (315–367 CE) regards the death of Christ as a classic example of an innocent sufferer paying the penalty for sins he had not committed. Hilary thereby introduced the thought of penal substitution, later occupying the sixteenth and seventeenth-century reformers.

Origen (185–254 CE) is credited with being the first Christian theologian to advance the "ransom theory" of atonement explicitly. In his view, the death

---

36. Kelly, *Early Christian doctrines*, 392.
37. Augustine, *Contra Faustum*.
38. Kelly, *Early Christian doctrines*, 383–384.

of Christ is a ransom paid to the Devil in exchange for human souls, forfeited on account of sin. For Origen, when Christ offered his soul as a ransom for human souls, the Devil could not withstand its perfect purity – having found it hazardous to enslave Christ's soul. Origen further asserts that the Devil was deceived into believing he could overcome Christ. However, the Devil later realized he could not bear the torment of holding Christ.[39] Gregory of Nyasa (335–395 CE) seized and further developed Origen's view of the atonement.[40]

This brief overview suggests that the "ransom" and "moral influence" view of atonement emerged during this period. It should be noted that nearly all Church Fathers, including Justin, Athanasius and Augustine, taught substitutionary atonement. However, specific interpretations of the meaning of the death of Christ differ. Athanasius and Augustine taught that through Christ's suffering on behalf of humanity, he overcame and liberated them from death and Satan. It was particularly Augustine's teaching that continued to be influential during the medieval period.

2.2.4 The Medieval Period

Anselm of Canterbury (1033–1109 CE) rejected Augustine's version of the ransom theory and proposed an entirely different model. Through Anselm, the satisfaction theory first came together as a coherent doctrine. This theory is articulated in his famous *Cur Deus Homo* (Why did God become human?). The more common ransom theory of the atonement held that Jesus died and thereby paid a ransom to the Devil, allowing God to rescue those under his bondage. For Anselm, this solution was inadequate. He, therefore, began his research by examining the idea of sin and the implications thereof on humanity's relationship with God. Anselm concluded that sin was a direct dishonouring of God, a betrayal of the Creator by humanity, not a cosmic battle between God and the Devil. He concluded that humankind owed God a debt of honour. For Anselm, owing this debt created an imbalance in the moral universe and could not be satisfied by God simply ignoring it. The rebellion of sin required repayment, for if left unpunished, it would create permanent disorder in the world God created.[41] Anselm thus concluded that

---

39. Kelly, 382.
40. Mozley, *Doctrine of the Atonement*, 109.
41. Anselm, *Cur Deus Homo*, 11–3.

the only possible way of repaying this debt was if a being of infinite greatness could act as a human being on behalf of humankind to repay a debt of honour owed to God. In this light, Jesus' death is seen not as a payment to the Devil but to God, His Father. Anselm did not expressly state whether Jesus' payment of the debt was for all of humanity or individuals. However, his rhetoric does indicate a stronger disposition for the former.[42] Later, Thomas Aquinas (1225–1274 CE) expressly attributes the scope of the atonement to be universal. Aquinas further argued that Christ's death satisfies the penalty owed by sin and that Christ's passion was explicitly needed to pay the debt of the sin of humanity.[43]

Peter Abelard (1079–1142 CE) offered a radical revision of the interpretation of the atonement. Abelard's response is a critique of the Anselmian view. Abelard's understanding of atonement was focused not on human rebellion or God's anger but rather on the loving nature of God. In his view, humanity is sinful, but this does not prevent God from caring for creation.[44] He thus rejected both the ransom theory, contending that Christ had come to pay a debt to the Devil and Anselm's theory that Christ had come to pay a debt to God. For Abelard, it is instead the plenitude of God's love that Jesus exhibited, and this love was ultimately expressed in Jesus' death. Jesus' death and innocent suffering offer a grand model to follow and help orient the will and love of humanity in the right direction. Abelard's position was later labelled as the "moral influence view."[45]

---

42. For a helpful guide on this discussion, see Hopkins, *Companion to the Study*, 187–214.

43. Kärkkäinen, 305.

44. Abelard, *Ethics: Book I*, 37–38.

45. Kärkkäinen mentions that: "This view of atonement was embraced by various later movements and thinkers who rejected the whole idea of vicarious satisfaction or penalty such as the Unitarian Socinians of the sixteenth century. Faustus and Laelius Socinus focused on the prophetic ministry of the early days of Jesus and highlighted his humanity. The Enlightenment thinkers found much to commend in the Moral Example view. It fit[s] well with Immanuel Kant's idea of Jesus as the moral ideal and our duty as human beings to elevate ourselves to this ideal of moral perfection." Liberal Protestants, similarly, considered this interpretation appealing, as evident in Schleiermacher's theology. While Schleiermacher's view often resembles the patristic position in highlighting the importance of the incarnation, the example motif seems to stand at the forefront. Another Liberal, Albert Ritschl, opposes vocally any notion of penal satisfaction even though he regards the death of Christ as the foundation for the establishment of God's kingdom. One of the most influential defenders of the Moral Example views in the early twentieth century is Hastings Rashdall, who speaks of the "moral ideal which Christ taught by His words, and illustrated by His life and death of love," the only "ideal given among men by which we may be saved." See Kärkkäinen, *Christ and reconciliation*, 304–305.

2.2.5 The Reformation Period

The Protestant Reformation saw many of the "Reformers" reject Abelard's moral influence theory in favour of Anselm's satisfaction theory.[46] The Reformers, particularly Martin Luther (1483–1546 CE) and John Calvin (1509–1564 CE) appreciated the Anselmian tradition and used this to develop this particular view of atonement even further. The Reformers' view is often labelled the "penal substitution" view, which implies its Anselmian basis coupled with the need for a sacrificial-expiatory death on the cross to deal with the condemned humanity's lot because of sin. Furthermore, they agree with Anselm that the atonement depended on God's initiative. Moreover, that the God-human is the only one who can make atonement; however, they recognize that God did not have to save fallen creation, but once God had committed to doing so, the death of Christ on the cross was the only way to do this. In this context, Christ's death perfectly satisfied the justice of God.

The one area where the Reformers reframed the discussion was by changing the language of sin as an insult to God's honour, to sin as the breaking of God's law. Herewith they stressed the guilt that results from transgressing the law. They also avoided Anselm's dilemma of the atonement using either satisfaction or punishment by pointing to the biblical teaching that Christ was a penal-substitute for, or representative of, humanity. Here Anselm's understanding of the satisfaction view should be distinguished from the penal substitution of the Reformers. Both are forms of satisfaction because both refer to the notion that Christ's death was satisfactory. However, Anselm's satisfaction and the Reformers' penal substitution offer different understandings of how Christ's death was satisfactory. For example, Anselm refers to humanity's sinfulness as defrauding God of honour due to Him. Therefore, Christ's death is seen as the ultimate act of obedience, which brings great honour to God because it goes beyond what was required from Christ. Christ gave more than what he was obliged to give. The merit of Christ's act and its surplus is, therefore, enough to repay humanity's deficit. This is why Christ's death is seen as substitutionary; he pays honour to God instead of humanity.

---

46. The "Reformers" in this context refer primarily to Martin Luther and John Calvin. But much could be said for others also considered Reformers. What is presented here as the Reformation period on the atonement also reflects theological development beyond the time of the first and second generation of Reformers. In other words, I am also reflecting on the insights of the Reformed Scholastics.

Penal substitution, on the other hand, differs because it views Christ's death not as repayment to God for lost honour but rather as paying the penalty of death that had always been the consequence of human sinfulness that was started with Adam. The main difference here is that for Anselm, satisfaction is an alternative to punishment, whereas, with the Reformers, it is the punishment that satisfies the demands for justice. The classical statement of Luther on the atonement is found in his commentary on Galatians 3:13. There he insists that Christ was the most cursed of all sinners, seeing that he assumed in his body the sins humanity had committed, to render satisfaction for them by his blood. Through the notion of penal substitution, this expression by Luther indicates a shift from the understanding of the atonement offered by Anselm. However, Luther was uncomfortable with the word "satisfaction" as it relates to the death of Christ.

Calvin also reflected on the atonement in two crucial chapters of the *Institutes*.[47] From this flowed the work of redemption, wherein hatred cannot be denied a place in God's just vengeance on sinful humanity. However, the most distinct aspect of his contribution on atonement involved the idea of election. For Calvin, Christ, through his death on the cross, did not pay a general penalty for the sins of humanity but suffered a specific penalty for the sins of individuals. This implies that Christ's atonement is limited in its effect only to those whom God has chosen to be saved.[48] Here Calvin draws on Augustine's work on predestination to construct his theory.

Calvin shifted from the idea of Aquinas that satisfaction was penance (which focused on satisfaction) to the idea of satisfying God's wrath, which is propitiated through Christ's death. Like Luther, Calvin also understood the atonement and satisfaction in terms of penal substitution; that is, Christ has borne our punishment through his death. For Calvin, Christ satisfied the demands of justice and appeased God's wrath in order for God to justly show grace. Calvin employs the language of sacrifice to explain the "how" behind the punishment. Calvin's theory of atonement was affirmed at the Synod of Dordt (1618–1619 CE).

---

47. See Wright, "Atonement in Reformation," 37–48, for a detailed investigation of all Reformation views, including the Catholic, with a focus on Calvin.

48. See Helm, *Calvin: A Guide for the Perplexed*, 83–85.

2.2.6 The Post-Reformation Period

The post-Reformation period debates on atonement were mainly in response to the satisfaction and punishment theories represented by Anselm and Calvin, respectively. These theories represented the two widely accepted notions of Western Christianity. The advocates of these views maintained that Christ died on the cross as a substitute for sinners. Christ did this in full payment for sins, which satisfied the righteousness of God. This was done for sinners to be forgiven without compromising God's righteousness. The sacrifice of Christ could thus be said to have satisfied divine justice.

The critical distinction between Anselm and Calvin is that for Anselm, satisfaction implies an alternative to punishment. The honour that was compromised must be repaid, or punishment should follow. Humanity avoids punishment through Christ satisfying their debt of honour to God. For Calvin, it is the punishment which satisfies the demands of justice; thus, he offers a specific explanation for the death of Christ rooted in the notion of substitutionary atonement.

While the idea of substitutionary atonement is prevalent in nearly all atonement theories, the specific idea of penal substitution became dominant only within the Latin Church. Nevertheless, the Reformers' view of penal substitution soon led to opposition. They experienced the first but less important opposition in Germany, among others, in the eighteenth-century writings of G. S. Steinbart, I. G. Tollner, G. F. Seiler, and K. G. Bretschneider.[49]

The most significant opposition occurred during the period of the European Enlightenment, where there was a shift to a focus on a rational, human-centred version of reality. Taking the philosophical concepts of the Enlightenment used by Immanuel Kant, René Descartes, and others, the theologians of the nineteenth century looked to find a more rational understanding of the atonement. With the advent of this modernist worldview, critical approaches were adopted towards theories of atonement, which included transcendent elements. Some of the rejected transcendent elements include the idea of a sacrifice that had some impact upon God, Christ dying to pay some penalty or of satisfaction required due to sin. The facets of the Enlightenment's notion of atonement can be summarized as follows: Firstly, the cross has no transcendent reference or value; its value relates directly to

---

49. McGrath, *Christian Theology*, 409.

its impact upon humanity. Thus the cross represents a "sacrifice" only in as far as it represents Christ offering his life. Secondly, the person who died on the cross was a human being, and the impact of that death is exerted upon other human beings alone. That impact takes on the form of inspiration and encouragement to model the moral example Jesus Christ set for human beings. Thirdly, an essential aspect of the cross is that it demonstrates the love of God for humanity. These approaches became enormously influential in rationalist circles throughout nineteenth-century Europe. Together with this, the model of a martyr, rather than a saviour, describes the attitude increasingly adopted towards Jesus within such circles.

Arguably, Friedrich Schleiermacher expressed the most significant challenge to the rationalist approach to the crucifixion.[50] Schleiermacher appealed for a religious rather than a purely moral understanding of Christ's death. In his view, Christ did not die to create or endorse a moral system; instead, he came so that the supremacy of a consciousness of God could be established in humanity. Schleiermacher's ideas, however, ultimately proved to be capable of being assimilated within a purely exemplarist understanding rather than posing a coherent challenge to that reductionist moralistic notion. In England, the most significant contribution to the exemplarist approach came from Hastings Rashdall in his 1915 Bampton Lectures.[51]

This brief overview indicates that there are several views on the atonement. These views are often nuanced. However, for clarity and brevity, I will discuss only the three main views as discussed by Gustaf Aulén in his 1931 monograph *Christus Victor*.

2.3 The Three Main Views of Atonement: An Overview of Aulén's *Christus Victor*

In this section, I provide some background information on Gustaf Aulén. This will be followed by a summary of the work of Christ that Aulén analysed in *Christus Victor*. The discussion will follow the structure of his analysis.

---

50. Schleiermacher, *Christian Faith*.
51. McGrath, *Christian theology*, 409.

2.3.1 Background

Gustaf Emmanuel Hildebrand Aulén (1879–1977 CE) was Bishop of Strängnäs in the Church of Sweden, a theologian and author of *Christus Victor: A Historical Study of the Three Main Types of the Idea of the Atonement*, first published in 1930 (English translation in 1931). From 1889 to 1915, Aulén was a student of Philosophy and Theology at Uppsala University and received the degree of Doctor of Theology in 1915. He began his academic career as a lecturer in Christian Dogmatics at Uppsala University in 1910 and later occupied the position of Professor of Systematic Theology at Lund University in 1913. Aulén was the president of the Royal Swedish Academy of Music from 1944 to 1950. As an avid music composer, he generously contributed to the Swedish hymnbook. Aulén was the author of several books and articles, including his most famous work *Christus Victor*, which still exerts considerable influence on contemporary theological discussions on the atonement.

In *Christus Victor*, Aulén distinguishes between what he identifies as the three main types of atonement. First, he highlights the "classic" type (drawing especially on Irenaeus) in which Christ's victory over the powers of evil is emphasized. Second, the "Latin" or Anselmian type in which Christ's satisfaction for guilt incurred by humanity is the focal point. And third, the "subjective" type draws on Abelard's subjective appropriation of Christ's atonement.[52] Aulén compares and contrasts the three main atonement theories around four key areas: sin, salvation, God and reconciliation.

2.3.2 The Ransom View (*Christus Victor* or Classic Theory)

The first model Aulén analyses is what he calls the *Christus Victor* view of atonement. This was established by the early Church Fathers, and it centres on the vivid imagery and mythology in much of the New Testament. For Aulén, the Christus Victor view of atonement is rooted in divine conflict and victory. Christ, the victor, battles against and triumphs over the evil powers of the world, the "tyrants" under whom humankind is in bondage. These

---

52. The names of the different models of atonement identified by Aulén are used in the following manner: the terms are used interchangeably; this, only as it relates to a specific model: First, referring to the "Ransom theory," Aulén also uses the notions such as *Christus Victor*, "dramatic" or "classic" approach to describe the model inspired by Irenaeus. Second, referring to the "Satisfaction theory," he also uses the notions of such as the "Latin" or "objective" view to describe the model inspired by Anselm. Third, when referring to "Subjective theory," he also uses notions such as "moral influence" (or exemplary) to describe the model inspired by Abelard.

evil powers that hold humanity in bondage serve as the executants of God's will.[53] Through Christ's decisive victory, God reconciles the world to himself. However, the redeeming work of Christ for humankind is not found in any sort of rational settlement but in a "drama" in which a decisive event occurs that fundamentally alters the relation between God and humanity.[54]

In what Aulén describes as the "classic" idea of atonement, sin is depicted as an objective power lurking behind humankind. In his view, the atonement of Christ entails God's triumph over sin, death, and the Devil.[55] Salvation, as defined, is a comprehensive term that highlights humanity's new relation with God. This idea of salvation maintains that Christ gained victory once and for all and that this victory is continuing in the work of the Holy Spirit. The victory of Christ is a present as well as a historical reality. Justification and atonement thus become one. God's love prevails over the curse of sin and death. Justification is simply the atonement brought into the present; thus, there is a close and inseparable connection between the incarnation and the atonement. Aulén contends that because salvation is understood as a divine victory, the incarnation is the necessary presupposition of the atonement. In this context, the atonement completes the incarnation.[56]

For Aulén, Patristic theology is dualistic in its nature. However, this dualism is not absolute. In the classic approach, God is depicted as intervening in conflict with evil on the stage of history. Yet, at the same time, God is also the all-ruler, the Sovereign. The hostile powers which hold humanity in bondage also serve as the executants of God's will, thus within divine control. The deliverance of humankind from the power of death and evil at the same time implies humankind's deliverance from God's judgment. Through the incarnation and death of Christ, God has taken away the evil forces' powers to harm humankind. Thus, God, through Christ, has overcome sin, evil and death and has reconciled humankind to himself.[57]

Irenaeus, according to Aulén, was the earliest Church father to provide a clear and comprehensive doctrine of atonement and redemption. Unlike some

---

53. This is linked to the view (see section of the early Church Fathers above) that God justly committed humanity to the power of the Devil when Adam sinned.
54. Aulén, *Christus Victor*, 4.
55. Aulén, 22–28.
56. Aulén, 28–34.
57. Aulén, 145–158.

of the more minor writings of the Apostolic Fathers and the Apologists, who treat the atonement in a relatively incidental way, Irenaeus' approach differed much; mainly because, in his work, the idea of the atonement recurs on a continual basis. In Aulén's words, "[Irenaeus'] basic idea [of the atonement] is in itself thoroughly clear and unmistakable . . . [marking] out a track which succeeding generations were to follow. [Thus] we may, then, feel satisfied that we have found in Irenaeus our true starting point."[58]

According to Aulén, the inseparability of the atonement and the incarnation is central in Irenaeus' articulation of the doctrine. In this context, the question posed by Irenaeus: "For what purpose did Christ come down from heaven?" becomes important.[59] Aulén contends the purpose of the incarnation is linked to Irenaeus' view that reflects God in Christ coming down from heaven so "that he might destroy sin, overcome death, and give life to [humanity]."[60] Here the work of Christ is first and foremost a victory over the powers which hold humankind in bondage: this includes sin, death and the Devil. The incarnation, therefore, is a necessary preliminary component of Christ's atoning work. In this sense, there is no trace of the separation between the incarnation and atonement, which, as Aulén argues, may be the case with the Latin theory.[61]

For Aulén, the divine victory accomplished in Christ stands at the centre of Irenaeus' thought. He contends that this is an essential element in Irenaeus' conception of *recapitulatio* (restoring and perfecting the creation). As well as this being the most comprehensive theological idea presented by Irenaeus. In this context, Irenaeus' recapitulation does not end with the triumph of Christ over the enemies which had held humanity in bondage but continues in the work of the Spirit in the church. This also includes the recapitulation that is not realized in this life, that which is eschatological.[62]

The role of sin, death and the Devil is important in Irenaeus' view of the atonement. Aulén suggests that Irenaeus opposed the moralistic view, which would have no other meaning for sin than as separate and individual acts of

---

58. Aulén, 17.
59. Irenaeus, *Against Heresies*, Book II, 14.7.
60. Aulén, *Christus Victor*, 19.
61. Aulén, 21.
62. On this point Aulén notes that: "Irenaeus' outlook is strongly eschatological, and the gift of the Spirit in this life is for him the earnest of future glory." See Aulén, 21–22.

sin. On the contrary, Irenaeus thinks of sin as affecting the whole of humanity. From one point of view, sin is an objective power under which humanity is in bondage and cannot set itself free. Moreover, from another perspective, it is something voluntary and wilful, which makes humanity debtors in relation to God. Because of this sinfulness, humankind is deemed guilty in the sight of God, and it is for this reason that fellowship with God is lost. This enmity between humanity and God for Irenaeus could only be taken away through the atonement, a *reconciliatio*. Through the atonement, the enmity created by the sin of humankind is abolished by God.[63]

According to Aulén, sin and death are inseparably associated in Irenaeus. Death is not merely associated with mortality and the loss of immortality. For Irenaeus, sinfulness is regarded as rebelling against God, and rebelling against God in this context essentially means death. For this reason, Aulén points to Irenaeus' interchangeable use of the concepts of sin and death. Thus, when Irenaeus speaks of salvation from death, his thought includes the idea of salvation from the state of sin. This way of thinking, Aulén suggests, is not unique to Irenaeus but "had already found its full and clear expression in the New Testament, particularly in the Pauline and Johannine epistles, where we find the most definite statements that salvation is life, in direct connection with the thought of Christ as Victor over sin and over death. In fact, the teaching that salvation is the bestowal of life holds the secret of the note of triumph which is characteristic of the Apostolic Christianity." [64]

Aulén also discusses the close connection between the Devil and Irenaeus's thoughts on sin and death. For Aulén, Irenaeus considers the Devil, the lord of sin and death. Through deception, humanity has fallen under the Devil's power. In this context, humanity is unable to escape the Devil's dominion, except through the victory of Christ. This victory, Aulén claims, is especially a victory over the Devil and, by implication, also sin and death.[65]

On the actual accomplishment of the work of atonement, Aulén observes that Irenaeus "traces a continuous line from the incarnation through the entire earthly life of Christ, and His death, to His resurrection and exaltation,

---

63. Aulén, 23–24.
64. Aulén, 25.
65. Aulén, 26.

and that no one point in this line claims anything like an exclusive emphasis."[66] In his view, Irenaeus appears to be free from the tendency which became common in theologies that appeared later. Some of these theologies tended to emphasize the death of Christ in such a way that it would ignore the rest of his earthly life. Irenaeus, Aulén argues, attached much significance to the obedience of Christ throughout his life on earth. Irenaeus showed how the one man's disobedience, which inaugurated the reign of sin, is answered by the one man who brought life. Through this obedience, Christ "recapitulated" and annulled disobedience. Obedience thus became the means of Christ's victory, annulling "the ancient disobedience that was committed at the tree."[67]

According to Aulén, using biblical images is another significant feature of Irenaeus' view of the atonement. Irenaeus, Aulén asserts, had a particular fondness for the image of ransom. This ransom is always paid to the powers of evil or the Devil. Through the paying of a ransom, the Devil is overcome, and his evil power over humanity is effectively brought to an end. For Aulén, this is an essential aspect of Irenaeus, mainly because once the atonement had taken place, a new relation between God and the world was established. In other words, God delivered humankind from the powers of evil and reconciled the world to himself through this. At this focal point, God is seen as both the reconciler and the reconciled.[68]

Aulén observes that the death of Christ is not an isolated occurrence in Irenaeus. Instead, "it is a death seen in connection, on one hand, with the life-work of Christ as a whole, and on the other with the Resurrection and the Ascension; the death irradiated with the light of Easter and Pentecost." Therefore, for Irenaeus, as Aulén further states, resurrection is "first of all the manifestation of the decisive victory over the powers of evil which was won on the cross; it is also the starting point for the new dispensation, for the gift of the Spirit, for the continuation of the work of God in the souls of [humanity] 'for the unity and communion of God and man.'"[69]

---

66. Aulén, 28.
67. Aulén, 29.
68. Aulén, 30–31.
69. Aulén, 31–32.

2.3.3 The Latin View (Anselmian or Penal Substitutionary Theory)

The second model Aulén analyses is what he calls the Latin view of atonement. According to him, it is in the work of Tertullian where the main ideas of satisfaction and merit in the Latin theory are to be found.[70] Aulén mentions that the Latin view appeared very early in the patristic period of the Western Church, but it never became the dominant view in the West. With some opposition, it gradually worked its way forward. For the most part, however, it was a silent, unchallenged advance.[71] Eventually, it was through Anselm's *Cur Deus homo?* (Why God became a Man), where the first systematic exposition of what became the Latin view of the atonement was made.[72] Anselm intended to replace what he regards as the old mythological account of Christ's work as the victory over the Devil.

The major limitation of the Latin view, according to Aulén, is the use of images and analogies taken mainly from the law courts. In this context, the legal order dominates the reconciliation between God and humankind. Aulén concedes that such analogies can also be found in the classic approach. However, he insists that, in the Latin type, legal order dominates the whole conception, and any violation of justice becomes unthinkable. This entails the payment of the required satisfaction. The continuity of divine operation is therefore lost. The satisfaction is offered by Christ as human, the sinless human, on behalf of sinful humanity.[73]

Comparing the classic and the Latin types on their conceptions of sin, Aulén contends that the classic type has a broader scope, while the Latin type concentrates only on sin and its accompanying guilt. In the classic type, sin entails a whole series of evil powers; this includes death, the Devil, law, and curse; the most constant is the grouping of sin and death. For Aulén, sin in the Latin type is reduced to a mere moralistic idea, and salvation becomes a mere remission of punishment. On the other hand, salvation in the classic type entails deliverance from sin and death, as well as an entrance into

---

70. Dillistone, *The Christian Understanding*, 190.
71. Aulén, *Christus Victor*, 38.
72. For a helpful discussion, see Hopkins, *Companion to the Study*, 187–214.
73. Aulén, *Christus Victor*, 146.

life. Thus, for Aulén, the classic understanding portrays salvation as positive instead of negative conceptions of the Latin type.[74]

Aulén also raises questions regarding the materialized view of sin in the Latin theory. The merits of the satisfaction delivered by Christ for humankind are treated by default as transferred onto humankind. Aulén argues that such a view obscures the personal relationship between God and the sinner. In this context, the very idea of satisfaction shows that the justice of God on humankind has not been fully met. So, in the payment of compensation for sin, or the endurance of punishment for sin, God's demand on humankind is not adequately expressed, nor is the idea of sin itself seen in its full personal significance.[75]

On the other hand, for Aulén, wherever the classic idea is dominant, the idea of sin is always positive, whether the actual terms used are the forgiveness of sins, union with God, the deifying of human nature, or some other. Thus, when Christ overcomes the tyrants who hold humankind in bondage, Christ's victory is accompanied by divine blessing, justification, grace, and salvation. Regarding the Latin doctrine, the natural tendency is for forgiveness to be regarded negatively, mainly because the satisfaction made by Christ remits the punishment humanity fully deserved.[76]

Aulén notes that the penitential system, on which the Latin type is based, is essentially moralistic. It deals with the issue of how a perfect God should deal with individual sinners. For Aulén, such an approach removes the atoning death of Christ from its immediate context. Christ's atoning work is meant to restore the broken relationship between God and humankind. The individual has sinned against God, against one another and nature as a whole. However, to dwell on this as a point of departure for the interpretation of the atoning work of Christ, as the Latin view does, is a distortion of the broader picture.[77]

On salvation, Aulén contends that the Latin doctrine provides a series of relatively loosely interrelated acts. The actual atonement consists of Christ's offering of satisfaction and God's acceptance. With this act, humanity has no input except in so far as Christ stands as their representative. Justification is

---

74. Aulén, 147–148.
75. Aulén, 90–91.
76. Aulén, 147–148.
77. Aulén, 92.

a second act in which God transfers or imputes to humanity the merits of Christ. Here again, Aulén argues, no direct relation seems to exist between Christ and humanity, with sanctification, the third act, having no organic connection with the preceding two acts.[78]

Aulén accuses the Latin type of failing to adequately explain the connection between the incarnation and the atonement. In this context, God is no longer viewed as the direct agent in the atoning work. Christ, as a human being, delivers atonement on behalf of humanity. For Aulén, the classic idea of atonement, as highlighted in the writings of the Church Fathers, is clear and decisive on this issue. The classic idea is based on the notion that Christ became human to accomplish God's redemptive work. In this sense, the incarnation is the necessary presupposition of the atonement. Moreover, the atonement is the completion of the incarnation. Aulén contends that incarnation and redemption belong indissolubly together. In other words, God in Christ overcomes the hostile powers that hold humanity in bondage. Also, the incarnation manifests God's goodness and the fulfilment of Christ's saving work in the flesh under the conditions of human nature. For Aulén, the continuity in the classic type appears to be missing in the Latin type.[79]

2.3.4 The Subjective View (Moral Influence Theory)

The third model Aulén analyses is called the subjective view of the atonement. This approach is generally associated with the work of Peter Abelard. It is also known as the moral influence theory. Like Anselm, Abelard also asks the question of "why" the incarnation in his "Expositions of the Epistle to the Romans."[80] Abelard disagreed with the ransom theory and the Latin theory, and his understanding of atonement focused not on human rebellion and God's anger but on the loving nature of God. Abelard insists that God indeed has a right of ownership over humanity and that it is perfectly appropriate to forgive without any "satisfaction," if God so wishes. Jesus' death provides a compelling example to follow. Jesus embodies God's sacrificial love, the perfect example, the ideal human being, and the realization of perfection. Rather than focusing on the original sin of Adam or the debt

---

78. Aulén, 90.
79. Aulén, 151–152.
80. Abelard, "Exposition of the Epistle", 276–278.

owed to God, for Abelard, sin consists of wrong and mistaken intentions and evil inclinations of the mind.[81] Abelard's emphasis is on true penitence that involves not just empty confessions about wrongdoings but an actual change in moral behaviour.[82]

Aulén notes that the consequence of the subjective type is that God's share in the process of salvation becomes secondary. The moral influence view does not regard the atonement as in any true sense carried out by God. Instead, reconciliation is the result of a process in human beings, such as conversion and amendment. If Christ is mentioned concerning the atonement, his efforts are not considered God's work for humankind's salvation. Rather, Christ is seen as the perfect example, the ideal human being, and the head of the human race. For Aulén, in so far as Christ's work can affect the relation between God and humankind, it is a matter of "from below upwards" and not an approach of God to human beings.[83]

Furthermore, for Aulén, the idea of sin has become altogether weakened in the subjective type. He highlights this weakness in the larger context of enlightenment theology which regarded sin as little more than infirmity. Aulén also notes that liberal Protestantism, which, he contends, serves as the framework for this type, generally has a truncated sense of sin. In his view, this humanistic interpretation of atonement fails to maintain the radical hostility of God to evil and God's judgment on sin.[84] For Aulén, although Abelard ignored the seriousness of sin which occasioned the atonement, he admits that one would still have to appreciate Abelard's renewed emphasis on love as the underlying motive of the atonement.[85]

On salvation, Aulén notes that Abelard stressed the accomplishment of the atoning work through the human nature of Christ. Accordingly, the emphasis on human nature becomes exclusive, and Christ is eventually treated simply as an ideal human being. According to Aulén, this ideal human becomes a sort of intermediary between God and humankind. The incarnation ceases to take a primary place in the moral influence theory. Aulén notes that the

---

81. As explained in Abelard, "Ethics, or Know Thyself," *Classic Moralists*, 186–191.
82. Dillistone, *The Christian Understanding of Atonement*, 324–325.
83. Aulén, *Christus Victor*, 146–147.
84. Aulén, 148.
85. Aulén, 133–44.

English theologians, who subscribe to the moral influence theory, interpret incarnation in a semi-Arian rather than a Nicene sense.[86] He further stresses that among continental liberal theologians, God is regarded as the ultimate cause of Christ's atoning acts. Through Christ, God sees humankind in a new light. In either case, the atonement is not in any true sense to be assumed the work of God.[87]

On the concept of God relating to sin, Aulén argues that the moral influence type does not view any opposition against God. He attributes this to the need to portray a "purified" and "simple" conception of God. In this sense, God's character is rooted in that unchanging love. However, Aulén surmises that this simplicity is won at the cost of obscuring the hostility of the divine love to evil. According to him, the conception of divine love has become humanized and, at the same time, rather obvious and stereotyped.[88]

Aulén contends that the subjective view must be seen against the background of the Latin theory. What Abelard proposed was essentially a response to Anselm. Above all, Abelard desired to uproot the "anthropomorphic" features and "relics of Judaism" from the conception of God, the idea of God that lay behind the Orthodox doctrine of atonement. In his view, this was inconsistent with the simple teaching of Christ and the love of God. Abelard, therefore, found it intolerable that God should be thought of as needing to be propitiated through a satisfaction offered. For Abelard, the death of Christ could not rightfully be interpreted in this way. The death of Christ was, among others, a seal set upon Christ's teaching, a vindication of the moral order of the universe, a lofty example, and a symbolic expression of God's readiness to be reconciled.[89]

The weakness of the subjective view, Aulén states, can be summed up in the context that the orthodox theologians may have been correct in noting that the only alternative to the satisfaction of God's justice was love, which spelt laxity. For Aulén, it was clear that the rejection of the orthodox doctrine of satisfaction involved a weakening of the idea of sin and a toning-down of the radical opposition to the will of God to that which is evil. Aulén thus

---

86. Semi-Arianism is a name that has been used for identifying a position that held to a version of the Nicene Creed that omitted the formula "of One Substance."
87. Aulén, *Christus Victor*, 153.
88. Aulén, 154.
89. Aulén, 133–134.

concludes: "If, then, we, for our part, have refused to accept the orthodox dilemma as valid, we can only do so because we have learnt to distinguish another idea of the atonement, which both orthodox Protestantism and the enlightenment had left out of count: the classic idea."[90]

To summarize Aulén's analysis, firstly, he contends that the classic view portrays atonement as a movement of God towards humankind. God is intimately and personally engaged in the work of humanity's deliverance. The classic type shows a continuity of divine operation and discontinuity in the order of merit and justice, while the Latin view is the opposite in both respects. In the classic type, the work of the atonement is accomplished by Godself, yet at the same time, the passive form also is used:

> God is reconciled with the world. The alternation is not accidental: He is reconciled only because He Himself reconciles the world to Himself and Himself with the world. The safeguard of the continuity of God's operation is the dualistic outlook, the divine warfare against the evil that holds mankind in bondage, and the triumph of Christ. But this necessitates a discontinuity of the legal order: there is no satisfaction of God's justice, for the relation of man to God is viewed in the light, not of merit and justice, but of grace.[91]

Secondly, with the Latin view, God seems to be more distant. Here the satisfaction is paid by a human being, in the person of Christ, to God. In the Latin type, the legal order is unbroken to the extent that any violation of justice becomes unthinkable. It is at this point,

> in the payment of the required satisfaction, that the continuity of divine operation is lost; for the satisfaction is offered by Christ as [a] man, as the sinless [human being] on behalf of the sinners. At the same time the atonement is still in some sense the work of God, since he is regarded as planning the atonement; therefore, also, the doctrine does not require that there is any change in God's attitude to men, even though this may often be taught.[92]

---

90. Aulén, 135.
91. Aulén, 146.
92. Aulén, 146.

Thirdly, in the moral influence view theory, God acts even more distantly. Here, no atonement is needed, and all the emphasis is on human movement to God, which is accomplished in the human world. In the subjective type, the atonement is no longer regarded as in any true sense carried out by God. Instead, the atonement is the result of some process that takes place in the individual.[93] Thus, in Aulén's *Christus Victor*, the essential Christian idea of God reaching out to humans, which dominates the classic type, is weakened in the Latin type and lost in the subjective type of atonement.

2.4 Responses to the Atonement Models as Outlined in *Christus Victor*

This section entails selected responses to the atonement models outlined. This includes selected theologians who have responded to this analysis of the victory achieved by Christ. The sources include the work of Colin Gunton,[94] Daniel Migliore,[95] Vincent Brümmer,[96] Gregory Boyd,[97] Joel Green & Mark Baker,[98] and Waldron Scott[99]. Individual theologians are chosen for their representative character in connection with their views on the atonement. The discussion will follow the structure of Aulén's analysis.

2.4.1 Responses to the Ransom View (*Christus Victor* or Classic Theory)

a) Colin Gunton

Colin Gunton was a British theologian and Professor of Christian Doctrine at Kings College, London, from 1984. He was involved in the United Reformed Church in the United Kingdom, where he had been a minister since 1972. Gunton was the editor of the *Cambridge Companion to Christian Doctrine* and the author of many influential publications, including, *The Actuality of*

---

93. Aulén, 146.
94. Gunton, *Actuality of Atonement*.
95. Migliore, *Faith Seeking Understanding*.
96. Brümmer, *Atonement, Christology and the Trinity*.
97. Boyd, "Christus Victor View."
98. Green and Baker, *Recovering the Scandal*.
99. Scott, *What about the Cross?*.

Atonement: A Study of Metaphor, Rationality and the Christian Tradition, published in 1988.

In *The Actuality of Atonement*, Gunton examines the Christian doctrine of atonement through various metaphors. Gunton's immediate focus is the three main views, particularly the classic theory, to which he seeks to respond. For Gunton, the classic theory (or ransom view) in its earliest forms was embedded with freighted accounts of devils and demons, which were vanquished by divine stratagems. From Gunton's perspective, Aulén recaptured the old theory in a new mode by employing the phrase *Christus Victor* to draw together interpretations of the cross as God's triumph over evil.[100]

With an emphasis on the use of metaphor as a central feature of theological language, Gunton examines some of the central metaphors for atonement. This includes the examples of the battlefield, the altar, and the law courts, which depict the ministry, sacrifice, and victory of Jesus Christ. He does this to demonstrate how some of these metaphors can be embodied in the daily reality of the Christian community. Gunton's examination of biblical material shows that the victory emphasized in the classic theory is not purely a past event or a cosmic battle but that it takes place within human history on an ongoing basis. The victory is seen to be continuous within the life of the individual Christian and the Christian community. Also, this is a victory that is as much human as it is divine.[101]

Gunton suggests that Aulén may have been justified in speaking of the victory of Christ over evil powers. However, it appears that Aulén primarily and almost exclusively based his analysis on Colossians 2:15. Moreover, it is at this point where Gunton disagrees with Aulén. Gunton argues that the emphasis on victory should instead come from a broader New Testament passage and an Old Testament background to make a more convincing case. From a New Testament perspective, Gunton cites several passages of Christ's victory over evil forces, particularly in the Gospels and Revelation.[102]

---

100. Gunton, *Actuality of Atonement*, 57–59.
101. Gunton, 57.
102. Here Gunton refers to "the Johannine literature and especially the book of Revelation, where it is the lamb bearing the marks of slaughter – a clear reference to the crucified and risen Jesus – who is confessed by the elders who stand round the throne of God: 'the Lion of the tribe of Judah . . . has conquered . . .' (Rev 5.5f). The theme of victory is taken up later in that book, when the birth of the male child is interpreted by a description of a war in heaven in which Satan, in an echo of Luke 10:18 ('I saw Satan fall like lightning from heaven'), is thrown down

Also, Gunton believes that the demons conquered by Christ are not mythological creatures to be set aside but appropriate metaphors for both personal and extra-personal aspects of sin. He argues that from both the Old Testament and the New Testament, the texts about demons "present us not with superhuman hypostases trotting about the world, but with *the metaphorical characterisation of moral and cosmic realities which would otherwise defy expression.*"[103]

Gunton explains that recent studies have cast doubt upon the use and interpretation of the text in Colossians. 2:15 (NIV: "And having disarmed the powers and authorities, [Christ] made a public spectacle of them, triumphing over them by the cross") often used by theologians such as Aulén. Gunton cites Wesley Carr, who in his book, *Angels and principalities. The background, meaning and development of the Pauline phrase, 'hai archai kai hai exousiai'* argues that the interpretation of victory in this particular text does not come from the New Testament, but rather from Origen, a major advocate of the ransom theory.[104] According to Gunton, the imagery used has traditionally been understood as a Roman triumphal procession where "powers and authorities" are believed to be Christ's opponents. However, it may be conceivable that the powers and authorities are not Christ's opponents but the "hosts of heaven cheering him on his way."[105]

Gunton concludes that in the light of scripture, Aulén's position of a victorious Christ is correct in terms of it being a victory. However, he contends that the victory of Christ is a passive and not a positive action. In his view, the synoptic gospels do not describe the ministry of Jesus as a victory as such. However, they see it as part of a conflict between God's authority represented

---

from heaven to earth (Rev 12.7ff). Similarly, though without using military imagery, John's gospel depicts the progress of Jesus to the cross as a movement of victorious conquest, certainly if it is right to interpret 19.30 ('It is finished') in the light of 16.33 ('Be of good cheer, I have overcome the world') as a cry of triumph. It is from such a perspective that we may interpret the encounter with and defeat of evil that are so much a feature of the synoptic accounts of the ministry of Jesus. Whatever we make of the language of demons and demonic possession – and that will concern us later - it is clear that a kind of victory over forces which hold human life in bondage is being described. When Jesus speaks of a sick woman as a 'daughter of Abraham whom Satan bound for eighteen years' (Luke 13.16) it seems clear that he is depicting the enslavement of parts of the world to an evil which it is the calling of Jesus and his followers to destroy." See Gunton, *Actuality of Atonement*, 56.

103. Emphasis in the original. See Gunton, 66.
104. Gunton, 66.
105. Gunton, 55.

by Jesus and the forces that deny it. He further explains that Jesus' victory over temptation was passive, and its outcome was in both the "spiritual" and "physical" worlds. For Gunton, no absolute distinction can be drawn with what may be termed the cosmic as opposed to the moral dimensions of the world.[106]

b) Daniel Migliore

Daniel Migliore is an American and Professor Emeritus of Theology at Princeton Theological Seminary. He is an ordained Presbyterian minister and a member of the Presbytery of New Brunswick. Migliore is the author of many influential publications, including the widely used textbook *Faith Seeking Understanding: An Introduction to Christian Theology* which was first published in 1991.

In *Faith Seeking Understanding*, Migliore also describes the three theories of atonement. Migliore suggests that the *Christus Victor* theory helpfully emphasizes the reality and power of evil that enslaved humanity and stresses the costliness and assurance of God's victory over evil. However, he also refers to a particular weakness in the *Christus Victor* theory. In his view, the theory is particularly misleading if the imagery emphasized is taken literally. This, he argues, results in reducing the humanity of Jesus to nothing more than a disguise to fool the Devil. Consequently, humanity is reduced to mere spectators of a cosmic battle that takes place beyond their reach and influence. He believes this undermines humankind's awareness to take responsibility for their sinfulness.[107]

However, Migliore maintains that at least two "deep truths" should be highlighted when referring to the *Christus Victor* theory. First, God's victory for the sake of humanity was done not through violent retaliation but rather through the power of God's divine love. God achieved the liberation and reconciliation of the world not by employing coercion or brute force but by the foolish wisdom of the cross. Second, the image of God's method of salvation through deceptive means is misleading, especially when interpreted literally. The idea of God's deception of the Devil frequently occurs in interpreting this theory. The analogies of the fish and the mousetrap are

---

106. Gunton, 59.
107. Migliore, *Faith seeking understanding*, 152.

often used in this regard: the fish (the Devil) unsuspectedly swallows the bait (Christ) on the fishhook.

Moreover, the mouse (the Devil) is enticed into the trap by the bait (Christ). Christ is the bait through which the Devil is caught. For Migliore, as morally offensive as the idea that God uses deception in the work of salvation may be, what the analogies of this theory intend to convey is that God's hidden or "foolish" way of redeeming humanity is by far wiser and more powerful than that of the evil powers.[108]

c) Vincent Brümmer

Vincent Brümmer is a South African-born Reformed theologian who was a Philosophy of Religion Professor at the University of Utrecht and Dean of the Theological Faculty until 1988. From 1991 until his retirement in 1997, he was the founding director of the Netherlands School of Advanced Studies in Theology and Religion (NOSTER). Brümmer is the author of many influential publications, including the *Atonement, Christology and the Trinity: Making Sense of Christian Doctrine,* published in 2005.

In *Atonement, Christology and the Trinity*, Brümmer investigates the different theories of atonement. Here he focuses on the patristic theories of recapitulation, ransom, and sacrifice. In his view, the Church Fathers never understood salvation as personal reconciliation with God. Instead, for them, salvation meant "divinization." He refers to Athanasius, who believed that Christ, through the incarnation, entered humanity so that we might be made divine.[109]

The first patristic theory Brümmer discusses is the recapitulation theory, which he suggests was predicated on the Platonic logic and was subsequently embraced by the early Church Fathers. In Irenaeus' theology of recapitulation, salvation makes humanity partakers of the divine nature of Christ (2 Pet 1:4). This "divinization" is achieved by the incarnation of Christ, an act propelled by divine love. Brümmer affirms that, in the context of Platonic logic, the early Church Fathers saw humanity as one entity in which all individuals participated. The Pauline parallel between Adam and Christ is also

---

108. Migliore, *Faith seeking understanding*, 188.

109. Brümmer, *Atonement, Christology and the Trinity: Making Sense of Christian Doctrine* (Aldershot: Ashgate, 2005), 46.

understood within the Platonic context. Just as Adam's disobedience plunged humanity into sin, Christ's obedience (the second Adam) brings about a new redeemed humanity.

The second patristic theory Brümmer refers to is the ransom theory. This is based on the idea that atonement was done by God and not to God. The question among the Church Fathers that then arose was: to whom was the ransom paid if it was not God? On this point, Brümmer suggests that the "obvious" answer to this question, in this case, would be to the Devil. He further notes that the ransom theory develops a speculative mythology explaining God's victory over the Devil, in which humanity was freed from the Devil's power.

Furthermore, some rejected this speculative mythology, especially by Gregory, since the notion of God paying a ransom to the Devil seemed blasphemous. Even though the ransom theory was rejected, Brümmer observes two "intuitions" concerning the ransom theory. First, the ransom theory perceives sin as an "objective personalized power" that keeps humanity in bondage. Second, it is God alone who can save humanity from this bondage. Brümmer asserts that in the contemporary context, these "intuitions" go against the grain of the notion that the evil actions of humanity not only affect but are also the source of evil in the world, and also that God's saving action requires the participation of humankind.[110]

d) *Gregory Boyd*

Gregory Boyd is an American theologian, pastor and one of the leading figures of the growing Neo-Anabaptist movement. Boyd is known as one of the leading proponents of open theism and a noted Christian anarchist. For 16 years, he was a Professor of Theology at Bethel University before resigning from this position but is still affiliated with this institution. Boyd is the author of many books and influential publications, including the first chapter

---

110. Brümmer cites Sallie McFague when she observes that, "In an era when evil powers understood to be palpable in contest with God for control over human beings and the cosmos, the metaphor of Christ as the victorious king and lord, crushing the evil spirits and thereby freeing the world from their control, was indeed a powerful one. In our situation, however, to envision evil as separate from human beings rather than as the outcome of human decisions and actions, and to see the solution to evil as totally a divine responsibility, would not be only irrelevant to our time and its needs but harmful to them, for that would run counter to one of the central insights of the new sensibility: the need for human responsibility in the nuclear age." See Brümmer, *Atonement, Christology and the Trinity: Making Sense of Christian Doctrine*, 26.

in an edited volume entitled, *The Nature of Atonement,* published in 2006. In the "Christus Victor View," Boyd reflects on the *Christus Victor* theory of the atonement.

Boyd suggests that the *Christus Victor* view of atonement needs to be observed within the broader context of the spiritual warfare motif that runs through the scripture. Boyd notes that the spiritual warfare motif describes the biblical narrative of an ongoing cosmic battle between God and the forces of evil, bringing victory over the hostile powers and human agents who threaten God's creation. Other atonement theories, he suggests, say very little (or nothing) about the cosmic victory and focus mainly on humanity and sin. Boyd briefly overviews the Old Testament depiction of the cosmic battle. It is seen as God waging war against hostile waters and vicious sea monsters holding the world captive. The ancient Israelite worldview was based on the notion that the spiritual happenings in the spiritual realm would affect events of history and nature. Therefore, poverty, injustice and natural disasters that befall humanity are considered the works of "rebel gods." The mythological imagery of hostile waters, cosmic monsters, and rebel gods stems from the Ancient Near Eastern language.[111]

For Boyd, this cosmic language adequately communicates that the earth and creation exist "in a cosmic war zone" and that ancient Israel depended on God's continuous battle against the hostile forces to preserve Israel. Furthermore, the consciousness that the earth is a war zone between the forces of good and evil intensified among the Jews. This is particularly the case for the two centuries leading up to the birth of Christ. It was in this environment that Jesus came, having one mission: to destroy the Devil's hold on humanity. Everything Jesus was about was centred on overcoming this empire – taking back the world that the Devil had seized and restoring humanity to its position as guardian over the earth.[112]

For Boyd, the theme of Christ's victory over cosmic foes pervades the entire New Testament. Psalm 110, he observes, is the most frequently cited passage in the New Testament and is always used in various ways to express the truth that Christ is Lord because he has defeated God's enemies. Furthermore, in contrast to the other theories, the *Christus Victor* model is the only model

---

111. Boyd, "Christus Victor View," 45–46.
112. Boyd, 27.

that emphasizes the cosmic significance of Christ's victory. Therefore, for Boyd to fully understand and appreciate the soteriological importance of the cross, one needs to understand it in the context of the cosmic significance of Christ's victory. For this reason, Paul discussed the cosmic significance of Christ's work and how He defeated the hostile powers.[113]

Boyd believes that victory over evil powers brings about reconciliation between God and humanity. Humanity is reconciled because the "rebel powers" have been defeated; because of this, humanity can be presented as "holy and blameless unto God." This particular aspect highlights the cosmic significance of Christ's work. In this context, the *Christus Victor* theory is the only view that makes this point explicitly. Also, much like Irenaeus' theology of recapitulation, Boyd believes that the divine victory is continuous within the life of the Christian community. The Christian community's personal and social victories are joined in Christ's cosmic victory.[114]

2.4.2 Responses to the Latin View (Anselmian or Penal Substitutionary Theory)

a) Colin Gunton

Gunton describes the Anselmian theory as forensic because it explains the God-man's substitutionary sacrifice as satisfying the requirements for justice. It demonstrates that there can be no restoration of relationships unless the nature of human sinfulness and universal justice is addressed at its roots. For the advocates of this theory, on the one hand, only a divine being could pay this enormous debt of human sin. On the contrary, only a human being (though also divine) could do so.

One of the problems with the Anselmian theory, as Gunton observes, is the overstressing of Christ's humanity and underplaying the role of the Triune God in history. For Gunton, this view of the atonement is more dipolar rather than Trinitarian. Here Anselm's emphasis on God's power rather than God's love and the seeming equation of salvation with the remission of punishment are highlighted. For Gunton, the Anselmian theory fails to take the suffering

---

113. Boyd cites Paul in (Col 1:21–22) when he states: "And you, who (like the rebel powers) were once estranged and hostile (to God) in mind, doing evil deeds, He has now reconciled in His fleshly body through death, so as to present you holy and blameless and irreproachable before Him." See Boyd, "Christus Victor View," 33.

114. Boyd, "Christus Victor View," 33.

of the Trinitarian God seriously and reduces atonement to merely a removal of guilt rather than a renewal of life by transforming humanity. From this perspective, the atonement is reduced to a transaction which remains external to the personal lives of people.[115]

For Gunton, criticism could be added to the non-biblical foundation of Anselm's key term of satisfaction. In his view, Anselm's understanding of cosmic order was based on the feudal structure of the society in which he lived. In this sense, Anselm made the error of mistaking a particular social system for the order of the creation itself. The scandal of the cross thus becomes eclipsed by fitting Christ's death into a pre-existing theological schema. Moreover, Anselm faces more serious questions, such as: "How far is the theology of satisfaction viable in a world which has so different a conception of human freedom . . . In what sense may or must we conceive God as the one responsible for universal justice?"[116]

Gunton also highlights what he considers positive aspects of Anselm's conception. In this context, the question of sin, as Anselm emphasized, broadens our soteriological understanding. For Gunton, Anselm's God is not an egotistical dictator who punishes all offences against God's honour. In fact, sin harms the creature more than the Creator. However, sin has to be dealt with because it disrupts the order and beauty of the universe.

Gunton's reading of Anselm indicates that sin cannot harm God because God is the transcendent, impassable Creator. Sin, therefore, has to be understood in a more comprehensive way than a personal offence to God. Because God is impassable, God cannot be offended by sin. In this sense, Anselm contributed significantly in helping to develop the understanding that sin disrupting the order and beauty of the universe has repercussions on the whole of the cosmic reality. Thus, for Gunton, even though the thought process begins with a legal metaphor, the argument leads humanity to see that it is more than a legal matter but has to do with a life lived in the world as a whole.[117]

For Gunton, broadening the parameters of the concept of sin tells us more about the nature of salvation. Gunton states: "If sin is cosmic disorder, then salvation is the action of God as he takes responsibility for the whole context

---

115. Gunton, *Actuality of Atonement*, 91–92.
116. Gunton, 94.
117. Gunton, 96.

of our lives, setting us free to live in the universe he does not allow to go to ruin."[118] In this regard, Anselm, using the satisfaction metaphor, broadened the parameters far beyond the legal and moral domains. For Gunton, Anselm may concentrate more than many would wish on sin as offence and salvation as remission of penalty.

Gunton notes that the concept of justice, as conceived by Anselm, goes beyond the narrow interpretations of his thought that are often emphasized. The God of Anselm exercises responsibility for the good order of the universe, not through settling scores but by accepting the gift of infinite value offered by the God-man. In this sense, justice, as conceived by Anselm, is not essentially punitive or retributive. It also includes restoration. Gunton suggests that if one continues to conceive of atonement in forensic terms, it is essential to view it not only as a legal transaction but also as the transformation of a relationship. He further argues that the advocates of the Anselmian theory do not convincingly make this connection to a doctrine of penal substitution.[119]

b) Daniel Migliore

On the Anselmian theory, Migliore explains that Anselm's reflections on justice arise from medieval thought and presuppose the then-current understanding of the law, offence, reparations and social obligations. For Anselm, God and humans are related, like feudal lords and their serfs. Any act of disobedience dishonours the lord, and satisfaction must be given. In this case, the satisfaction due to God on account of human sinfulness is infinite. While humanity must provide this satisfaction, only God can provide it. God, therefore, becomes human in Christ and through his obedience unto death, satisfaction is rendered, and justice is done. The result is forgiveness for sinful humankind.[120]

As Migliore further explains, the trouble with Anselm's theory is that it seems to set God in contradiction to himself. Anselm draws from the juridical metaphors of the New Testament in a way that brings mercy and justice into collision. The Anselmian theory renders the act of forgiveness something of a problem for God. Here grace is made to be conditional on satisfaction.

---

118. Gunton, 96.
119. Gunton, 99.
120. Migliore, *Faith Seeking Understanding*, 152–153.

Migliore thus questions whether conditional grace is grace at all. In his view, in the New Testament, it is not God but humanity who needs to be reconciled. God is not so much the object as the subject of reconciliation in Christ.[121]

Also, the Anselmian theory does not adequately distinguish between a substitute and a representative. Here, Migliore employs the thoughts of Dorothee Sölle, who highlights the critical distinction between a substitute and a representative in the book Christ Our Representative (1967).[122] In his view, Sölle makes this point quite convincingly. The world of substitution is the impersonal world of replaceable things. A new part can be substituted when something wears out, like a machine part. However, representation belongs to the world of persons and personal relationships. For Sölle, the representative stands for humanity on a provisional basis but does not divest humanity of responsibility. Usually, the parent-child relationship works on a similar basis. The parent can represent their children until their maturity or until they can act and speak on their own behalf. In this context, the atoning work of Christ is more faithfully and understandably interpreted as an act of personal representation rather than a work of mechanical substitution.[123]

c) *Joel Green and Mark Baker*

Joel Green is an American theologian, and Associate Dean for the Center for Advanced Theological Studies and Professor of New Testament Interpretation at Fuller Theological Seminary in Pasadena, California. He is also an ordained elder of the United Methodist Church. He is a prolific author of a range of topics in theology. Mark Baker is an American theologian and Mennonite Missionary. He currently serves as an Associate Professor of Mission and Theology at Fresno Biblical Seminary in Fresno, California. Green is the author of numerous publications, including *Recovering the Scandal of The Cross: Atonement in New Testament and Contemporary Contexts* (2000), which he co-authored with Joel Green.

In *Recovering the Scandal of The Cross*, Green and Baker examine the strengths and weaknesses of Anselm's model of atonement. In their view,

---

121. Migliore, *Faith Seeking Understanding*, 153.

122. See Sölle, *Christ Our Representative*, as quoted in Migliore, *Faith Seeking Understanding*, 153.

123. Migliore, *Faith Seeking Understanding*, 153.

Anselm set out to present a logical model of atonement in which he explains the necessity of the death of Jesus on the cross. Anselm managed to achieve this by using imagery taken from the feudal system of his time. This is in contrast to the evidence presented in Paul's letters. Anselm, they argue, gives an interpretation of the cross which his contemporaries could easily understand. His experience of medieval life and culture is identified as the framework of this particular atonement model. This is also evident with examples such as "vassal" or "satisfaction," which according to Green and Baker, come not from biblical language but a medieval conception. Anselm's usage of certain images gives the cross and atonement a meaning very different from that found in the New Testament, for example.[124]

For Green and Baker, Anselm's emphasis on the debt of sin rather than removing sin is another issue that has its roots in medieval life and culture. They believe his view of sin is somewhat limited. They argue that it may be rational but falls short of the view of sin presented in biblical writings. Here the biblical concept of salvation focuses not so much on the debt of sin but on the removal thereof. Salvation is rooted in the removal of these sins and the reconciliation of humanity with God. The atonement work of Christ is rooted in the notion of freedom from indebtedness, which includes the New Testament conception of freedom from slavery, including the slavery to sin.[125]

Anselm's conception presents further problems. Green and Baker argue that since it is a model of atonement deeply rooted in his culture and the penance system, he promotes a distorted view of God's character. For Anselm, God assumes the guise of a Lord or King to which the payment of satisfaction has to be made. This distortion, they argue, leads to a character of God which is likened to a feudal lord. This also diminishes God's active role in reconciling humanity to Godself.

Another problem is Anselm's acceptance of the Greek understanding of an impassable deity. Green and Baker assert that this acceptance causes Anselm to separate Christ's divinity from His human suffering, resulting in Anselm not placing sufficient emphasis on Jesus being a representative of God to humanity. Anselm, they argue, keeps the human Jesus at arm's length from God, which contributes to a sense of division in the Trinity and limits the

---

124. Green and Baker, *Recovering the Scandal of the Cross*, 131.
125. Green and Baker, 133.

emphasis Anselm can place on Jesus serving as a representative of God to humanity. By basing his model of the atonement on the feudal system and Greek philosophy, Anselm repeatedly reinforces the image of God being an angry, distant and demanding God.[126] Here, Green and Baker employ the thoughts of Leonardo Boff in *Passion of Christ, Passion of the World: The Facts, Their Interpretation, and Their Meaning Yesterday and Today* (1987), when he observes that Anselm's God would bear little resemblance to the father of Jesus. Rather:

> He epitomizes the figure of an absolute feudal lord, the master with the power of life and death over his vassals. God is endowed with the traits of a cruel, bloodthirsty judge, bound and determined to exact the last farthing owed by any debtor in justice. A horrible cruelty prevailed in Saint Anselm's time regarding payment of debts. This sociological context is reflected in Anselm's theological text, unfortunately contributing to the development of an image of a cruel, sanguinary, vindictive God, an image still present in many tormented, enslaved Christian minds.[127]

For Green and Baker, Anselm seeks to grant understanding to the atonement theory by looking at it not from a biblical point of view but rather from within a legal and social context. This rootedness in culture and social context results in Anselm's theory of atonement having both strengths and weaknesses.

d) Vincent Brümmer

Brümmer interprets the satisfaction theory as a "theology of merit" on the basis that sinners have the opportunity to make satisfaction. The satisfaction required is to restore the balance of rights and duties between God and humanity. Since it is Christ who makes adequate satisfaction on behalf of humankind, restoring the imbalance between God and His creation, all credit goes to him and not humanity. Brümmer adds that salvation must still be earned by Christ rather than by humanity. In other words, *Soli Christo Gloria!*[128]

---

126. Green and Baker, 160.
127. See Boff, *Passion of Christ*, as quoted in Green and Baker, 160.
128. Brümmer, *Atonement, Christology and the Trinity*, 399.

Brümmer notes that Anselm places much emphasis on the condition of humankind and their failure to give honour to God, which constitutes a weight, a debt, a doom upon them. In light of this notion, the satisfaction theory in today's context appears immoral since it asserts that God punishes the "innocent" on behalf of those guilty of sin. Brümmer affirms that the only way to understand this teaching and make moral sense of it is to view it through the eyes of a feudal concept of honour. Christ is, therefore, the only perfect human who could make the required satisfaction in order to satisfy God's honour. For Brümmer, such feudal honour may have been well understood in the twelfth century, but it goes against modern-day thinking to view Christ as a feudal lord who demands honour.[129]

Brümmer believes that in the light of human relationships and love, the theory of penal substitution will go against the understanding of what may be considered modern-day thinking. In his view, many human relationships today are based on each person striving to know and serve the genuine interest of the other. By serving the other's interest as their own, people display a love for the other, which they have for themselves. This love relationship differs from business relationships in which people accept certain rights and obligations from each other. One renders a service, and the other pays for it. The relationship and value are based merely on the service rendered. Brümmer considers the feudal concept of honour to be like this. God's honour needs to be satisfied. "If this is the type of relationship we have with God," says Brümmer, "then it means that we do not love God for Himself alone, but merely as a provider of eternal happiness. In turn, this means that God values our service more than God values us."[130] Therefore, according to Brümmer, it would not matter to God whether it was humanity or Christ in their place who provided the satisfaction as long as God's honour was satisfied. Also, love cannot be earned or coerced. Modern-day thinking accepts a God who loves people for who they are and not for what they render unto Him. This notion goes against the teaching of penal substitution. The value of humanity is based on the love of God and not on the service they render to God.

Brümmer identifies another problem with penal substitution: the view that the "divine-human relationship" is insufficient for divine forgiveness.

---

129. Brümmer, 400.
130. Brümmer, 401.

According to penal substitution, the forgiveness of sin is seen as treating sin lightly. Similarly, as in the case of damaged human fellowship, the necessary and sufficient conditions for reconciliation with God are not punishment or satisfaction or condemnation but repentance and forgiveness.[131]

On the issue of God's justice, Brümmer considers penal substitution as satisfying the demands of retributive justice rather than restorative justice. He argues that since sin causes estrangement between God and humanity, retributive justice only removes the guilt of sin. It fails to restore and reconcile humanity with God. Therefore, in his view, this theory is not a theory of atonement "in the sense of at-one-ment."[132]

2.4.3 Responses to the Subjective View (Moral Influence Theory)

a) Colin Gunton

For Gunton, the subjective view of the atonement is theologically associated with Abelard and philosophically with Kant.[133] He contends that this view characterizes the attempts of rationalism to reduce Christ to a perfect role model. Christ is the ultimate example of genuine human life in a fallen world. This view of atonement depicts redemption as an achievement human beings can reach themselves. Gunton argues that Abelard sought a more humane idea of atonement and rejected Anselm's doctrine of penal substitution that proposed a notion of retributive punishment.[134]

However, the New Testament indicates why the subjective view is inadequate for Gunton. First, it takes the biblical message about Christ out of context. This theory tends to emphasize the human character of Christ without taking proper cognizance of his divine nature. The imitation aspect emphasized by Abelard may be more apparent in terms of Christ's human character but hangs in the air with regard to the divine.

Gunton's second critique is implied in the first. Here he argues that Christ is an example because he and he alone is the incarnate Son who, by the enabling of the Holy Spirit, remained unfallen, whereas humanity is flawed in

---

131. Brümmer, 400.
132. Brümmer, 401–403.
133. This view of atonement fits well with Kant's idea of Jesus as the moral ideal and our duty as human beings to elevate ourselves to this ideal of moral perfection.
134. Gunton, *Actuality of Atonement*, 156–7.

their sinfulness. Christ's humanity is only what it is because it is that of the one sent by the Father through the Holy Spirit. "As the only human victory, the life of the one just man, the only true offering of free obedience to the Father, *this particular* humanity is what it is because it is his who is sent by the Father to save lost [humankind]," Gunton observes that there is no treatment of the person of Christ in the New Testament which does not place it in the context of its end in the redemption of the creation, the reconciliation of all things in Christ.[135]

Third, for Gunton, the subjective view is the only model that does not make the death and resurrection of Christ the pivot of events in which the reconciling action takes place. The fact that the ministry and mission of Christ led to his death dominates the Christian narrative in most of its forms. This is the case to such an extent that no treatment of Christian theology of salvation which wishes to be faithful to scripture, is possible apart from it. Here Gunton insists that the death of Christ is, first of all, to be understood as part of the divine purpose of redemption. All other things associated with Christ depend on the divine purpose of redemption. This would include the fact of him becoming human.[136]

b) Daniel Migliore

For Migliore, the subjective view contrasts the other two theories. In the subjective type, God reconciles humanity not by some cosmic battle nor by some legal transaction but by showing God's love to humanity in such a compelling way that they are constrained to respond in wonder and gratitude. Migliore mentions that the strength of the moral influence theory lies in emphasizing the unconditionality of God's love and highlighting the importance of the human response. He further mentions that while attending to the subjective side of atonement, this theory might be developed to recognize "the objective power of the revelation of God's sacrificial love that shines into our sin-darkened world."[137]

Migliore also warns of the serious weaknesses of the moral influence theory. The most important is what he calls the tendency of the proponents of

---

135. Gunton, 158.
136. Gunton, 158–159.
137. Migliore, *Faith Seeking Understanding*, 154.

this view to sentimentalize God's love while simultaneously underestimating the power and tenacity of evil in the world. This is highlighted in its emphasis on merely following Christ's good example without taking the nature of evil and human sinfulness seriously. Gunton employs the work of H. R. Niebuhr in his book *The Kingdom of God in America* (1959), Richard Niebuhr highlights this point. Niebuhr refers to the subjective type of atonement as falling victim to a naïve form of liberal theology in his country: "A God without wrath brought people without sin into a kingdom without judgment through the ministrations of a Christ without a cross."[138]

c) *Waldron B. Scott*

Waldron B. Scott is an American theologian who formerly served as General Secretary of the World Evangelical Alliance. Scott is the author of numerous publications, including *What about the Cross: Exploring Models of the Atonement*, published in 2007.

Scott suggests that the very subjectiveness of this moral influence theory appeals to the modern mind. In his view, the classic and satisfaction models acknowledge the love of God as motivating the atoning act. Abelard goes much further in noting that God's love does not merely motivate the atonement but is the atonement. God's love is what brings the alienated parties together and keeps them together. Also, through God's love, true liberty is achieved through the unique gift of grace to humanity. For Abelard, it is Christ's life and death that inspires humanity's love in a way that God is no longer served out of fear. Abelard's conception thus encompasses justification and sanctification and, by implication, ultimate glorification.[139]

Scott also identifies some problems with Abelard's approach. Here he highlights the view that Abelard does not deal adequately with the holiness of God and the issue of sin. In this model, God does not appear to hold human beings accountable for sin. Here it is believed that original sin has such effects on the human character that humanity cannot respond adequately to the appeals of Christ's example, no matter how powerful it may be. Scott does, however, warn that it is not Christ's inspirational example that atones but God's active love, which is embodied in the incarnate Word. In his view,

---

138. See Niebuhr, *Kingdom of God*, as quoted in Migliore, *Faith Seeking Understanding*, 154.
139. Scott, *What about the Cross?*, 89.

God's love graciously overpowers the effects of original sin, thus awakening the potential of humanity to change accordingly.

In highlighting another shortcoming, Scott employs the work of J. Denny Weaver in *The Non-Violent Atonement* (2001), arguing that the moral influence theory features no change in the order of things until individual sinners perceive the loving death and respond positively to God. According to Weaver, the balance of power between good and evil in the universe has been decisively changed by the atonement and validated by the resurrection of Christ, whether or not acknowledged by sinful humanity. Scott suggests that scholars like Weaver believe that Abelard's emphasis on inward subjective change is prioritized at the expense of an objective change in the cosmic order.[140]

2.5 Closing Reflections

The theories of atonement all carry strengths and weaknesses. As I have already mentioned, it is not my intention to critique or offer my evaluation of these theories. The aim is to give an overview of the analysis of these main atonement theories as Aulén and others understand them. The review is intended primarily as a soteriological map to engage with at least three different ways Christ's work of atonement may be understood and its implications for the discourse on reconciliation in South Africa. So, while the review of Aulén's work is directly related to reconciliation in Christ, I now appropriate this typology in order to make them more fruitful for reconciliation from a pneumatological perspective. This applies less to reconciliation in Christ and more to the implications of Christ's atoning work for the ministry of reconciliation in South Africa. In other words, this overview served as a map for the construction of my hypothesis, in which I will now identify at least three distinct discourses on how reconciliation is understood in the theological discourse in South Africa.

---

140. See Weaver, *Non-violent Atonement*, as quoted in Scott, *What about the Cross?*, 90.

CHAPTER 3

Justice through Reconciliation in Jesus Christ

3.1 Introduction

This chapter describes and analyses a particular way reconciliation has been understood in South African discourse, namely, based on an Anselmian, Lutheran, and Calvinist notion that the reconciliation of humanity with God in Jesus Christ implies a ministry of reconciliation. In this approach, it is assumed that the reconciliation of humankind with God in Jesus Christ entails a ministry of reconciliation in a country divided by race, class, and culture and that this necessitates a concern for social justice and, therefore, restitution. This is evident in the *Message to the People of South Africa* (1968), the *Belhar Confession* (1982/86) and the statement of the *National Initiative for Reconciliation* (1985). Rhetorically, this was aimed at apartheid theology and its assumptions about the fundamental irreconcilability of people.

This chapter has three main sections. The *Message to the People of South Africa* in 3.2, the *Belhar Confession* in 3.3, followed by the statement of affirmation for the *National Initiative for Reconciliation* in 3.4. The description and analysis will be done on the basis of the literature that emerged as a result of these initiatives.

3.2 The Message to the People of South Africa (1968)

This section entails a brief survey of literature emerging from the publication of the *Message to the People of South Africa*. Of course, the *Message to the People of South Africa* cannot be understood apart from the events leading to it, which will be addressed in summary form.

3.2.1 Cottesloe

"Apartheid" was the electoral slogan which brought radical Afrikaner nationalism to power in South Africa in 1948.[1] This year also marks the beginning of a legislated policy of racial segregation, known as "apartheid," a policy promoted by the ruling National Party after their stunning election victory.[2] While 1948 marks the beginning of the apartheid era, the history of racial discrimination reaches back to the start of the colonial period.[3] At least until 1960, much of the discriminatory practices applied by the apartheid government were mirrored by the country's institutions, including the Christian churches.

However, 1960 also marks the beginning of what Saul Dubow calls "seismic upheaval in South Africa." It started with the death of 437 men (all but six were black) in a pit collapse at Coalbrook coal mine south of Johannesburg on 21 January. The cause of the accident is linked to engineering negligence brought about by the reckless pursuit of profit. On 21 March, police fired more than 1,000 rounds of ammunition at a crowd of black protesters in what became the infamous Sharpeville massacre. In the end, 69 protestors were shot and killed, and as many as 180 people were wounded. Many of them were shot while running away. In contrast to the Coalbrook disaster, the Sharpeville massacre resonated as an iconic symbol of cruelty and popular resistance against the apartheid government.[4]

---

1. The "apartheid" concept first emerged in the context discussions by Dutch Reformed Church missionaries in the 1930s, only gaining wider political currency in the 1940s. The word literally translates as "apartness" or "separateness."

2. Dubow, *Apartheid: 1948–1994*, 1.

3. Hendriksson, *Journey with a Status*, 28–33.

4. Sharpeville, together with the fatal shooting of protestors in Langa, a black township in the Cape, represents a watershed moment in the anti-apartheid resistance movement. Together with those killed and injured in Sharpeville, in Langa two protestors were killed and as many as 49 were injured. See Dubow, 74, 82.

The intensification of protest action resulting from Sharpeville prompted the Nationalist government to declare a state of emergency on 30 March 1960. This gave the security forces significant powers to arrest and detain. Parliament voted in favour of banning anti-apartheid organizations like the African National Congress (ANC) and the Pan-Africanist Congress (PAC), citing their alleged revolutionary objectives. By the month of May, more than 2000 political leaders and activists were arrested, including notable figures like Albert Luthuli (ANC) and Robert Sobukwe (PAC), who were taken into custody under emergency regulations.[5]

Hans Engdahl suggests:

> In addition to a viable opposition holding their moral high ground, the Sharpeville massacre had made the world pay attention to South Africa and her policies. The global impact of media was becoming a reality now, other political leaders worldwide and the United Nations took note and acted, as did also the churches especially through the World Council of Churches (WCC). Finally, the wind of change had reached also the southern tip of Africa, with nation states in Africa already starting to set dates for their independence. The absurdity of the system of apartheid was there for all to see.[6]

Formal talks between the WCC and its South African member churches occurred after Sharpeville in 1960. At this time, the WCC General Assembly at Evanston in 1954 had already passed a resolution on race relations, which undoubtedly had a bearing on the unfolding racial policies in South Africa. Among other things, the resolution at Evanston stated: "that any form of segregation based on race, colour or ethnic origin is contrary to the Gospel and is incompatible with the Christian doctrine of man and with the nature of the Church of Christ."[7] Amidst the tension, the WCC General Secretary, Willem A. Visser't Hooft, sent a personal representative to South Africa to plan and facilitate a fellowship mission. What was envisioned was a consultation, if possible, with the eight-member churches and the WCC representatives.

---

5. Dubow, 81

6. Engdahl, *Theology in Conflict*, 36–37.

7. Report on the World Council of Churches Mission in South Africa April – December 1960. Geneva, April 1961, 10, quoted in Engdahl, *Theology in Conflict*, 38.

This was made all the more significant given the accusations that the white Dutch Reformed churches, the Nederduitse Gereformeerde Kerk (NGK) and the Nederduitsch Hervormde Kerk (NHK), were in cahoots with the apartheid government.[8] The WCC-sponsored consultation took place in the Johannesburg suburb of Cottesloe in December 1960. This meeting became known as the landmark Cottesloe Consultation. However, the Anglican Archbishop of Cape Town, Joost de Blank, almost jeopardized the initiative by sending a letter to the WCC demanding a clear word from the white Dutch Reformed churches regarding apartheid. De Blank demanded: "Unless the Dutch Reformed Churches are prepared to forsake their support for apartheid and to condemn the government for its ruthless action, [they] can no longer remain as fellow members of the World Council of Churches with them. Either they must be expelled or [the Anglicans] shall be compelled to withdraw."[9] The WCC representative, Robert Bilheimer, was utterly dissatisfied with the Anglican response in his report back to the World Council.[10] In the end, the consultation did take place, comprising 80 delegates from the eight South African WCC member churches. This included the Bantu Presbyterian Church, the Presbyterian Church, the Anglican Church, the Congregational Union, the Methodist Church, the NGK Transvaal Synod, the NGK Cape Synod and the NHK. Not including the six WCC representatives, 86 participants plus an observer. Peter Walshe critically observes that,

---

8. Since the inception of apartheid, the policy of "separate development" drew support from the white Dutch Reformed churches. At a church conference in Bloemfontein in 1950, the NGK resolved that "total separation" and "separate economic development" could only be achieved by the "gradual movement toward territorial separation between whites and the Bantu." In an effort to mobilize support for the separate development of black nations, the NGK convened a series of conferences during 1951 and 1952. In keeping with the National Party government's policy of "retribalization," the NGK invited representatives to separate "ethnic" conferences. A conference for the "Sotho" was held in 1951, one for "Xhosa" in 1952 and another for "Zulu" in the same year. Since separate development required the creation of new ethnic and national identities, the NGK represented early experiments in the building of black ethnic nationalisms. See Chidester, *Religions of South Africa*, 202.

9. Correspondence Visser't Hooft: De Blank – SA Bishops, 9.4. 1960, 8, quoted in Engdahl, *Theology in Conflict*, 38.

10. Bilheimer reported that, "The Anglican Church, to put it very bluntly, needs a big reform of attitude at the above point (apartheid issue), and in regard to their attitude to the [Dutch Reformed Church]. They speak and act as the Church, not only on theological grounds, but on historical-cultural grounds. They do not try to consult with the [NGK], and are too greatly isolated from them." Billheimer Collection: "Confidential Report from Bilheimer," quoted in Engdahl, *Theology in Conflict*, 38.

although the consultation was ecumenical and multiracial, only 17 out of the 80 delegates were black. In his view, it was essentially a white affair where "a group of anguished white clerics [set] out to listen to each other and to pay polite attention to the small minority of their black colleagues."[11]

Elfriede Strassberger observes that the consultation reflected a clear division between English-speaking and Afrikaans-speaking churches.[12] For example, the English-speaking churches showed apartheid to be unacceptable, whereas the Afrikaans-speaking churches showed an implicit acceptance of apartheid if it was implemented fairly.[13] In this sense, Afrikaans-speaking churches supported the principle that each racial group should maintain its separate path to the future. They warned, however, that this should not be confused with the damaging practice of discrimination. On the other hand, the English-speaking churches were opposed to the idea and opted instead for a multiracial future within one shared state.[14]

Despite some disagreements, the consultation outcome was surprisingly positive, and a high level of consensus was reached. Except for the more conservative NHK who rejected the resolutions, the Transvaal and the Cape Synods of the NGK signed the final resolution with minor reservations.[15] In fact, most of the Cottesloe resolutions were memoranda prepared by the Cape Synod of the NGK.[16] The resolutions were not far-reaching but were quite radical from an Afrikaner perspective. At the end of the consultation,

---

11. Walshe, *Church Versus State*, 36.

12. De Gruchy observes that the designations, "English-speaking" or "Afrikaans-speaking" churches is "somewhat clumsy and untheological." However, in exploring the churches' response to apartheid it seems, as he puts it, "impossible to avoid the phrase or find a satisfactory alternative." Suffice to say that these phrases do not refer in any primary sense to some common doctrinal or liturgical commitment and practice, nor does it include all those churches in the country who use English or Afrikaans as their main language of communication and worship. These terms were devised not by the churches themselves but by the mass media, politicians, other churches, and by the general populace in order to make the distinction among those who opposed or supported apartheid. For example, the English-speaking churches were known to oppose the racial policy of the Nationalist government, whereas the Afrikaans-speaking churches were known to support these policies. See De Gruchy and De Gruchy, *The Church Struggle*, 84.

13. Strassberger, *Ecumenism in South Africa*, 222–227.

14. Walshe, *Church versus State*, 12

15. Matters of concern were: mixed marriages, migrant labour and job reservation, the right to own land, the right of collaboration in the government of the country and direct representation of Coloured people in Parliament. See Lückhoff, *Cottesloe*, 58–63.

16. Vosloo, "Christianity and Apartheid," in: Bongmba, *Routledge Companion*, 411.

the resolutions (in the form of a statement) in which many of the basic principles of apartheid were rejected were made public.[17] David Chidester adds, "although its condemnation of racism would later appear fairly moderate, the Cottesloe resolutions marked a departure from apartheid theology for the delegates of the [NGK]."[18] However, soon after the meeting was concluded, the Prime Minister of South Africa, Hendrik Verwoerd, referred to the Cottesloe Statement in his 1961 New Year's message, in which he rejected and downplayed its significance. Verwoerd stressed that the NGK, the Transvaal, and Cape Synods, in particular, were yet to respond to Cottesloe. In his view, the NGK delegations that supported Cottesloe did not have the authority to do so, and it was only with the approval of their respective constituencies that they could support the consensus reached at Cottesloe.[19] He further called on the churches to get rid of the "betrayers" and distance themselves from those who did not repudiate the consultation. In concert with the government, apartheid theologians ensured that the NGK Synods formally rejected the Cottesloe Statement.[20] The NGK delegates who supported Cottesloe were severely reprimanded; some were even stripped of their synodical responsibilities. Thus, what could have been a breakthrough, the beginning of a process of moving away from apartheid, resulted in the white Dutch Reformed churches separating themselves from the wider ecumenical community in South Africa. This was also the case when the NGK and the NHK withdrew their membership from the WCC in 1961. This self-imposed ecumenical isolation lasted for more than three decades.

Regardless of its outcome, Cottesloe marks the beginning of an important shift in church relations in South Africa. For De Gruchy, this signals the beginning of the period commonly referred to as the "church struggle" in South Africa. At the heart of this struggle "is a theology of reconciliation that fundamentally challenged both the politics and theology of racial separation. God's will, as expressed in the gospel of Jesus Christ, was not apartheid but the reconciliation of the people of the country into one nation."[21] Cottesloe's

---

17. For a detailed description and evaluation of the document, see Van der Borght, "Unity that Sanctifies," 318–320.
18. Chidester, *Religions of South Africa*, 202.
19. Dubow, *Apartheid*, 82.
20. Chidester, *Religions of South Africa*, 202.
21. De Gruchy, *The Church Struggle*, 33.

final statement was by no means a radical document. However, it was entirely different from anything that had come from the churches before 1960, mainly because it challenged the fundamental basis of apartheid in a new way. Johann Kinghorn's discussion on the significance of Cottesloe is helpful here. Kinghorn mentions that, although the consultation did not plead the course of general integration, its resolutions conflicted with Prime Minister Verwoerd's policy of total, territorial separation of "nations" in South Africa. In this sense, it was quite different from the anti-modern discourse that characterized statements of Afrikaner leaders of that era. As if Cottesloe's resolutions were not bad enough for the ruling establishment, what made matters worse was that most of the resolutions in the final statement originated from the NGK Cape Synod.[22]

Eddy Van der Borght mentions that in the Cottesloe resolutions, "justice," for the first time, became the hermeneutical key to evaluating apartheid policies.[23] The insistence on justice is based on apartheid's racial separation and associated discrimination. From a theological perspective, justice, on the basis of reconciliation in Jesus Christ, became crucial in assessing the situation. Concerning De Gruchy's assessment of the beginning of the "church struggle," Cottesloe is characterized by the belief that "God's will, as expressed in the gospel of Jesus Christ, was not apartheid but the reconciliation of the peoples of South Africa in one nation."[24] This is mentioned in Cottesloe's two references to reconciliation – first, in terms of reconciliation between the churches and second, the call to the ministry of reconciliation in Jesus Christ. However, these ideas are not further developed theologically. It is only in the *Message to the People of South Africa* a few years later where more attention was given to the reconciliation concept.

3.2.2 Cottesloe in Perspective

The post-Cottesloe environment proved to be hostile for some of the NGK delegates. Some were ostracized for being "betrayers" of the church and the Afrikaner community. In this context, the WCC encouraged members of the NGK to start ecumenical study groups. One NGK leader, who

---

22. Kinghorn, "Modernization and Apartheid," 148–151.
23. Van der Borght, 318.
24. De Gruchy, *Reconciliation*, 33.

continued supporting the Cottesloe resolutions, was the acting moderator of the Transvaal Synod, Beyers Naudé. Chidester mentions that "as son of a founding member of the Broederbond [a secret, exclusively male Afrikaner Calvinist organization, dedicated to the advancement of Afrikaner interests], Naudé had impeccable Afrikaner nationalist credentials. After 1960, however, Naudé resigned from the Broederbond [and] denounced the theology of apartheid."[25] After Cottesloe, Naudé and a group of sympathizers started a campaign to promote the Cottesloe resolutions. This was done by organizing Bible study groups and producing a monthly journal called *Pro Veritate* (For the Truth). *Pro Veritate* first appeared in May 1962, with Naudé as its editor. From its very first issue, the journal was instrumental in challenging the theological basis of apartheid. The aim was to debunk the "biblical justification of apartheid by citing biblical texts which emphasized the unity of the Christian Church."[26]

One year later, in December 1963, under the leadership of Naudé, a multiracial-interdenominational institute called the Christian Institute of South Africa (Christian Institute) was established. Drawing their inspiration from the German church struggle and the witness against Hitler and Nazism of figures such as Martin Niemöller and Dietrich Bonhoeffer, and documents such as the Barmen Declaration of 1934, the establishment of the Christian Institute was aimed at creating a confessing movement, with Beyers Naudé writing several articles along these lines in *Pro Veritate*.[27] Moreover, it tried to counter apartheid racial separation by promoting "one-ness" in church and society.[28] Initially, its core function was to foster dialogue between the English and Afrikaans-speaking churches and advocate for justice and reconciliation in society. Heeding the call of the WCC, the aim was to "search for a deeper insight into the will of Christ for his church through study circles and discussion groups and to strengthen the witness of the church by holding courses and conferences."[29] Moreover, as Daryl Balia puts it, "to equip Christians for a life of doing, a life committed to reconciliation and to

---

25. Chidester, *Religions of South Africa*, 202–203.
26. Ryan, *Beyers Naudé – Pilgrimage*, 68–70.
27. Vosloo, "Christianity and Apartheid in South Africa," 412.
28. Chidester, *Religions of South Africa*, 203.
29. Ryan, *Beyers Naudé*, 77.

witnessing more clearly to the Kingdom of God in South Africa." For Naudé and others, "the spirit of Cottesloe" was undoubtedly a motivating hope in the formation and work of the Christian Institute.[30] The NGK responded by removing Naudé from his role as a minister, but he continued to pursue an alternative ministry through various study projects, conferences, and publications of the Christian Institute.[31]

The Christian Institute worked closely with the Christian Council of South Africa (Christian Council).[32] Formed in 1936, the Christian Council was a Protestant ecumenical body for inter-church cooperation, and it was set up mainly as a means for ecumenical coordination in South Africa. Their membership also included the Roman Catholic Church – after Vatican II (1962–1965), the Roman Catholic Church was brought into much more direct contact with other churches, including the Christian Council. As the political situation deteriorated in the country, the Christian Council found itself increasingly having to mediate the tensions between the South African churches. This continued in the aftermath of Cottesloe. Without a credible political opposition, the partnership between the Christian Institute and the Christian Council became increasingly important. In fact, given the political vacuum left by banning the liberation organizations, these organizations were beginning to function more like a movement of opposition against the apartheid state.[33] Moreover, through their combined efforts, the Christian Institute and the Christian Council (renamed the South African Council of Churches in 1968) became the instruments for prophetic leadership in South Africa.[34]

The WCC-sponsored Geneva Conference on Church and Society in 1966 proved vital for the Christian Institute and the South African Council of Churches (SACC). The meeting was unique in the history of the ecumenical

---

30. Balia, *Christian Resistance to Apartheid*, 21.

31. After years of intimidation by the security police the Christian Institute was banned in 1977. Many of its staff were arrested or fled into exile. Naudé was banned, forbidden by government to write, publish or be in the presence of more than one person at a time. See Chidester, *Religions of South Africa*, 203.

32. By the time the plans for Cottesloe were underway the Christian Council was a relatively ineffective organization. This continued in the aftermath of Cottesloe. The Christian Council changed its name to the South African Council of Churches in 1968.

33. De Gruchy, *A Theological Odyssey: My Life in Writing* (Stellenbosch: Sun Media, 2014), 21–22.

34. De Gruchy, *The Church Struggle*, 113–115.

movement. Not only did it set the agenda for considerable theological debate and social action for the WCC, but it also detailed a response to the problem of racism and oppression worldwide.[35] The conference highlighted the need for the churches to encourage the legitimate aspirations of suppressed majorities and minorities and to "support all practicable measures aimed at changing any political and economic order which reflects the denial of political rights or economic opportunity, segregation, discrimination, or other suppression."[36] This conference was significant for the South African delegation. Among them, the director of the Christian Institute, Naudé and the General Secretary of the Christian Council, Bill Burnett, returned challenged by the urgent necessity for the churches to strive for the scriptural demand of social justice and peace. On their return, they facilitated regional conferences in Durban, Port Elizabeth, and Cape Town to consider the recommendations of the Geneva Conference. This led to the National Consultation on Church and Society held in Johannesburg in February 1968.

The National Consultation on Church and Society presented Christian activists with the leaders of the Christian Institute and the SACC with an opportunity to articulate an alternative to what was happening in South Africa. Walshe posits that the hope was that this would be the first "halting attempt to outline an alternative to apartheid – a comprehensive Christian social ethic."[37] An appointed ecumenical committee was tasked to create a theological critique of apartheid. The objective was to create a document that would be irrefutable on biblical grounds and serve as a basis for further study and action. The result was a document entitled the *Message to the People of South Africa (The Message)*.[38] It was issued jointly by the Christian Institute and the SACC. De Gruchy mentions that *The Message* was prepared by people representing various theological positions. He further states,

---

35. The Geneva Conference confronted the churches with the reality of millions of oppressed people, particularly those in the so-called "Third World," with a call for justice. It was at Geneva that the question regarding Christian participation in the revolutionary struggles was first raised. This was the first time that this issue was raised at a high-level meeting of the Christian church. It was here where the controversial WCC Programme to Combat Racism of 1970 (discussed in the following chapter) was first envisioned.

36. World Conference on Church and Society, Official Report. 137.

37. Walshe, *Church Versus State*, 58.

38. Theological Commission of the South African Council of Churches, *A Message to the People of South Africa*, January 1969. [Online]. Available: https://onlinelibrary.wiley.com/doi/10.1111/j.1758-6623.1969.tb02249.x. [Accessed: May 23, 2024].

the two dominant theological approaches which influenced *The Message* were Anglican social thought and that of the Dutch theologian A. A. van Ruler, an interesting if a somewhat unlikely blend of two distinct traditions. These traditions found considerable commonality in seeking to relate the gospel to apartheid. What bound the drafters of *The Message* together was not only a common ideological and political enemy but a Christology which stressed our common humanity in both son and redemption, a Christology which confessed the reconciling power of the cross and implications for society.[39]

3.2.3 *The Message to the People of South Africa*: An Overview

In *The Message*, like Cottesloe, justice is the hermeneutical key through which apartheid policies are evaluated.[40] However, *The Message* goes further than Cottesloe by not only identifying apartheid as a social problem but defining it as a false faith, a novel gospel that is built on a theory of racial separation.[41] Using a theology of reconciliation as a starting point, the authors build an argument on the belief that, in Christ, God has reconciled the world to himself and therefore made reconciliation between people both possible and essential to the Christian faith.

The document itself consists of five sections. The first, entitled "What the Christian Gospel says," draws out the implications of the atoning work of Christ in terms of South African society. It suggests that in Christ, "God has broken down the walls that divide God and humanity and, therefore, that which divides human beings."[42] It further maintains that Christ is the truth that sets humanity free from all false hopes of grasping freedom for themselves and liberates humanity from pursuing false securities. It further states that the resurrection followed the crucifixion of Christ. With this, it is implied that God's purpose shapes history, giving rise to the expectation of a

---

39. De Gruchy, "From Cottesloe to the," Paper presented at the Annual Meeting of the Theological Society of Southern Africa held at the University of Port Elizabeth, 29–31 August 1990, In: Loots, *Listening to South African*, 8.

40. *The Message*, Available: https://onlinelibrary.wiley.com/doi/10.1111/j.1758-6623.1969.tb02249.x

41. *The Message*, Section 2: Our Concern.

42. *The Message*, Section 1: What the Christian Gospel Says:

new heaven and a new earth in which righteousness dwells. This, it maintains, is manifested in the kingdom of God that is presented in Christ's atoning work and realized at present through the Holy Spirit.

The second section, entitled "Our Concern," insists that salvation in Christ offers hope and security for all areas of human life. This is to be understood in the context of the individual person or in a sacramental and ecclesiastical sense within the church context.[43] However, salvation in "Christ is to be understood in a cultural, social (and therefore political), cosmic and universal sense."[44] It further posits that the Gospel of Christ should not be reduced to an object of hope for the future only, but rather that it should be experienced as a reality in the present. Christians are therefore called to be witnesses to the significance of the gospel in the particular circumstances of the time and place in which they find themselves. On the basis of salvation in Christ, *The Message* proceeds to the South African situation in what it calls the situation where a policy of racial separation is being deliberately imposed with increased rigidity. In the light of the salvation to be found in Christ alone, it labels the "doctrine of racial separation" as "truly hostile to Christianity." It suggests that such a doctrine of racial separation is based not on Christ but on a "false offer of salvation."[45]

Furthermore, this false offer of salvation is based on the notion that the separate development of race groups is a way for the people of South Africa to save themselves. Because it is based on a false offer of salvation, *The Message* labels apartheid a "false faith" – it claims to be offering peace and happiness through "the preservation of racial identity" in the name of Christianity. *The Message* concludes that the hardship derived from implementing the doctrine of racial separation "can serve only to keep people away from the real knowledge of Christ."[46] For this reason, it is believed that the church has a duty to enable people to discriminate more carefully between what may be demanded of them as subjects or citizens of the state of South Africa and what is demanded of them as disciples of Jesus Christ.

---

43. The Message, Section 2: Our Concern.
44. The Message, Section 2: Our Concern.
45. The Message, Section 2: Our Concern.
46. The Message, Section 2: Our Concern.

The third section, entitled "The Gospel's claim," reaffirms the conviction that "The Christian Gospel declares that there is no other name than that of Christ whereby humanity must be saved."[47] It also highlights the belief that salvation in Christ exposes the falsity of hope of salvation through any other means. It notes that first Christians, Jews, and Gentiles alike "discovered that God was creating a new community in which differences of race, nation, culture, language and tradition no longer had the power to separate human beings." It thus stresses that Christians "are under obligation to assert this claim and live by it." It furthermore postulates that Christians "are under an obligation to assert that the most significant features of a human being are not the details of his genetic inheritance, nor the facts of his ancestry but the characteristics that make him a disciple of Christ." It further maintains that an (over)emphasis on racial identity denies the Gospel. In other words, it is in opposition to "the Christian understanding of the nature of human being and community." This, therefore, puts an arbitrary limit on a person's ability, "to obey the Gospel's command to love its neighbour as itself."[48]

The Message attributes the demand for racial separation to human sin. It argues that any scheme proposed for rectifying human disorders must take account of this essentially sinful element in the divisions between people and between groups of people. Furthermore, any scheme which claims to be Christian must also take account of the reconciliation already made for humanity in Christ.[49] It thus concludes that the doctrine of racial separation does not take the gospel truth manifested in Christ seriously. It further states that the doctrine of racial separation promises peace and harmony between the people of South Africa not by a faithful and obedient pursuit of the reconciliation wrought by Christ but through separation, which is the opposite of reconciliation. Racial separation, it maintains, is a demonstration of unbelief and distrust in the power of the gospel. In *The Message*, any demonstration of the reality of reconciliation, as highlighted in Christ, would endanger the doctrine of racial separation. Thus, the supporters of apartheid would "inevitably find themselves opposed to the church if it seeks to live according

---

47. The Message, Section 3: The Gospel's Claim.
48. The Message, Section 3: The Gospel's Claim.
49. The Message, Section 3: The Gospel's Claim.

to the gospel and if it shows that God's grace has overcome hostilities."[50] The consequence, therefore, is that "a thorough policy of racial separation must ultimately require that the church should cease to be the church."[51] This section concludes by stating that the doctrine of racial separation rejects the good reconciliation and fellowship God gives to humanity through Christ as undesirable. It further seeks to limit the limitlessness of God's grace by which all human beings may be accepted in Jesus Christ. In other words, it seeks to confine the operation of God's grace within the barriers of human distinctions and reinforces divisions that the Holy Spirit calls the people of God to overcome. *The Message* thus states that the doctrine of racial separation is a form of resistance to the Holy Spirit.

In the fourth section, entitled "Our Task," *The Message* is much more introspective.[52] Here the focus is on the role of the church in society. It states that society as a whole should be able to see in the church an inclusive fellowship in Christ. In other words, society should be able to see the power of God at work in the church, changing hostility into love. The problem with this, however, as *The Message* suggests, is that "even in the life of the church, there is conformity to the practices of racial separation; and the measure of conformity is the measure of the Church's deviation from the purpose of Christ."[53] Here also, *The Message* maintains that the church's task is to work for the expression of God's reconciliation here and now.

The final section, entitled "We must obey God rather than men," affirms the conviction that Christ should be at the centre of the life of any Christian.[54] Here *The Message* affirms the position that Christ should be the criterion for everyone, including different racial or interest groups. *The Message* warns that if the church does not consider this, it too "fails to witness to the true gospel of Jesus Christ." In other words, the church "will find itself witnessing to a false gospel."[55] It states that "if the church seeks to reconcile Christianity with the so-called 'South African way of life,' (or any other way of life) the church shall find that it has allowed an idol to take the place of Christ." In

---

50. The Message, Section 3: The Gospel's Claim.
51. The Message, Section 3: The Gospel's Claim.
52. The Message, Section 4: Our Task.
53. The Message, Section 4: Our Task.
54. The Message, Section 5: We Must Obey God Rather Than Men.
55. The Message, Section 5: We Must Obey God Rather Than Men.

other words, if the church "abandons its obedience to Christ, it ceases to be the church." In this context, the church breaks the link between itself and the kingdom of God. *The Message* asserts that those calling themselves Christians "are under an obligation to live by the Christian understanding of human beings and community, even if this is contrary to some of the customs and laws of South Africa." Therefore, Christians in the country will have to face the question: "to whom or to what are you truly giving your first loyalty, your primary commitment? Is it to a subsection of humankind, and ethnic group, a human tradition, a political idea; or to Christ?"[56]

3.2.4 *The Message* in Perspective

The Message was officially adopted by several of the member churches of the SACC. Like the Cottesloe resolutions, this also was not radical in its approach. It merely stated that on the basis of the Gospel, it is a sin to keep people apart due to social markers such as race. If the church were not allowed to preach and live this Gospel, "the church would [essentially] cease to be the Church."[57] Nonetheless, it evoked an immediate reaction from the government. Vosloo indicates that the South African Prime Minister, John Vorster, strongly criticized the document, warning clergy not to delve into politics and not to imitate what Martin Luther King Jr. did in the United States. Church leaders and ecumenical leaders such as the Anglican Archbishop Selby-Taylor, Bishop Bill Burnett, and Beyers Naudé responded by writing an open letter to the Prime Minister, signalling the intensification of the conflict between the churches and the apartheid state.[58]

Moreover, *The Message* was crucial in helping Christians to reflect more critically on the South African situation. However, compared to Cottesloe, it categorically rejected apartheid as a false gospel. It was not the first church statement to be critical of apartheid, but it was the first extensive theological rebuttal of the system. Whereas apartheid focused on separateness and segregation, *The Message* draws on the atoning work of Christ as a means of reconciling people to each other. God reconciles the world to himself, and this has implications, first of all, for the church and then, by implication, also

---

56. The Message, Section 5: We Must Obey God Rather Than Men.
57. De Gruchy and De Villiers, *Message in Perspective*, 14.
58. Vosloo, "Christianity and apartheid in South Africa," 412.

for the society in which it exists. The kerygmatic tone of *The Message* points to the work that has already been achieved in Christ. Thus, when compared to Cottesloe, *The Message*

> was much more of an overtly theological document . . . with the result that it has much greater theological coherence . . . [w]hat bound the drafters of *The Message* together was not only a common ideological and political enemy, but a Christology which stressed [their] common humanity in both sin and redemption, a Christology which confessed the reconciling power of the cross and its implications for society, over against an ideology of ethnic division, dominating power and material interests.[59]

Apart from this particular focus on reconciliation, *The Message* reflects a position that stopped short of understanding the gospel as a call for blacks to take the future into their own hands. While espousing a social gospel of reconciliation, the document was essentially paternalistic. It was a call to whites to establish justice for blacks. From this vantage point, it was directed mainly to those in positions of privilege and power.[60] De Gruchy agrees, saying that at this stage in history, the discussion was primarily among white Christians, reflecting the theological divide between conservatives and liberals.[61] This is highlighted by the fact that the document was not widely accepted within the white constituency of the SACC member churches. In fact, some white Christians were somewhat reluctant to mix politics and religion, which, according to Balia, was the standard pretext for avoiding the practical implications of the initiative altogether. In the end, *The Message* offered a clear denunciation of apartheid but failed to provide any ideological annunciation or direction. Balia thus concludes that it was of little relevance to the black community.[62]

To sum up, at the heart of *The Message* is a theology of reconciliation that rejects apartheid as a false gospel. Apartheid is further branded as false salvation. Over and against apartheid, *The Message* proclaims the Lordship of Christ. It refers to attempts to justify apartheid through the use of scripture,

---

59. De Gruchy, "From Cottesloe," 8–9.
60. Walshe, *Church versus state*, 54.
61. De Gruchy, *Reconciliation*, 34.
62. Balia, *Christian Resistance to Apartheid*, 35–37.

in particular through the idea of an order of creation. It concludes that any political scheme claiming to be Christian has to be based on reconciliation already achieved in Christ. It develops the idea of reconciliation by focusing on the implications for the church. The doctrine of separation, when enforced on the churches, means the destruction of the church since it is not based on the reconciling work of Christ. For the authors, support for a doctrine of separation implies distrust in the gospel of Jesus Christ. In this context, *The Message* represents the beginning of something that would, as explained in the following section, become the most serious theological judgment against apartheid. For De Gruchy:

> It is important to keep in mind, for the message of reconciliation at that moment in the church struggle against apartheid had a power and significance which it was going to lose. At [this] stage, however, the message of reconciliation was a fundamental rejection of apartheid and not, as it was later described in the theology of *The Kairos Document*, a way of escaping fundamental change in society.[63]

3.3 The Belhar Confession (1982/1986)

This section entails a brief survey of literature emerging from the *Belhar Confession* (1982/1986). Of course, the *Belhar Confession* cannot be understood apart from the events leading to it, which will be addressed in summary form.

3.3.1 *Ras, Volk en Nasie en volkeverhoudinge in die lig van die Skrif*

The report, *Ras, Volk en Nasie en volkeverhoudinge in die lig van die Skrif* in 1974, represents the NGK official response to the possible faith relationship between apartheid and a Christ-centred understanding of reconciliation.[64]

---

63. De Gruchy, "From Cottesloe," 8.

64. It was translated into English under the title "Human Relations and the South African scene in the light of Scripture." For the purpose of clarity, the original Afrikaans title will be used, simply because the English title does not quite capture what exactly is at stake. One may even argue that the English title is not an accurate description of its original Afrikaans version.

Johan Van der Merwe observes that the roots of the document can be traced as far back as Cottesloe in 1960. The developments at Cottesloe prompted the NGK, in 1961, to appoint a permanent commission to formulate a response to the race issue. In 1965, this commission tabled a report on race relations and this "became the vehicle which transported the call from the Cottesloe Consultation from synod to synod and kept the discussion about race and relations between races in the [NGK] on the agenda."[65] The commission's work also formed the basis of a report tabled at the NGK General Synod of 1966 before another revision was tabled at the General Synod of 1969. Between the synodical reports of 1966 and 1974, the Dutch Reformed Church also issued a report entitled, *A Plea for Understanding: A reply to the Reformed Church in America* in 1968.[66] Better known as the "Landman Report," this document came in the wake of intense criticism from the Reformed Church in America about the NGK's support for apartheid. The response came in the form of a publication. The hope was that the publication would provide American colleagues with an understanding of the desire of the NGK to come to a better understanding of Jesus Christ concerning the tensions in South Africa. Though admitting the situation was not perfect, the NGK appealed for a more sympathetic understanding of the situation as it strove to listen anew to what the Word of God had to say about race relations in a plural society. In 1970, the General Synod decided to appoint a permanent commission to study race and ecumenical issues. The report of this commission was presented and approved at the General Synod in 1974. In 1975 it was published under the title *Ras, Volk en Nasie en volkeverhoudinge in die die lig van die Skrif.*[67]

The report itself is extensive, and its authors claim that it is an attempt by the NGK to listen anew to what the Word of God had to say about race relations in a plural society. The report's authors assume the Bible to be normative on all matters of race relations. They posit that the concept of race is not well developed in the Bible. The report states that neither the Old Testament nor the New Testament outline the "modern scientific understanding" of terms such as "people," "nation," "population," and "ethnos." It nevertheless turns to the Babel story in Genesis 11 to build a case.

---

65. Van der Merwe, "Dutch Reformed Church," 53.
66. Landman, *Plea for Understanding*.
67. Van der Merwe, "The Dutch Reformed Church," 54.

J. A. (Bobby) Loubser suggests that the Babel story is associated with a significant thread in Dutch Reformed theology. This approach is linked to the work of Stephanus. J. du Toit, an early advocate of "people's theology," who argued that the unity of different nations followed directly from the appearance of distinct tongues.[68] Using this as a starting point, the report states that the scriptural lesson about distinct tongues is not just for language differentiation but a calling for the separate development of peoples. It asserts that God called nations into existence, each with their own language, history, and church and that the salvation of all peoples should thus be sought in a sanctified way befitting the particularity of the group. Accordingly, the authors believe that the unity of God's creation marks a divine calling to enact ethnic differentiation, allowing all races to fulfil their own destiny.[69]

They further suggest that human attempts to unify distinct languages were a sign of arrogance by those who sought only to "make a name for themselves." It is therefore concluded that interventions to change the pluriformity of creation could only be effected by God, not by human beings. Humanity should thus be urged to abide by the pluriformity of God's creation. The notion that the Afrikaner people are a select race is rejected. Instead, the authors drew from the story of Babel to claim that language is the natural-historical expression of a complex divine interest of differentiation. It states, "The diversity of the races and peoples to which the confusion of tongues contributed is an aspect of reality which God obviously intended for this dispensation. To deny this fact is to side with the tower [of Babel] builders."[70]

The cultivation of difference is held as justification for separate development. However, the authors deny that this would be a warrant for racism. Instead, they declare that the church's responsibility is to serve a "prophetic, priestly and kingly function toward the people" and to respect the "intrinsic cultural possessions" that constitute the "identity of each people."[71] Furthermore, this obligation does not require a "people's church" but one that allows every group to give expression to their own identity. With this distinction, the authors shifted the focus on separate development away from race

---

68. Loubser, *Apartheid Bible*, 24.
69. Loubser, *The Apartheid Bible*, 24.
70. DRC, *Human Relations*, 18.
71. DRC, 65.

and more towards the notion that separate development was an opportunity for all God's creatures to realize their unique potential. The different groups join a larger unity based on Christ but only as a future eschatological reality.

The authors further claim that separate development is underwritten by the norm of love that holds the potential for reconciliation. The report states, "The message of Holy Scripture must remain the fundamental basis for the determination of relationships between people. Because [human beings are] created in the image of God, the basic concepts and norms for this life are love, justice, truth and peace. These arise from his reconciliation with God in Christ, by regeneration and renewal (2 Cor 5:17). On this basis, the faithful are called upon to erect the signposts of the kingdom of God even in this dispensation, including the sphere of social relations."[72] When stated differently, the logic of reconciliation appeals to unity in diversity in the social context. It contends that it is only in the next life that various peoples would experience that which unites them. However, reconciliation is only possible in the present through adherence to God's created order. In other words, reconciliation is realized only through racial separation in the present. Moreover, justice is based on reconciliation in Jesus Christ but concretely separated from each other. The NGK call for reconciliation, as presented in the report, is thus a promise of a relationship that cannot exist in the present. Instead, it refers to an abstract notion of forging a relationship in the future – an eschatological reality.

3.3.2 *Ras, Volk en Nasie* in Perspective

The release of the report proved to be quite controversial. Internationally, Protestant churches were quick to express their disapproval.[73] This included

---

72. DRC, 63.

73. The main point of critique was the fact that the report sanctioned the political policy of separate development and gave it a biblical foundation. The Swiss Federation of Reformed Churches invited an NGK delegation to a conference in Le Louverain. The conference revealed that the main criticism was linked to the NGK's (i) interpretation of scripture; (ii) the prophetic calling of the church; (iii) separate development; (iv) the dualism between theology and practice as outlined in the report. From Switzerland the NGK Delegation went to Germany to meet with delegates of the Reformierter Bund. The Reformierter Bund responded by declaring, *Ras, Volk en Nasie* as theological confirmation of not only separate development but in actual fact the apartheid system itself. In practice the separation of races (apartheid) meant the dominion of the one and the discrimination, denial of rights and exploitation of the other. See Van der Merwe, "The Dutch Reformed Church from Ras," 55–56.

a response from the Gereformeerde Kerken in the Netherlands. The NGK had very close ties with the Gereformeerde Kerken, but this relationship was severed when the Dutch denounced the report. This finally led to a break in relations in 1978.[74]

In South Africa, conservative Afrikaner groupings viewed the report as a "liberal" shift away from the 'true' biblical perspective and the well-known policy of the church. Those with a more liberal perspective criticized the report for its theological endorsement of apartheid. These debates continued in the years following the publication of the report. For example, in the *Koinonia Declaration* (1978), some white Calvinist ministers argued that if separate development had to exist, as the church insists, it had to extend equal rights and afford blacks an adequate share in negotiating their political future.[75] Prominent theologians made a similar appeal in the *Reformation Day Witness* (1980), a statement appearing in *Die Kerkbode*, the official news organ of the NGK.[76] The *Reformation Day Witness* challenged the church "to carry out its divine calling of reconciliation on a meaningful and credible basis." The statement also warned against mutual estrangement and exclusivity among Christians.

Furthermore, it encouraged Christians "to work against the divisions of the church which shame the communion of saints." Members of the church were invited to eliminate "loveless and racist attitudes and actions which cause hurtful incidents" and move towards "a form of church unity in which the oneness of believers adhering to the same confessions can take a visible form."[77] The book *Stormkompas* (1981), co-edited by prominent Dutch Reformed theologians, is another attempt that highlights the challenges faced by the church.[78] The 44 statements in the book highlight the injustices against blacks

---

74. De Gruchy, *Church Struggle*, 80.
75. This view is most evident in the *Koinonia Declaration*, prepared by a group of white ministers of the Gereformeerde Kerk in Potchefstroom. The statement was privately circulated and also published in the *Journal of Theology for Southern Africa*, September 1978. The statement received a warm reception in some English-speaking churches but was not well received in the NGK and the Gereformeerde Kerk. See De Gruchy, *The Church Struggle*, 80–81.
76. The "Reformed Day Witness" was signed by C. F. A. Borchardt, H. J. B. Combrinck, B. A. Muller, W. P. Esterhuyse, J. A. Heyns, W. D. Jonker, H. W. Rossouw and A. B. du Toit and appeared in *Die Kerkbode* on 5 November 1980.
77. "Reformation Day Witness," in: Serfontein, *Apartheid Change*, 270.
78. Smit, O'Brien, Meiring, *Stormkompas*.

and allude to the inevitable collapse of white rule. This initiative was followed by an *Open Letter* (1982) one year later. It was signed by 123 white ministers and theologians of the Dutch Reformed churches and criticized apartheid legislation. It called for reconciliation in Christ to be realized. The authors of the *Open Letter* stressed that "it is the inalienable privilege of the church to proclaim the message of reconciliation between God and [humanity]." It further argued that "it is the inalienable privilege of the church to proclaim simultaneously the message of reconciliation between people – even between those who had formerly been enemies." The letter states that "the calling of the church extends beyond the ministry of reconciliation within the four walls of the church . . . reconciliation includes a prophetic witness in relation to the entire life of society and therefore the church dare not remain silent on those matters of moral decay, family disintegration and discrimination." With a veiled reference to *Ras, Volk en Nasie* it states that "the church will always bear witness that an arrangement of society based on the fundamental irreconcilability of individuals and groups cannot be accepted as a basic point of departure for the ordering of society."[79]

Thus, having to contend with dissident voices inside the church, the NGK leadership was compelled to re-open the discussion on separate development. During its General Synod in 1982, the church decided to revisit *Ras, Volk en Nasie* – appointing a commission to start this process and present its findings at the General Synod of 1986. The new report, *Kerk en Samelewing*, resulted from four years of intense discussions.[80] Most importantly, *Kerk en Samelewing* signals a departure from the extreme views of *Ras, Volk en Nasie*. This includes retracting the theological justification for apartheid.[81]

For Kinghorn, the difference between *Ras, Volk en Nasie* and *Kerk en Samelewing* is the difference between 1974 and 1986. In his view, this reflects the difference between a self-assured ideology and an ideology under siege. With the new report, there was an awareness not to emulate the extreme doctrinal approach of the past. The result is a document that takes theological and ethical considerations much more seriously. Kinghorn warns that *Kerk*

---

79. Open Letter in Els, "Reconciliation in Southern Africa," 85–86.
80. The English translation of the report is entitled *Church and Society*.
81. De Gruchy, *Church Struggle*, 195.

en Samelewing also has serious shortcomings, noting that this report also fell short of taking the ethical implications of apartheid seriously. He states that:

> Having rejected the 'application of apartheid', [*Kerk en Samelewing*] nowhere, not even remotely, tries to ascertain if and how apartheid was applied in such a way that injustice was done to other people. No consideration is given to even the possibility that apartheid might inherently be a *system* of injustice. It is inconceivable that this fact simply escaped the attention of those who drafted [*Kerk en Samelewing*] . . . it is impossible that the [NGK] could be unaware of it. The omission . . . points to the fact that the [NGK] was not prepared to question its own fundamental assumptions, nor was it prepared to question the fundamental assumptions of the policy of apartheid . . . Thus the [NGK's rejection of apartheid] was not the system of apartheid, but only some of the *effects* of apartheid.[82]

De Gruchy arrives at a similar conclusion arguing that *Kerk en Samelewing* was nothing more than a theological rationalization of the government's attempt to reform apartheid. Further stating that: "apartheid was beyond reform; it was a heresy that had to be rejected as contrary to the gospel of Jesus Christ. There could be no compromise, no 'cheap reconciliation', only the dismantling of apartheid and everything that sustained it."[83]

Ras Volk en Nasie, and *Kerk en Samelewing*, significantly impacted the relationship between the NGK and its so-called "daughter" churches. It should be remembered that the relationship between the NGK and the "daughter" churches was always intertwined, mainly because the "daughter" churches were financially dependent on the NGK. Its superior financial standing granted the NGK significant influence on what was happening in the "daughter" churches. However, following *Ras, Volk en Nasie*, the relationship between the "mother" church and her "daughter" churches became much more strained. This resulted in the "daughter" churches asserting their independence more purposefully. Among other things, "daughter" churches joined the SACC and established informal links with the Christian Institute.

---

82. Kinghorn, "On the Theology of Church," 21–36.
83. De Gruchy, *Church Struggle*, 195.

The development of anti-apartheid arguments in the "daughter" churches came especially from an organization called the *Broederkring* established in 1974.⁸⁴ This organization was formed mainly by black ministers of the NG Kerk in Afrika to facilitate anti-apartheid responses within the Dutch Reformed family of churches. They were soon joined by colleagues of the Nederduitse Gereformeerde Sendingskerk (NG Sendingskerk). With close ties to the Christian Institute, the reasons for the formation of the *Broederkring* included the establishment of "a seriously considered and concerted effort to organise for a biblical, Reformed and relevant witness in the struggle for justice, liberation and reconciliation within the DRC family context."⁸⁵ In a show that symbolizes a break in relations between the Dutch Reformed family of churches, the "daughter" churches, through organizations like the *Broederkring*, publically rejected apartheid. This was in contrast to the "mother" church which maintained that the apartheid system was not inherently wrong if it were to be implemented honestly. In this context, even some of the longstanding assumptions for terms such as "mother" and "daughter" churches were being challenged by those in the black missionary churches.⁸⁶ It was especially those in the predominantly coloured NG Sendingskerk who challenged this relationship.⁸⁷ The NG Sendingskerk eventually formulated

---

84. The *Broederkring* was later renamed the the *Belydende Kring* in 1983.

85. Mokgoebo, "Broederkring. From 1974 to . . .?," 14.

86. In a series of interviews with black NGK clergy conducted by Walshe, he observes that for some it appeared as if it was the "mother" church rather than the "daughter" churches that was in need of guidance. Among other things, those in the "daughter" churches "were asking whether black churches did not have a missionary responsibility to convert the white DRC's from their corrupting racism . . . Whites were often in black pulpits; why not a regular flow of preachers in the opposite direction? How could segregated churches witness common humanity? Why were black and white, African, Coloured and Indian congregations not sharing *nagmaal* (communion) together? Why was there not a Federal [NGK] Synod that was more than advisory, a Synod in which black churches, under black control, would exercise considerable power? Why was the [NGK] cutting itself off from the wider Christian community, from the SACC, the WCC and even isolating itself within the Alliance of Reformed Churches? Why was the Christian Institute being persecuted by white [Dutch Reformed churches] and the state? Was apartheid a blasphemous attack on the process of building Christian fellowship? Was the segregated structure of the [NGK] itself blasphemous?" See Walshe, *Church versus State*, 187–188.

87. Pauw traces the problematic relationship between the NG Sendingskerk and the NGK to a much earlier date. Already at the establishment of the NG Sendingskerk In 1881 the missionary Paulus Teske of Beaufort West objected to the constitution of the NG Sendingskerk as it endorsed submission to the NGK. *Ras, Volk en Nasie* was thus not the sole reason why the NG Sendingskerk challenged its relationship with the NGK but rather the culmination of

an anti-apartheid response aimed at greater unity within the Dutch Reformed family of churches. This started with the NG Sendingskerk, General Synod of 1978, where for the first time since *Ras, Volk en Nasie*, the mission church officially opposed apartheid policies, both in church and society.

Christoff Pauw mentions that the NG Sendingskerk General Synod of 1978 declared that the Church should not design or prescribe party political policy. Moreover, the Church is obliged to criticize and object when the state follows a policy that is contrary to the gospel's demands – especially when the state claims to be inspired by Christian values. The General Synod further expressed the conviction that apartheid (or separate development) is contrary to the gospel:

1. Because over and against the Gospel of Christ's directness on the reconciliation of human beings with God *and* with one another, the forced separation of people on the grounds of race and colour is based at the deepest level on the conviction of the fundamental irreconcilability between people who are thus separated;
2. Because the system that has arisen out of such a policy necessarily had to and did lead to an increasing polarisation between people, especially since the practice has irrefutably shown that within the system one population group, namely the whites, is advantaged and that consequently the gospel's demand of justice for all is not fulfilled; and
3. Because thereby the human dignity of not only the disadvantaged populations but the human dignity of all involved is affected.[88]

The General Synod's final determination was that apartheid (or separate development) could not stand the test and requirements of scripture and was, therefore, a sin.[89] This eventually led to the 1982, World Alliance of Reformed Churches (WARC) assembly in Ottawa, officially rejecting apartheid. The WARC statement read: "We declare with black Reformed Christians in South

---

what Chris Botha calls a "century-old protest." See Pauw, "Anti-apartheid Theology", 163; Botha, "Belhar: Century-old Protest", In: Cloete and Smit, *Moment of Truth*, 67.

88. *Acta Synodi NGSK* 1978, 399–400; 559; 618–619 quoted in Pauw, "Anti-apartheid Theology," 185.

89. *Acta Synodi NGSK* 1978, 399; 505 quoted in Fortein, "Allan Boesak and the Dutch Reformed," 305–306.

Africa that apartheid ('separate development') is sin, and that the moral and theological justification of it is a travesty of the Gospel and, in its persistent disobedience to the Word of God, a theological heresy."[90] For those at the WARC assembly, the theological justification of apartheid meant that the credibility of the gospel itself was at stake and that this necessitated the declaration of a *status confessionis*. Holding out for something more progressive than *The Message*, prominent figures within the NG Sendingskerk, including Allan Boesak, argued that racism was a sin that apartheid had entrenched within a "system of domination." Its antidote, therefore, is a struggle orientated towards reconciliation. This was done based on the theological conviction that the sin of apartheid called the church to work towards realizing the reconciling work of Christ. This meant calling the church to confession.[91]

Boesak's role in these developments cannot be overstated. Some black theologians from the Dutch Reformed family of churches studied in the Netherlands; among them was Boesak, who, upon his return, was instrumental in articulating a theology of resistance against apartheid. Drawing on the insights of Black Theology and his Reformed tradition, he played a leading role in the establishment of the Alliance of Black Reformed Christians (ABRECSA) formed in 1981, which urged the WARC to scrutinize the NGK justification of apartheid carefully and see where it contradicted the truth of the gospel. Boesak was elected President of the WARC in 1982, urging the alliance and its members to disassociate themselves from such false interpretations of the gospel.[92]

Among other things, the WARC assembly had two significant consequences for the Dutch Reformed family of churches. Firstly, it led to further ecumenical and international isolation of the NGK and the NHK. And secondly, WARC affirmed the conviction by some prominent figures in the

---

90. De Gruchy and Villa-Vicencio, *Apartheid is a Heresy*, 170.

91. In the 1980s, Boesak was a popular figure of the liberation movement. Among other things he was the Moderator of the NG Sendingkerk as well as the President of the World Alliance of Reformed Churches (WARC). It was during the WARC assembly in 1982 where Boesak called the ecumenical body to take a "more active role in the struggle against racism" by issuing a broad-based condemnation of apartheid. More precisely, it was Boesak who urged the WARC assembly to declare a *status confessionis* and suspend churches that failed to denounce the apartheid state. See Allan Boesak, "He Made Us All But . . .," in: De Gruchy and Villa-Vicencio, *Apartheid is a heresy*, 3–4.

92. For Boesak's autobiographical accounts see Boesak, *Running with Horses*.

NG Sendingskerk that the sin of apartheid prompted the need for a *status confessionis*. This led to the drafting of the *Belhar Confession* at the NG Sendingskerk, General Synod of 1982 – a confession that was ratified by the General Synod of 1986 (thus being the first document accepted as a confession since the 17th century) and which declared the existence of a *status confessionis* on the grounds that apartheid was "diversity in despair of reconciliation."[93] It offers a profound theological articulation affirming the Lordship of Christ, focusing on the process on the notions of unity, reconciliation, and justice.[94]

3.3.3 The *Belhar Confession*: An Overview

According to Piet Naudé, the Accompanying Letter of the *Belhar Confession* is crucial in understanding the contextual nature of the document itself. The letter consists of four paragraphs in which: a) the need for a *status confessionis* is explained; b) Christ is highlighted as the central motive in confessing, including calling for humility in doing so; c) personal confrontation is allayed, stressing that it is an ideology and not a particular person or church that is confronted and d) the implications of the confession are underlined, warning that repentance, remorse, and confession may involve pain and fear, but that the aim is reconciliation and unity, and ultimately salvation – it stresses that the process of reconciliation demands the pain of repentance, remorse and confession.[95]

The confession itself is relatively short – less than 1,200 words – consisting of five articles in which articles 2–4 deal with the issues of "Unity," "Reconciliation," and "Justice," respectively. Article 1 is a short introduction that describes how the confession relates to faith in the Triune God. Article 5 highlights that in obedience to Christ, the church has to confess in this way and live according to it, regardless of the authorities' response.

The article on "Unity" says that unity rooted in Christ's work of reconciliation has to become visible and manifested in many ways, but that can only

---

93. The full text of the *Belhar Confession* can be found in De Gruchy and Villa-Vicencio, *Apartheid is a Heresy*, 175–182; Cloete and Smit, *Moment of Truth*, 1–6; Hofmeyer, Millard and Froneman, *History of the Church*, 342–349.

94. On the origin, reception and relevance of the *Belhar Confession*, see Cloete and Smit; Botha, and Naudé, *Good News to Confess;* Naudé, *Neither Calendar nor Clock;* Plaatjies-Van Huffel on "Reading the Belhar Confession," 329–345.

95. Naudé, *Neither Calendar nor Clock*, 1–5.

be established in a situation characterized by freedom. It states that: "Christ's work of reconciliation is made manifest in the Church as the community of believers who have been reconciled with God and with one another (Eph 2:11–22)." Here the emphasis is on the work of Christ, reconciling people with God as well as those considered enemies, i.e. Jews and Gentiles, circumcised and uncircumcised, as highlighted in the Ephesians text. According to this text, these parties are now reconciled "in one body" through the cross of Jesus Christ.[96] Among other things, the confession "rejects any doctrine which absolutizes either natural diversity or the sinful separation of people in such a way that this absolutization hinders or breaks the visible and active unity of the church." It further states that this unity is "both a gift and an obligation." It is a gift of the Holy Spirit, built on the unity of and in God (Eph 4:4–6). Moreover, it is a mission and an obligation to which the church should apply itself, something that must be earnestly pursued and sought (Eph 4:3–4). From this perspective, the unity motive is at the very core of the commission of the church, whereas disunity contradicts the very nature of the church. Thus, in this article, the unity of the church is inextricably tied to and is a manifestation of, Christ's reconciliation. Smit, on the logic of this article, suggests that credible unity in the church presupposes true reconciliation. In his view, it was impossible for the NG Sendingskerk to accept the structural or organizational unity in the Dutch Reformed family (and more widely) without true reconciliation. Credible church unity implies that the Dutch Reformed family become reconciled with one another; this means they have to get to know one another and learn to accept one another. In light of their painful history, this includes the reconciliation with their past. Church unity on which the past is silenced and where fellow believers are kept at a distance so that true reconciliation cannot occur will not suffice. The many ways the unity must be made visible, evoked by biblical associations in the first article, contradict any unity that is merely administrative or institutional.[97]

The next article, on "Reconciliation," calls the church to take up the message of reconciliation "in and through Christ" to share it in a country "which professes to be Christian, but in which the enforced separation of people on a racial basis promotes and perpetuates alienation, hatred and enmity." Russel

---

96. Naudé, *Neither calendar nor clock*, 8.
97. Smit, "Reformed Confession and Ecumenical," 367.

Botman mentions that the authors of the confession develop an understanding of reconciliation that goes beyond ecclesiological divisions and connects it directly to the notion of justice.[98] Reconciliation is placed at the centre of its critique against the injustices of apartheid. Moreover, the church is challenged to assume its responsibility as the reconciling community in the world. For example, the article refers to 2 Corinthians 5, where the church is entrusted with the ministry of reconciliation. Christ's work on reconciliation must be implemented in practical terms. How? "By being the salt and the light of the world (Matt 5:13–16), by being peacemakers (Matt 5:9), by living in the world with godliness and dedication (2 Pet 3) so that the promises of the future – the righteousness in particular (Rev 21–22) may be realized in the present." Thus, the reconciliation invoked has both a soteriological as well as an eschatological dimension. It is further maintained that God, by his life-giving Word and Spirit, has conquered the powers of sin and death and, therefore, irreconciliation, hatred, bitterness and enmity. The ministry of Jesus illustrates how he struggled against these forces and how he conquered them on the cross (Col 2:13–19). Through this victory, he is Lord "of all creation" (Col 1:15), and Christians are exhorted to put on the armour, even while they know that the victory has already been attained (Eph 6). The powers of irreconciliation and hatred, bitterness and enmity, therefore, no longer have a hold over humanity because of the victory of the cross. This victory gives humanity new possibilities in life, society, and the world. The church is therefore called to play a central role in providing hope to society in search of meaning beyond the confines of irreconciliation, hatred, and bitterness.

With an indirect reference to the situation in the country, the article challenges the legitimacy of any authority claiming to be Christian, especially when its policies suggest otherwise. It states that "the enforced separation of people on a racial basis promotes and perpetuates alienation, hatred and enmity," which, if taken seriously, contradicts Christ's victory on the cross. Instead, through the enforced separation of people on a racial basis, the "forces of estrangement" that were conquered in Christ are kept alive. The article, therefore, rejects any doctrine which sanctions, in the name of the gospel or of the will of God, the forced separation of people on the grounds of race and colour. This, it posits, weakens the ministry and experience of

---

98. Botman, "Church Partitioned," 110.

reconciliation in Christ. Any ideology that contradicts Christ's reconciliation in the name of the gospel must be considered a false doctrine. Such a doctrine, it maintains, cannot be based on the victory in Christ because it is based "out of prejudice, fear, selfishness and unbelief" and therefore denies the reconciling power of the gospel. Without mentioning apartheid explicitly, the article concludes that any approach that presents enforced racial separation as gospel or as the will of God must be rejected because it fundamentally undermines the church's ministry of reconciliation in the world.

The final article of the main section, "Justice" and peace, are introduced as central in defining the character and purpose of God. This justice, it suggests, is granted especially to the vulnerable and those from whom justice is withheld in society. In this context, the church is called to follow God in bringing justice to practical effect in the world. Much of what follows in the article tries to capture the nature of God as outlined in Bible verses. This includes scriptural references such as He brings justice to the oppressed (Isa 1:16–17). He gives bread to the hungry; he frees the prisoner and restores sight to the blind (Ps 146:7–8). God raises those who are bowed down (Ps 146:8) and exalts the lowly (Luke 1:52). God showers the poor with good things (Luke 6:20; 16:19–31).

Regarding the practical implications for the church, the following guidelines are suggested. First, the church must choose to stand where Christ stands because he is the source of justice – and because he stands with the victims of injustice. As followers of Jesus, as people in the service of God (Rom 6:13), the church is called to uphold the year of grace, the year of reparation. Second, the church is called to testify against injustice and for that which is right. Here the article refers to the church having a responsibility to witness against the powerful and privileged that selfishly seek their interest and thus control and harm others. Third, for the church to be faithful to its calling, it must reject any ideology that legitimates any form of injustice and any doctrine which is unwilling to resist such an ideology in the name of the gospel.

The *Belhar Confession* concludes that the "Church must therefore stand by people in any form of suffering and need, which implies, among other things, that the Church must witness against and strive against any form of injustice" and must therefore "reject any ideology which would legitimate forms of injustice and any doctrine which is unwilling to resist such an ideology in the name of the gospel."

3.3.4 The *Belhar Confession* in Perspective

Erik Doxtader's analysis on the reception of the *Belhar Confession* is helpful. While it is deemed virtually "impossible to differ" with the conclusions of the confession, some issues remain unresolved. For example, the *Belhar Confession*'s call to recover reconciliation did not resolve whether its significance simply replicates the divisions it opposes. The confession produced a call for reconciliation that appeared both to oppose and constitute identity. Doxtader notes that:

> For the present, reconciliation's potential was a (be)coming into relation, an event that refigured individual experience in the name of forging collective identifications that could turn the differentiations of separation toward unity of difference. Against the heresy of law's emergency, this exceptional potential was a fragile power; synthesis risked a lapse back to the very identitarian logic of the system being opposed. For its faith to work, reconciliation had to stand and pivot between the creation of self-certainty and the creative contingency of collective (inter)action.[99]

Jaap Durand further observes that with the reception of the *Belhar Confession*, one gets the impression that the parting of ways within the Dutch Reformed family was inevitable.[100] In a sense, *Ras Volk en Nasie* and the *Belhar Confession* represent the culmination of what could be interpreted as two irreconcilable positions. The confession represents a turning point in what essentially became a contest for the Reformed identity in the country.[101] Whereas previously, the NGK had regarded itself as the custodian of the true Reformed faith, it was now accused of supporting injustice and having become heretical in the process.[102] Durand further argues that:

> The new confession presents a hitherto unknown challenge for the [NGK] which put its very being in the balance. Its ecclesiastical policy and practice in respect of racial and national

---

99. Doxtader, *With Faith in the Works*, 70.
100. Durand, "Crisis in the Dutch," 119.
101. See for example, De Gruchy, *Liberating Reformed Theology*.
102. De Gruchy, "Contest for Reformed," 26–36.

relations are rejected confessionally as being in conflict with some of the central tenets of Christianity. If it were to persevere in its policy, the result could only be that the [NG Sendingskerk] severs its ecclesiastical ties with the [NGK], if, that is, the [NG Sendingskerk] is true to the gospel and to itself. The original communications gap between the [NGK] and the [NG Sendingskerk thus becomes] a confessional one.[103]

Under increasing ecumenical and social pressure, the NGK was compelled to review its policy on race. As mentioned above, the official response came a few years later, but at this point, the church was still not ready to accept the *Belhar Confession*.[104] Piet Naudé's analysis suggests that the acceptance of the *Belhar Confession* is hampered by a few aspects (or theses), as he calls them. Firstly, this includes the persistence of an intensified "hermeneutic of suspicion." He argues that for many in the NGK, the *Belhar Confession* is not a deviation from the existing confessions of the church. Yet, what functioned more explicitly from the start was the perception that the confession and its rejections were aimed at the NGK specifically. This is despite the accompanying letter suggesting that the *Belhar Confession* is not directed against specific persons, church or churches.

Given the circumstances, the confession is often interpreted as a direct attack, thus explaining the defensive stance of the NGK. This may also be attributed to the deep suspicion that still exists today. The second aspect is linked to the "pietistic spirituality" in the NGK. Naudé mentions that issues such as "reconciliation," "justice," and "unity," so explicitly addressed in the *Belhar Confession*, were in direct contrast to a worshipping trend among many Afrikaans-speaking ministers. Here this "pietistic spirituality" is associated with the strict separation of politics and church. In this context, the distance between this "pietistic spirituality" and the *status confessionis* was too much of a divide, thus contributing to its rejection as a common confession. Thirdly, Naudé suggests that church unification, where the dialogue partners operate from different social locations, hamper the possibility of a common confession. He argues that: "Confessions like Dort, which addresses

---

103. Durand, "Crisis in the Dutch," 119.

104. As mentioned previously, the official response came in 1986 with the policy statement entitled *Kerk en Samelewing* in which the church changed its stance on apartheid.

Arminian heresies, and the Belgic Confession, which deals with Marcionism, Arianism, Epicureanism, and Pelagianism, are by implication closer to the heart of the [NGK] faith than a contemporary expression in simple language about unity, reconciliation, and justice." In this context, the NGK revealed "a theological stance in contrast to the continued reformation of the church and a fundamental orientation toward European theology, specifically its anti-liberal tradition, where debates sounded more like sixteenth – or rather seventeenth-century Europe, than the twentieth century in Africa." And lastly, the acceptance of the confession is further hampered because the dialogue partners understand themselves as ecumenically isolated "denominational" churches. In this context, the problem has less to do with confessional differences. Nor does it derive from major or minor disagreements over the content of the confession. Instead, it has more to do with the preservation of Afrikaner identity. This becomes even more problematic when an ecumenically isolated church struggles to preserve its identity. In this sense, the *Belhar Confession* served as a counter-narrative that could not be accommodated in the identity of the NGK. The cumulative effect of these factors led to what Naudé suggests is its non-reception in the NGK.[105]

The *Belhar Confession* also had a notable effect on relations between the missionary churches. In 1987 the NG Kerk in Afrika and the NG Sendingskerk met a number of times to prepare for the unification of the churches. The remaining missionary church, the Reformed Church in Africa, never responded to the invitation. And the NGK only attended initial discussions but later withdrew from the process.[106] Thus, unification talks consisted of the NG Sendingskerk and the NG Kerk in Afrika only. By 1990 a proposed church order was drafted, and after deliberation, it was decided to include the *Belhar Confession* as the fourth confession of the new church. The NG Kerk in Afrika was requested to make the necessary changes to its church policy to accommodate the confession and circulate it among its congregations for further study. In doing so, it became the first church to include the *Belhar Confession* in its Standard of Faith.[107] Later in April 1994, the NG Sendingskerk and the NG Kerk in Afrika signed the charter of unification,

---

105. Naudé, *Neither calendar nor clock*, 139–148.
106. Pauw, "Anti-apartheid Theology," 96.
107. Plaatjies-Van Huffel, "The Belhar Confession," 17.

and with this, the Verenigende Gereformeerde Kerk in Suider-Afrika was formally constituted. The name was chosen to express that the seats of the other two in the Dutch Reformed family of churches, the NGK and the Reformed Church in Africa, were still empty.[108]

To sum up, the *Belhar Confession* represents a theological deepening of the reconciliation concept. This was prompted by the theological justification of apartheid in *Ras, Volk en Nasie*. It places reconciliation at the theological centre of its critique against apartheid. And then develops an understanding that goes beyond ecclesiological divisions and connects it directly to the issue of justice in society. Reconciliation is seen as God's work in and through Christ. In turn, Christ's work of reconciliation is manifest in the church as a community of believers who have reconciled with God and one another. That done through Christ's reconciliation must now be the guiding principle of unity in the church and towards working for justice in society. The authors of the *Belhar Confession* assume that the reconciliation of humanity with God in Jesus Christ entails a ministry of reconciliation.

3.4 The *National Initiative for Reconciliation* (1985)

This section entails a brief survey of literature emerging from the *National Initiative for Reconciliation*. Of course, the *National Initiative for Reconciliation* cannot be understood apart from the events leading to it, which will be addressed in summary form.

3.4.1 The Rise of Neo-Pentecostalism

The beginning of the *National Initiative for Reconciliation* is traced back to the 1960s. During this period, neo-Pentecostalism (or the charismatic movement) emerged within mainline churches. This started in the United States

---

108. The unification of the NG Sendingskerk and the NG Kerk in Afrika has since been met with some resistance from (former) NG Kerk in Afrika congregations. The congregations from both the Phororo Synod and the Free State Synod have since disassociated themselves from the newly constituted Verenigende Kerk in Suider-Afrika. Both claim to be a continuation of the NG Kerk in Afrika and that there were legal problems with the unification process that justified them continuing as such. The NGK as well as the Reformed Church in Africa remained separate churches. The Reformed family of churches have in the meantime started the process of unification initiated by the leadership of Verenigende Kerk in Suider-Afrika and the NGK. This development was still unfolding by the time this study was completed. See Pauw, "Anti-apartheid theology in the Dutch Reformed family of churches," 96.

and soon spread to other parts of the world, including South Africa, where it spread widely among ministers and laity. In South Africa, it was mainly among the white and coloured constituencies of the major denominations that this movement gained momentum. In the process, some members left their churches to join the new Pentecostal denominations, while others decided to form new independent charismatic-type congregations. The majority of people, however, remained in the mainline denominations. In the 1970s, there were significant charismatic groups in the Anglican, Methodist, Presbyterian, Roman Catholic, Baptist, and Congregationalist churches, including some in the Dutch Reformed Church. De Gruchy mentions that the charismatic movement was significantly strengthened when prominent figures like Bill Burnett, the Anglican bishop of Grahamstown and, later, Archbishop of Cape Town, together with several other church leaders, joined the movement. He further suggests that the emergence of the charismatic movement came about mainly as a reaction to the social and political activism that was taking place in the mainline churches. "Thus, while [the charismatic movement] had a significant impact upon the life and worship of many congregations, it also led to a spirituality of withdrawal from socio-political involvement, as well as to dissension and the formation of independent charismatic churches."[109]

Charismatics and conservative evangelicals in various denominations concentrated their attention more on evangelism and church growth. They generally stood apart from ecumenical cooperation, especially on political matters. Motivated by the claim of political neutrality, the increased focus away from politics significantly contributed to the life and worship of many congregations. However, this meant white charismatics and evangelicals supported the *status quo*, whereas blacks often accepted their oppression.[110]

In 1973 the first attempt was made to relate the "evangelicals" to the "ecumenicals" at the Congress on Mission and Evangelism in Durban. The meeting was meant to create a platform where these groups could integrate their concerns. The meeting was jointly sponsored by the SACC and the Africa Enterprise, an evangelical organization founded in the 1960s by an Anglican evangelical, Michael Cassidy. The meeting brought together an array of church groups, including some from the Pentecostal movement as well as Roman

---

109. De Gruchy, "Christianity in Twentieth-century," 101.
110. De Gruchy, 101.

Catholics. The idea was to create an environment where these groups could discuss the many issues facing the churches. In one sense, the meeting was crucial in getting groups together and setting the tone for further deliberations and cooperation. At the same time, the meeting also revealed the extent of the racial and theological polarization. According to De Gruchy:

> This was demonstrated in the response of many whites to black theologian Manas Buthelezi's address entitled 'Six Theses on Evangelism in the South African Context'. Buthelezi argued that the time had arrived for blacks to take the initiative in the life of the church and in the church struggle against apartheid. Indeed he declared, it was now necessary for blacks to evangelise whites and enable them to be set free from their racism.[111]

At this point, it was clear that whites were prepared to work towards eradicating racial discrimination. However, the question of black liberation and blacks taking the lead in the process remained a challenge that many whites were unwilling to face.

Following the 1973 meeting, the Africa Enterprise attempted to bring the various church constituencies together at the South African Leadership Assembly (SACLA) meeting in July 1979. Following the Soweto uprising in 1976, the purpose of the meeting was to consider ways of responding to the crisis in the country.[112] Among its achievements, SACLA helped generate a more radical evangelical witness among student participants leading to the establishment of the Student Union for Christian Action.[113] However, as was the case with the Congress on Mission and Evangelism in 1973, SACLA also was too theologically diverse and politically divided to reach a consensus.

---

111. De Gruchy, 101.

112. The Soweto Uprising of 16 June 1976 took place after thousands of black schoolchildren began protests against the compulsory use of the Afrikaans language in their schools. It began with a youth march in Soweto, but spread to townships across the country. As tensions rose, more security police were deployed and youth became a symbol of bravery against armed soldiers. This protest gained significant local and international attention when police opened fire on a gathering of scholars marking one of the most significant events in the struggle against apartheid. The detail of the Soweto Uprising will be discussed in the following chapter of this study.

113. The Student Union for Christian Action is a non-racial student body that sought to engage in direct acts of Christian witness against the growing crisis of apartheid and rising resistance. It sought to respond to the ecclesiastical, political, social and economic challenges in the post-1976 political environment.

According to De Gruchy, this meeting revealed the extent to which the church had become even more polarized by politics, particularly regarding appropriate political action. For some, the way to overcome apartheid was through gradually changing people's hearts and minds through spiritual conversion and the renewal of the church. For others, apartheid had to be opposed by direct political action and, if need be, by participating in the armed struggle against the state.[114]

In response to the political instability, the Africa Enterprise, under the leadership of Michael Cassidy, launched the *National Initiative for Reconciliation* (NIR), calling together a large church conference in Pietermaritzburg in September 1985. Consisting of some 400 church leaders from 47 denominations, the primary purpose was to convene a conference to pray and discuss how the church could respond to the political crisis. It attracted church leaders of different denominations and races to reconcile with one another and implement this practice in their respective churches and communities. Desmond Tutu, who had recently been elected Anglican archbishop of Cape Town and the University of South Africa, Professor David Bosch, among others, were some of the main speakers.[115]

3.4.2 The Theological "Third Way"

Anthony Balcomb notes that alongside the aims of the NIR, it also had a qualifying statement claiming that the initiative was ideologically free and politically neutral. "The proposed gathering of togetherness," it said, "does not have political origin." Instead, the intention was to "wait and listen for the voice of God." It noted, however, that it is hard to achieve this mainly because "Christians are highly politicised" and "trapped by group loyalties and interests" so that "pre-understanding, biases, and agendas become the filter through which everything is received." Moreover, it asserted that "any particular political agenda do not influence these gatherings of Christian people" and that "at the heart of this movement is an ideological freedom which does not project any particular economic or political solution for South Africa." It further stressed that "there is no purpose, secretly obscured, either to preserve the status quo or enhance revolutionary objectives." It admitted,

---

114. De Gruchy, "Political Landmarks," 19.
115. See Nürnberger and Tooke, *Cost of Reconciliation*.

however, that "socio-political solutions" must be found but that this could happen only through "Christian repentance, reconciliation, reflection and resolution." According to the NIR, what was needed was a "third way" forward between a "violent and repressive peace" and a "violent and destructive revolution or civil war." Out of this "third way" could come "considerable social and political consequences," which would help in moving the nation towards "peaceful and just solutions."[116]

For the organizers, the church provided an excellent opportunity to facilitate dialogue because it had representatives on both sides of the socio-political divide. The idea was that the presence of Christians, connected by their faith, could counterbalance the political instability. In order to achieve this, the conference proposed two strategies. The first had to do with a general reconciliatory and conscientizing nature. And the second was focused on exerting pressure for change. Among the recommendations of the first strategy was the need to continue to "proclaim and witness to the good news of Jesus Christ," to "continue in prayer and fasting for renewal of the Holy Spirit and reawakening of the church of Jesus Christ and for peace and justice," to "create concrete opportunities for meaningful worship, fellowship and discussion with people of differing racial and cultural groups," to "help remove ignorance of events in South Africa and prepare people for living in a changed and totally non-racial land," and to "share the South African reality of suffering by extending and accepting invitations to experience the life of fellow Christians in the townships."[117] The second strategy was intended to place pressure on government and to meet the demands to, among other things, a) end the 1985 state of emergency; b) to remove the army and emergency police forces from townships; c) release all political prisoners and withdraw charges against those accused of treason for fighting apartheid; d) begin talks immediately with the authentic leadership of the various population groups with a view towards equitable power-sharing in South Africa; e) begin the process of introducing a common system of education; and f) take the necessary steps towards the elimination of all forms of legislated discrimination.

---

116. Unpublished *National Initiative for Reconciliation* document, private collection found in Balcomb, *Third Way Theology*, 83.

117. Balcomb, *Third way theology*, 85.

The meeting further asserted that these objectives could only be achieved if a position of political and ideological neutrality was taken.[118]

According to Balcomb, there were at least four reasons why those behind the NIR felt that they needed to remain neutral: a) all perspectives on the political situation in the country reflected an ideological bias which meant that most (if not all) views were fundamentally distorted; b) to take sides politically meant the church would jeopardize its potential to act as a mediator in the conflict; c) the violence committed by the state for the sake of "law and order" as well as the violence committed by those who revolted against the state was basically the representation of the two dominant political views, so, for the sake of neutrality it simply had to distance itself from these polarized positions; d) the NIR was convinced that it was able to exercise its unique understanding of and make its contribution to the situation, without seeing itself accountable to political positions.[119]

In order to disseminate the conference proceedings, the organizers planned to publish a series of readers with relevant materials on justice and reconciliation to be used by study and action groups. The most important, *The Cost of Reconciliation in South Africa*, published in 1988, deals specifically with reconciliation as a theological concept.[120] De Gruchy notes that its "Statement of Affirmation," also published in national newspapers at the time, focuses on the reasons for the initiative and reveals the commitment to work towards reconciliation. At the same time, it warns that reconciliation without removing the causes of injustice is counter-productive. They further understood that reconciliation without linking it to justice (in society) was highly problematic. Following the "third way" of the gospel, reconciled communities (i.e. the churches) provided the key to overcoming the political crisis. This proved to be an attractive proposition for many conservative church leaders. At the same time, many outside this initiative called for a more radical response.[121]

---

118. Nürnberger and Tooke, *Cost of Reconciliation*, 83–85.
119. Balcomb, *Third way theology*, 87.
120. Nürnberger and Tooke, 1.
121. De Gruchy, *The Church Struggle*, 196; De Gruchy, *Reconciliation*, 35.

3.4.3 The NIR, Statement of Affirmation: An Overview

Apart from a detailed analysis of socio-political challenges, the NIR reader, *The Cost of Reconciliation in South Africa*, deals specifically with reconciliation as a theological concept. It states that "Christian reconciliation is based on the fact that God reconciled us to himself in Christ. Christ suffered our iniquity on the cross, restored us to his fellowship with God and with each other, and involves us in God's act of reconciliation by the power of the Spirit. Forgiveness, acceptance, redressing the causes of the conflict and forbearance all imply the willingness to sacrifice and suffer for the sake of justice, peace, fellowship and cooperation." It further suggests that those "who have been reconciled to God, the new life in fellowship with God constantly puts to death their sinful nature and involves them in God's redeeming love for others. As God's agents of reconciliation and transformation, they share God's suffering acceptance of the unacceptable. That is the human meaning of the cross of Christ."[122]

The NIR expands the meaning of reconciliation to include reconciliation between God and humanity and how the concept is to be understood for human relationships. It states, "Reconciliation between people implies the active commitment to achieve justice." In this context, justice is the hermeneutical key to evaluating human relationships. Justice becomes the means through which reconciliation as a theological concept is understood. In other words, justice is the ordering of social relationships in such a way that both the benefits of the relationship and the sacrifice necessary to maintain the relationship are shared equally between those concerned as far as this is possible and conducive to the relationship. Furthermore, reconciliation between people occurs when conflicting parties are willing to confess and redress wrongs they have inflicted on each other, forgive each other and restore full fellowship with each other. To confess, redress and forgive wrongs implies suffering. This suffering is interpreted as participation in the cross of Christ. In this context, reconciliation takes place when the parties concerned: a) acknowledge, regret and undertake to put to an end the abuse of power and all injustices in society; b) agree to cooperate in redressing the structural imbalances and maladjustments concerned by instituting social mechanisms that balance out power and privilege in society and; c) are willing to tolerate

---

122. Nürnberger and Tooke, *The Cost of reconciliation in South Africa*, 84–85.

differences of race, culture and conviction within the common society and ban any discrimination on these grounds.[123]

The NIR further suggests that:

> Reconciliation which serves to conceal or play down injustices, which condones the abuse of power at the expense of others, which appeases the wronged party, which expects of the victims of structural imbalances to accept their fate, which serves to avoid the suffering necessary for the restoration or development of just relationships, or which assigns to one party more of the benefits and to another more of the sacrifices is a fraud and stands condemned in the eyes of God and human morality. It will make no contribution to the resolution of the conflict and undermines the credibility and effectiveness of the church's message of reconciliation in the society.[124]

The NIR reader concludes the section on reconciliation by affirming the view that God has reconciled humanity to himself and to one another through the death of Christ. Through this act, Christians are invited to form the body of Christ on earth. This unity does not remove difference; instead, it is a higher reality that relativizes worldly divisions. For this reason, Christians cannot regard any other Christians as their enemies. On the contrary, Jesus commands that when Christians realize that other Christians have anything against them, they should postpone everything to "go and be reconciled" to the others (Matt 5:24). In South Africa, this means that Christians who have many grievances against one another should continually be going across the boundaries for the sake of reconciliation. Christians are further called to listen to one another to understand the pain of the other on a personal and social level. This understanding, the document further asserts, should lead to a new perspective for the privileged to see the social structures that benefit them and deprive others. The inevitable result, it further claims, will be that the privileged start acting to promote social justice. This would include social action for justice as part of true reconciliation. Those belonging to the oppressing groups have to be willing to confess their collective guilt, and the

---

123. Nürnberger and Tooke, 85–86.
124. Nürnberger and Tooke, 87.

oppressed should be willing to forgive them. The former will then show the genuineness of their repentance by their actions. Reconciliation without actions is false reconciliation which deepens the divisions in society.[125]

The NIR asserts that it is not a viable option to be neutral mediators in the conflict. In this context it is necessary to take a position in favour of the poor and the weak. However, this does not mean that:

> Christians automatically have the right to become instigators of war against the system. They refuse to give their absolute loyalty to any side because it belongs to Christ and his body. Essentially they are not war-makers but peacemakers, and therefore they are very critical against the powers of hostility building up on both sides. It is very clear that all will have to refuse co-optation by the oppressive forces but [their] solidarity with the poor will also have to be critical as their struggle is also not free from sin.[126]

The document's authors suggest that Christians have the responsibility to "open the road towards peace" by not surrendering to the "powers of hostility." In this context, the powers of hostility refer to individuals or groups who give loyalty to any side in an absolute manner – thus, becoming agents of division rather than reconciliation. It further forewarns that those who refuse to give their exclusive loyalty to either side will experience painful rejection, which highlights the costliness of working towards reconciliation.[127]

3.4.4 The NIR in Perspective

The organizers of the NIR placed much emphasis on its ideological neutrality. In response, Balcomb argues that the black constituency found this so-called neutrality or "third way" approach difficult, if not impossible, to comprehend. At the same time, the white constituency believed that a position of neutrality was essential to maintain the kind of objectivity appropriate for the church. The problem with this, according to Balcomb, is that even at church events, blacks continued to see themselves as victims of oppression. This made it difficult for them to suspend their convictions for the sake of neutrality. Just

---

125. Nürnberger and Tooke, 87–88.
126. Nürnberger and Tooke, 88.
127. Nürnberger and Tooke, 89.

as blacks formed themselves into political groupings to assert their common will outside the church, the declaration of black demands also had to be considered when mapping a way forward for the NIR. This was not the case, and it is, for this reason, that the prospect of neutrality remained elusive. In reality, even the NIR could not escape the politicization of the time, and this made the claim of political neutrality highly problematic. It soon became apparent that the NIR proceedings themselves became a microcosm of the struggles that were taking place in the broader political context. He further stresses that an attempt was made to imbue the initiative with a kind of spirituality that transcended the political environment. It was hoped that this would bring about a kind of political "objectivity" in which the issues could be more "reasonably" and "calmly" discussed. He asserts, however, that this particular approach highlights a "liberal" agenda in which political differences are minimized as much as possible and political processes are harmonized as much as possible.

In contrast, this was very different from a "liberation" agenda, which maximized political differences and promoted confrontation. These differences are typical of the entire character and process of liberal and liberation politics, each of which has its own tradition, agendas, style, and aims – essentially ideological and political in character. In this context, the NIR's "third way" was a profoundly political process with distinguishable political aims, despite its convenors' claims of neutrality.[128]

Martin Prozesky suggests that the convenors of the NIR may have underestimated the difficulty of working towards reconciliation.[129] This was further exacerbated by the continued injustices taking place in the country. He argues that the convenors grossly underestimated the extent to which society, including the church, was polarized. However, he admits that the convenors may have successfully created an environment where conflicting parties could engage each other. As he puts it, the NIR created an environment where "a white [NGK] minister may well embrace a politically radical black bishop." However, the more important question remained: how would this embrace materialize in a divided society? Prozesky argues that:

---

128. Balcomb, *Third Way Theology*, 89–90.
129. M. Prozesky, "Can Christians Overcome Apartheid," 53.

> The real challenge is to make reconciliation work in the big, bad and unrepentant world outside, and that is another story altogether. Helping it happen is a challenge worthy of the best in Christianity, but do those who have begun this initiative recognize how huge the task ahead is? Do they know just how crucially they are putting the credentials of Christianity as a force for significant social change on the line? As a minimum requirement, they must now get the Treurnichts and the Boesaks – fellow Christians in the same Dutch Reformed tradition – to find political brotherhood, and not just spiritual agreement."[130]

Critically, for Prozesky, the burden of the legacy of apartheid could not be wished or even prayed away. In his view, something more than the "easier reconciliations" highlighted by the NIR was needed. What was required was the reconciliation between bitterly and absolutely alienated people, reconciliation "between the Tambos and the Terre Blanches." In this context, the NIR faced the real danger of believing "deludedly" that it had achieved a genuine breakthrough.[131]

Balcomb argues that the NIR's commitment to the goal of reconciliation seems to obscure some important societal challenges. Here he refers to how reconciliation is understood in relation to the dynamics of power and justice in society. In his view, the convenors did not sufficiently recognize that reconciliation was impossible while one party was aggrieved, marginalized and oppressed.[132] This is similar to the views expressed in the *Kairos Document* (discussed in the next chapter). In this context, the NIR is accused of making reconciliation an absolute principle that must be applied in all cases of conflict and dissension. However, this does not mean the initiative ignored the justice issue. Instead, the NIR process illustrates that when it came to the actual dynamics of the power struggle, "its lot fell not to the side with the most claim to justice but to the side with the most hold on power." In other words, the pressing demand for the "absolute principle of reconciliation" as articulated by the NIR superseded the pressing demand for the "absolute principle" of justice as articulated by blacks involved in the process.

---

130. Prozesky, "Can Christians Overcome Apartheid," 53–54.
131. Prozesky, 53–54.
132. Balcomb, *Third Way Theology*, 115.

Balcomb further suggests that here the demand for reconciliation cannot be adequately understood unless one takes seriously the power struggle that occurred at the meetings of the NIR. In this sense, reconciliation must be understood within the context of these vested interests. In his view, the convenors themselves had vested interests in seeing their reconciliation initiative succeed. Consequently, these interests were an added dynamic to the negotiation processes around black demands. He further submits that "the tendency to locate the notion of reconciliation, as a theological category, outside the dynamics of power struggle, obscured these interests and therefore soon exposed the NIR at best to co-option by the state and at worst to legitimation of the state's political agenda."[133] This power struggle gave reconciliation a particular character that contradicted the claims of neutrality. The fact that the demand for reconciliation superseded black demands for justice made it especially susceptible to manipulation. The use of reconciliation as a theological category without taking the power struggles in society seriously further complicated matters. In this context, De Gruchy argues that the NIR failed to connect the church and the political situation in the country. In this regard, slogans such as, "Let the church be church" were often used to escape political commitment for the sake of neutrality. He adds that:

> The good news that God has reconciled the world to himself in Jesus Christ is the foundation of Christian faith and action. Reconciliation is an act of God in Jesus Christ, it is something which is given. At the same time, Christians are called to be reconciled to their neighbours and their enemies through suffering, love and forgiveness. Reconciliation to God is inseparable from reconciliation with one's fellows. Such reconciliation requires repentance and change, not just a change in attitude, but fundamental change which affects the very structures of existence. In South Africa it is possible for individuals of different races to discover the deep significance of Christian reconciliation. But as long as apartheid structures continue, the genuine reconciliation of social groups remains elusive, and therefore peace remains elusive. Both whites and blacks are chained, and the liberation

---

133. Balcomb, 115.

of the one is necessary for freedom of all. 'Cheap reconciliation', and therefore negotiation prior to a genuine commitment to change, only prolongs the bondage.[134]

To sum up, the NIR reflects a deep commitment to reconciliation and justice in South Africa. However, based on the political situation in the country, the convenors may have underestimated how difficult this task would be. Focusing on neutrality, the convenors may have overlooked the power struggles within the church. In this context, they may have underestimated the extent to which the church was politicized. Balcomb warns that the NIR must not be seen as a deliberate and calculated attempt to mislead people. On the contrary, he judges it to be a genuine attempt at responding to the crisis in the country. In this sense, the integrity of those who called for the NIR is not in question.[135] However, taking a particular approach to the situation in the country, they exposed a particular theology used to legitimize a certain kind of political analysis and action. This was done on the premise of neutrality. However, instead of being neutral, it reflected a liberal character that precluded acknowledging its ideological bias.[136] The NIR claim of neutrality should therefore be treated with suspicion. Nevertheless, at the heart of the initiative was the longing for Christ's work of reconciliation to manifest in the church as the community of believers who have been reconciled with God and with one another. In other words, that which was done through Christ's work of reconciliation must now be the guiding principle for working towards justice in society.

3.5 Closing Reflections

It is essential to highlight that the *Message to the People of South Africa* in 3.2; the *Belhar Confession* in 3.3; as well as the *National Initiative for Reconciliation* in 3.4 employ what may be referred to as deductive logic.[137] In other words, all of the above initiatives move from reconciliation with God to the ministry of

---

134. De Gruchy, "Church and the Struggle," 203–204.
135. Balcomb, *Third Way Theology*, 115.
136. Prozesky, "Can Christians Overcome Apartheid," 53.
137. See my discussion on the deductive logic as an approach to the doctrine of reconciliation in Chapter 1. This approach is borrowed from Conradie, "Reconciliation as One Guiding", 17–21.

reconciliation in society. According to this logic, the fruits of reconciliation in South Africa are contingent upon reconciliation with God. This approach assumes that no lasting solution to social conflict can be found without addressing the deep roots of such social conflict. In this case, social conflict is linked directly to our alienation from God. Ultimately this can be overcome (only) through God's gracious forgiveness of sins. From a classic Reformed perspective, such forgiveness is appropriated through justification, sanctification and the vocation of believers. Furthermore, such reconciliation in Christ enables and requires reconciliation with one's brothers and sisters, regardless of the social markers that may separate them ("We are all one in Christ"). According to this "deductive" logic, the ministry of reconciliation in church and society is only possible based on reconciliation in Christ. In this sense, the ministry goes beyond the requirements for social cohesion, and its primary focus remains firmly rooted in reconciliation with God. It is only through reconciliation in Christ that social conflict can be addressed adequately. Without this, reconciliation remains superficial, if not misplaced, thus opening itself to renewed conflict. In other words, reconciliation in society springs from the celebration of the Holy Communion. God's reconciliation in Jesus Christ thus becomes the basis for Christians to reject any social system that assumes the fundamental irreconcilability of people.

The emphasis on the cross is of particular importance when observing this particular approach to reconciliation. Here the Anselmian or penal substitutionary theory comes to mind. As mentioned, the *Message to the People of South Africa*, the *Belhar Confession*, and the *National Initiative for Reconciliation* proceeds from the premise that the injustice of apartheid cannot be addressed unless the roots of the predicament are also identified. Here the roots of human suffering are typically traced back, at a more ultimate level, to our alienation from God. In this context, it is stressed that we not only need to overcome the consequences of sin (evil) but also address the roots of evil (sin). On this basis, human sin is the root cause of contemporary manifestations of evil.

Moreover, salvation is understood at the ultimate level as reconciliation between God and humanity. From an Anselmian perspective, such reconciliation is only possible based on God's liberating word of forgiveness. However, forgiveness alone will not suffice and is dependent on a complex and reciprocal interaction between God and human beings where human sin is not merely condoned (which would be to condone injustice) but is addressed in such a way that reconciliation becomes possible. In this context, Christians typically find the clue to such reconciliation in the cross and not so much in the resurrection of Jesus Christ – the latter, which is the case in the approach to reconciliation found in the *Kairos Document*.

CHAPTER 4

Justice and Reconciliation after Liberation

4.1 Introduction

This chapter describes and analyses a particular way reconciliation is understood within the context of liberation theology in South Africa. In this approach, the need for political, economic and cultural liberation is emphasized. It is assumed that social justice can only follow upon liberation and that reconciliation is only possible on the basis of following justice. This approach is evident especially in the *Kairos Document*, in comments on reconciliation in the context of Black Theology and in critical engagements with the proceedings of the TRC. It is still found in current forms of prophetic theology. Rhetorically, this approach was aimed primarily at what the *Kairos Document* describes as "church theology" and "state theology." One may suggest that the question addressed here is how reconciliation between people relates to the victory established by Christ over the forces of death, destruction, and oppression. This leads to a different notion of the relationship between justice and reconciliation.

The description and analysis of this chapter will be done based on selected literature emerging after Cottesloe in 1960 and leading up to the *Kairos Document* in 1985.

4.2 Historical Background to the *Kairos Document*

This section entails a survey of literature emerging from the publication of the *Kairos Document* in 1985. Of course, the *Kairos Document* cannot be understood apart from the events leading to it, which will be addressed in summary form.

4.2.1 The Study Project on Christianity in an Apartheid Society

The rejection of apartheid as a "false gospel" was discussed in *The Message*. The Christian Institute, together with the SACC, were shown to be key contributors in formulating what became the first extensive theological rebuttal of the system. However, after its release, the question concerning the social implications of *The Message* simply had to be addressed. As a response, the Christian Institute and the SACC launched the programme, the Study Project on Christianity in Apartheid South Africa (SPRO-CAS), in 1969. The five biblical principles of SPRO-CAS were inherited from the theology of *The Message*. Walshe suggests that "these principles also provided the foundations for an indigenous development of liberation theology – a theology that had been gestating within the Christian Institute and was simultaneously maturing as Black Theology within the Black Consciousness movement." The first principle of change (2 Cor 5:7; Gal 6:16; Rev 21:5) focused on personal redemption but also referred to the historical evolution of society. Christians were called to be "active collaborators" in seeking a "new world." For this to happen requires a concern for life (Matt 11:4–6; 15:32, 25:36), which is the second principle. Here the focus is on the poor and oppressed, including the sick, exploited, deprived and alienated. In this context, to love one's neighbour implies a responsibility for public affairs, including government policies. With this understanding, a third principle is revealed, namely that of Christian participation (Luke 10:1; John 15:15; Matt 23:8) in the sharing and ordering of society which was the antithesis of racial domination. This implies the fourth principle, which focuses on stewardship (Matt 25:14; 1 Cor 4:2; 1 Pet 4:10). Here stewardship refers to both the individual being a steward to his or her own life as well as being a steward of the country and its resources. This also includes the stewardship of social processes that govern the political economy. The fifth principle is guided by the belief that every human person is created in the likeness of a loving God (Luke 12:6; Eph 2:10;

Gal 3:28). This principle rejects any notion seeking to humiliate, oppress and exploit those created in God's likeness; this includes any social arrangement that strives to alienate the human person from its fellows.[1]

The novelty of SPRO-CAS was its open-ended, exploratory mode and its willingness to move from the realm of religion to the secular worlds of sociology, politics, education, and economics.[2] Under the directorship of Peter Randall, a teacher and writer and Assistant Director of the South African Institute of Race Relations, SPRO-CAS, a public policy think-tank, represents a bold attempt to envision a society beyond apartheid. Its various initiatives were designed to present practical as well as ethically acceptable alternatives to the government policy of apartheid. Alf Stadler mentions that the programme had two phases, with SPRO-CAS I focusing on providing an extensive analysis of the situation and SPRO-CAS II focusing on formulating strategies for change in South Africa.[3] Over four years, SPRO-CAS established six major commissions (on economics, education, law, society, politics and the church) consisting of more than 130 leading South Africans of different racial and cultural groups. White, English-speaking participants were predominant, with black and Afrikaner leaders also represented.[4] They included people from various disciplines, such as academics, politicians, lawyers, clergy, teachers, and theologians. Walshe critically observed that "all ethnic groups and a wide range of occupations were to be represented. However, in practice, the white professional class and particularly university faculty were pre-dominant, with no more than token black representation on the commissions: the black/white member ratios were 5:26 in the Church Commission, 1:20 Economics, 1:14 Education, 1:13 Legal, 1:24 Political and 5:22 in the Social Commission."[5] Dubow further suggests that through SPRO-CAS I, an older generation of white liberals had direct contact with a rising new generation. Moreover, with SPRO-CAS II in 1972, the initiative became much more action orientated and committed to the idea of black leadership.[6]

---

1. Walshe, *Church Versus State*, 103–104.
2. Dubow, *Apartheid*, 167–168.
3. Stadler, "Anxious Radicals: SPRO-CAS," in: *Journal of Southern African Studies*, 102–108.
4. Naidoo, *Island in Chains*, 86–87.
5. Walshe, *Church Versus State*, 102.
6. Dubow, *Apartheid*, 168; Also see Walshe, *Church versus State*, 108.

The SPRO-CAS findings and recommendations were not particularly theological. Instead, its recommendations "were designed to produce a common, non-racial society structured around the dignity of the human person. The hope was that it would stimulate discussion in government circles and within political parties as well as in the churches by offering a humane range of alternatives to Christians and non-Christians alike."[7] These recommendations were outlined in the SPRO-CAS reports: *Education beyond Apartheid* (1971); *Towards Social Change* (1971); *Power, Privilege and Poverty* (1972); *Apartheid and the Church* (1972); *Law, Justice and Society* (1972); *South Africa's Political Alternatives* (1973) as well as a coordinated report entitled, *A Taste of Power: The Final Spro-Cas Report* (1973).[8] Though they lacked a single direction, the reports were quite thorough and their recommendations very specific – they were polemical in intent and reflected a significant understanding of the challenges facing the country.[9]

This was also reflected in the Church Commission's report, *Apartheid and the Church*, which focused on how apartheid affected the churches.[10] The report highlighted discrimination, denominationalism, segregation and paternalism as factors undermining the church's witness. Churches were called to move beyond ecclesiastical self-concern, pragmatic pietism and clericalism to become more faithful to the demands of the kingdom of God. The report further emphasized the failure of the multiracial churches "to promote inter-racial contact, communication and dialogue on a large scale," calling for symbolic acts of protest against racial discrimination – including welcoming persons of different races as worshippers into the various congregations.[11] Most importantly, in Walshe's estimation, was the report's focus on crash training programmes for black clergy and laity – with the aim of taking over leadership responsibilities. In his view, this was "the beginning of a shift towards an acceptance of black predominance in the life of the church." The encouragement of black leadership in the churches and wider society was further outlined in the final SPRO-CAS report, *A Taste of Power*. "This not

---

7. Walshe, *Church versus State*, 102.
8. Randall, *Taste of Power*.
9. Randall, *Taste of Power*, 117; 146.
10. Randall, *Apartheid and the Church*.
11. Randall, *Apartheid and the Church*, 71.

only encouraged whites to work for the emergence of black leadership but recognised that South Africa was at a turning point in its history in that a white control model for change had become an outmoded strategy, an unrealistic hope destroyed by white intransigence."[12]

Notwithstanding its "white liberal" outlook, SPRO-CAS initiated a shift in highlighting the importance of black participation and leadership – this, despite its critics, among them the black consciousness leader, Steve Biko, arguing that the initiative was constrained by its desire to find "an alternative acceptable to the white man."[13] Through its director, Peter Randall and his co-directors, Beyers Naudé, Bill Burnett and Alan Paton, the boundaries began to be tested. For Walshe, those involved in SPRO-CAS started to think more courageously, "rather than seeing black pressures for change as a problematical and even alarming reality that had somehow to be coped with, they were slowly coming to see such pressures as the sociological basis for Biblically-inspired hope."[14] This statement should be considered in light of the emergence of Black Theology within the Black Consciousness movement, a development acknowledged in the *Apartheid and the Church* report.[15]

In addition to bringing people from various backgrounds into urgent conversation, SPRO-CAS allowed the Christian Institute and the SACC to strengthen their ties with Black Consciousness groupings. But its diverse membership meant that those involved in the initiative could never fully agree on what apartheid was, let alone create consensus about how to end it. However, for De Gruchy, SPRO-CAS represents a decisive turning point in the work and witness of the Christian Institute. By 1972, when the programme was completed, the Christian Institute (with support from the SACC) rapidly

---

12. Walshe, *Church versus State*, 109; Also see Randall, *Apartheid and the Church*, 71–72.

13. Biko, *I Write What I Like*, 90–91.

14. Walshe, 108.

15. The report states that "the basic purpose and tendency of 'Black Theology' is to be welcomed. For this is basically an attempt to indigenize the Gospel in terms of the cultural forms, the general situation and the specific needs of blacks. It is an attempt to translate the Gospel much more radically into black ways of thinking and in relation to black problems so that Christ will no longer be seen through the eyes of [white people]. One of the causes that has helped prompt the rise of black theology is evangelistic concern about the general drift of blacks from the Church today. It is felt that one of the reasons for this is that the traditional Churches have been more adapted to the spiritual needs of the [whites] than to [blacks]. Underlying Black Theology, and necessary for it, is the emergence of a sense of black identity. It realises that the understanding of God must come through life experience and for the black person this means his black experience." See Randall, *Apartheid and the Church*, 51–52.

expanded its work and became more involved in the black struggle.[16] Walshe describes this change in the stance of the Christian Institute as a parting of ways with "the old liberal illusion that change could be effected solely by education and moral appeals directed at the privileged." He further posits that the Christian Institute

> began to encourage the resurgence of Black Consciousness as a source of renewed dignity and potential for the poor. This involved the judgement that black initiatives would be crucial in pressing for change; that whites could and should no longer expect to control such initiatives; that the [Christian Institute], by increasing its black membership and witnessing to the essential human community above color, could assist in the emergence of a new generation of black leaders.[17]

4.2.2 The World Council of Churches Programme to Combat Racism

On the ecumenical front, the WCC launched its controversial Programme to Combat Racism (PCR) in 1971. This came in the aftermath of the WCC-sponsored Geneva Conference on Church and Society in 1966. As stated elsewhere, the developments at the Geneva Conference significantly impacted the South African delegates, eventually leading to *The Message* in 1968.[18] Also, at this meeting, the controversial issue of Christian participation in revolutionary struggles was tabled. This resulted in the WCC Executive Committee's decision to recommend the formation of an ecumenical PCR. Their decision formed part of the WCC's broader response to the predicament of human sin – described as the struggle against the deeply entrenched "demonic forces" of "racial prejudice" and "hatred" that operate in the social, economic and political structures of the time. They further called upon the churches to move beyond charity grants to "relevant and sacrificial action" that would lead to new "relationships of dignity and justice" among all.[19] With this in mind, the WCC Executive Committee unveiled a five-year programme providing

---

16. De Gruchy, *The Church Struggle*, 106.
17. Walshe, "Church versus State," 462.
18. See Chapter 3, section 3.2.2.
19. Van der Bent, *World Council of Churches'*, vii.

guidelines for a special fund which was to be used to financially support liberation movements struggling against racism in different parts of the world, notably in Southern Africa. This includes grants to the liberation movements in South Africa, including the ANC.[20] David Thomas notes that the WCC insisted that a distinction be made between expressing "solidarity" with the oppressed and "support" for violence – the grants represent the former, not the latter. However, this subtle distinction was quickly brushed aside in the debates that followed.[21]

The news of the special fund caused considerable controversy in South Africa. Generally, blacks welcomed the grants while many whites rejected them – this polarized reaction created serious tension within the churches.[22] For many whites in South Africa, the WCC was now identified as a "terrorist organisation" simply because it aligned with the liberation movements and their struggle.[23] This further intensified the debate on using violence (as opposed to a non-violent approach) in the liberation struggle. For the most part, the WCC leadership was seen to be in support of violent revolution. The ecumenical body was also accused of giving up hope in the churches' own struggle for change through working towards justice and reconciliation.[24] These problems were further compounded through government propaganda, pressuring member churches to leave the ecumenical body. In the end, none

---

20. "FRELIMO, in control of approximately one-fifth of Mozambique, received $15,000 for social welfare as its first development plan set out to expand the number of schools and clinics, to foster agriculture co-operatives and encourage exports of groundnuts, rye, cashew nuts, tobacco and rubber. SWAPO (The South West African Peoples Organisation) received $5,000, ZANU (the Zimbabwe African National Union) and ZAPU (the Zimbabwe African People's Union) $10,000 each, the MPLA (Popular Movement for the Liberation of Angola) and GRAE (the Revolutionary Government of Angola in Exile) $20,000 each, and UNITA (the National Union for the Total Liberation of Angola $10,000. The ANC received $10,000 to launch a Luthuli Memorial Fund which, it was hoped, would influence world opinion through exploring alternatives to apartheid. Five thousand US dollars were allocated to the Angola Committee and Dr. Eduardo Mondlane Foundation for a joint venture: a Foundation for the Promotion of Information about Racism and Colonialism. These were modest sums and all recipients gave assurances that the funds would be used not for military purposes but for educational or organisational needs which included establishing social infrastructure in liberated areas." See Walshe, *Church versus Sate*, 111.

21. See Thomas, *Councils in the Ecumenical*, 73.

22. De Gruchy, "Christianity in Twentieth-century", 100.

23. Thomas, *Councils in the Ecumenical*, 73.

24. De Gruchy, *Church Struggle*, 127.

of them did, but the churches' ambiguous synodical statements reflected the differences of opinion on the matter.

The SACC leadership immediately distanced itself from the WCC decision. Walshe suggests that the SACC, with its predominantly white leadership, failed to comprehend the "carefully marshalled arguments" of the WCC. In his view, the SACC "made the instinctive and tendentious leap from the WCC's support for the publicity and welfare activities of the liberation movements to the assumption that this support involved a commitment to the use of violence for change in Southern Africa."[25] De Gruchy's assessment of the SACC is more generous. He posits that:

> While the [SACC] expressed their critique of the grants to liberation movements, they also expressed their support for much of the rest of the work of the Programme to Combat Racism. This support needs to be underlined. The churches were unanimous in affirming the programme. The only significant point of difference was on the grants made by the Special Fund to liberation movements using violence to achieve their ends. In rejecting the support, whether implicit or explicit, of violence as a way to solve racism, they were not opting for the status quo. They had long been committed to change that, at least in theory.[26]

The Christian Institute also committed to a pacifist stance and distanced itself from the WCC decision. However, its leadership insisted that South Africans had no right to criticize the WCC while structural violence characterized the country's political, economic and social life. They further contended that, given the circumstances, law and order should not be sacralized at the expense of justice and liberation. On the use of violence, Beyers Naudé argued that Christianity traditionally offers two options: "The first point of view is that the Church and the Christian have under no circumstances the right to approve or use violence. The other point of view is that when all other means have failed, a Christian has the right to use violence to change a situation of unbearable injustice and to bring about a situation of greater justice."[27]

---

25. Walshe, *Church versus State*, 115
26. De Gruchy, *Church Struggle*, 127–128.
27. International Commission of Jurists, *The Trial of Beyers Naudé*, 116.

In this context, Naudé's stance was closely aligned with the WCC. Walshe postulates that for both Naudé and the WCC the matter was judged to be more complex than simply reducing it to "violence versus non-violence." For instance, the use of violence (structural and otherwise) was a well-established reality, so whether Christians could avoid this is problematic. In Naudé's case, the dilemma was to "reduce the sum total of violence in the situation and to liberate human beings for just and peaceful relations with each other."

In the same way, the WCC leadership judged their support for the liberation movements as an attempt to address the broader societal deficiencies. The main aim was to minimize violence and injustice. The accusation that the WCC was pro-violence is thus incorrect. Although Naudé and the Christian Institute adopted a pacifist position, they also held the view that action against injustice was needed to reduce the sum total of violence both in interpersonal relations and social structures – in this sense Naudé and the Christian Institute was closely aligned with the position taken by the WCC leadership.[28] Baldwin Sjollema, the first director of the PCR, also calls attention to the WCC's long tradition of condemning racial discrimination and when all peaceful means have been exhausted to do more to ensure the greater good is realized. He insists that the grants to the liberation movements did not imply the unqualified endorsement of their specific tactics. Instead, it was an indication of the WCC's support for the long-term goals of a more just society. In the case where some believed that they had no other option but to resort to violence, they were no longer automatically excluded from the moral and practical support of the WCC. Moreover, the WCC leadership maintained they would "continue to work for reconciliation, for an end to the violence of the oppressors as well as the violence of the oppressed."[29]

4.2.3 The SACC National Conference at Hammanskraal

The concern over the use of violence resurfaced when the SACC National Conference met at Hammanskraal, a black township north of Pretoria, in 1974. However, at this stage, the situation in the country had deteriorated

---

28. Walshe, *Church versus State*, 116–117. This position, Naudé later explains that their support for the grants had consequences (both personally and for the Christian Institute) which he describes in an article, "The parting of the ways": *"Die tyd vir vroom woorde is verby"* (the time for pious words is past) he wrote in *Pro Veritate*. See *Pro Veritate* 9, 6 October 1970.

29. Sjollema, *First Answer to Comments Received*.

significantly.³⁰ De Gruchy remarks that the attempts to resist apartheid by the Christian Institute, the SACC and the Black Consciousness movement (discussed below), as well as by the churches, had been severely countered by the state. This included the arrests, deportation, and banning of many individuals. The South African government also intensified its efforts to suppress SWAPO, the liberation movement in Namibia, and increased its involvement in the civil war in Angola. In the process, the South African state became heavily militarized.³¹ Delegates to the conference knew how combustible the situation was, which created an expectation (especially among blacks) that the SACC would reconsider its stance on non-violence as the only viable Christian response. Whites, on the other hand, were aware that despite all the resolutions and programmes, little had been achieved to resolve the problems arising out of apartheid. In De Gruchy's words:

> There was the feeling that while the position adopted by the churches on the grants to liberation movement was correct, insofar as violence was rejected as a solution, the churches had not really come to grips with the growing militarism of South Africa. Yet, both issues hung together. This provides the background to the challenge to SACC members which required a response as costly for whites as resolutions had normally been for blacks.³²

The SACC response came in the form of the controversial Resolution on Conscientious Objection against compulsory military service for whites.³³ With this resolution, whites were encouraged to refuse military service, given the injustice and violence committed by the South African government.

The idea of "conscientious objection" was first proposed by Douglas Bax, a white Presbyterian minister. Bax contributed to the SPRO-CAS report on

---

30. According to some there was a mood of desperation in the air. Some even suggest that the country was entering a state of civil war. See for instance Walshe, *Church versus State*, 118; Balia, *Christian Resistance to Apartheid*, 55–60.

31. De Gruchy, *Theological Odyssey*, 24–25.

32. De Gruchy, *Church Struggle*, 135.

33. "Conscientious objection" is an indigenous phenomenon that was encouraged by the success of the peace movement in the United States which opposed the war in Vietnam. A 'conscientious objector' is a person who claimed the right to refuse to perform military service on the grounds of freedom of thought, conscience, or religion. This point became particularly important during the SACC National Conference because by law white adult males were required to perform military service. See Regehr, *Perceptions of Apartheid*, 265.

Apartheid and the Church, and it was there that the idea of conscientious objection was first raised. Walshe describes the Resolution on Conscientious Objection as "an effort to find a 'third way' – not that of defending the *status quo* as 'law and order', nor that of countering the violence of unjust social structures and repression with revolutionary force. The hope was that a way could be found between the violence of white domination and the force of black liberation – a way of non-violence with conscientious objection and passive resistance as major components."[34] The SACC member churches were further reminded that the taking up of arms could be justifiable, "if at all, only to fight a just war," but that this excluded "war in defence of a basically unjust and discriminating society." Since the South African government was unjust, any attempt to defend it was deemed questionable. In addition, church leaders were encouraged to call on their members to "identify with the oppressed" and consider "becoming conscientious objectors."[35]

Due to its controversial nature, the Resolution on Conscientious Objection drew considerable public attention. The opponents of the SACC used the opportunity to accuse those who considered conscientious objection the same as those who supported the WCC grants to "terrorists." For De Gruchy, "The fact that the [conscientious objection] statement explicitly indicated that violence was [criticised] as a means to solve problems, and did not, therefore, justify the black use of violence, was lost from sight. Most people did not want to know the full position of the churches, which was submerged beneath a plethora of press publicity and propaganda."[36] Walshe adds that leaders of the NGK accused the SACC of committing treason and called on South Africans to defend the country's borders. Even the United and Progressive Parties, which were known to have a liberal orientation, condemned the Resolution on Conscientious Objection for what they believed was undermining the security of the country. This view was echoed by many whites, who, through state propaganda, believed that South Africa was under threat from a foreign attack. In their opinion, the SACC acted irresponsibly by not outright condemning foreign and domestic military aggression against the state.[37]

---

34. Walshe, *Church versus State*, 120.

35. See the resolution on conscientious objection in Thomas, *Councils in the Ecumenical*, 114.

36. De Gruchy, *Church Struggle*, 137.

37. Walshe, *Church versus State*, 121.

The response from white parishes remained largely apathetic. The attempt to encourage a white movement of conscientious objectors never gained the support needed. In reality, the Resolution on Conscientious Objection caused some white South Africans, who were generally opposed to apartheid, to distance themselves from the SACC and the Christian Institute. During this period, the modest white membership of the Christian Institute diminished. At the time, Naudé suggested this was "simply because many whites who are willing to be 'liberal' are unwilling to be liberated."[38] In Walshe's words, "liberal whites would not relinquish control. In principle, they were prepared to move away from racial discrimination and permit blacks to enter the established economic and political structures under white leadership; but they balked at the risks involved in empowering the poor and oppressed majority."[39] Naudé maintained, however, that the Christian Institute had "no option . . . but to continue to portray to the church and society its understanding of liberation as proclaimed and exemplified by Christ."[40] In the aftermath of Hammanskraal, the Christian Institute moved into much closer cooperation with black organizations. As a result, it became much more activist-orientated, significantly increasing its black membership. More importantly, the Christian Institute, under Naudé, gained the trust of the black protest movements that were forming inside the churches and the Black Consciousness movement.[41]

4.2.4 The Emergence of the Black Consciousness Movement

The SPRO-CAS call to action resulted in two different initiatives. One was called the White Community Programme (WCP), and the other the Black Community Programme (BCP). The WCP, later renamed the Programme for Social Change (PSC), never gained the support needed to be sustainable.[42]

---

38. Christian Institute, *Director's Report August 1, 1973 to July 31, 1974*, 8.
39. Walshe, *Church versus State*, 122.
40. Christian Institute, *Director's Report August 1, 1973 to July 31, 1974*, 8.
41. Walshe, *Church versus State*, 122.
42. The WCP was "intended to raise white consciousness; that is, the responsibility of well-meaning whites was now seen to be in their own community." Here, "the task was to release individuals from their race and class biases, to free them from the morally stultifying grip of their own privilege so that they might respond creatively to black initiatives." However, the WCP never gained the support needed. "As the Christian Institute suspected, even as the [WCP] was being launched, there was insufficient yeast – no critical mass. Certainly the dough did not rise, despite the efforts of a few brave individuals." This trend continued when the WCP was renamed PSC. See Walshe, *Church versus State*, 140–145.

By mid-1975, it had exhausted its budget. Moreover, its white staff members found the initiative to have lost its relevance to effect any meaningful change.

In contrast, the BCP had the "easier" task of harnessing black discontent to gain support. However, Walshe cautions against exaggerating the impact of the BCP. In his view, the BCP did not initiate a new protest movement. Instead, it set out to support the much broader Black Consciousness movement, which had independent origins in the late 1960s.[43] Here the resurgence of African nationalism, usually described as the Black Consciousness movement, is traced to the University Christian Movement (UCM) formation in 1966 – this, by black and white students committed to a Christian witness against apartheid. Soon after its formation, the UCM was challenged by internal tension between its black and white members.

Driven by an emerging sense that blacks should take the initiative for their own liberation struggle, it soon became apparent that the (white) liberal model of the non-racial student organization could not withstand the level of black discontent.[44] It was argued that despite its facade of non-racialism, the UCM was primarily a "white-dominated," organization.[45] This made cooperation across racial lines increasingly more difficult, eventually leading to the formation of a black caucus with Steve Biko and Barney Pityana at its centre.[46] Those in the black caucus were determined to understand the long history of black protest in the country and find creative ways of addressing existing challenges. They did this by focusing on the radical writings of black American scholars like James Baldwin, Stokely Carmichael, Eldridge Cleaver and James Cone – particularly, their concern with Black Theology as a vehicle for examining the predicament of the poor and the oppressed.[47]

In the meantime, talks were already underway on the importance of forming a black organization. This led to the establishment of the South African Students' Organisation (SASO) in 1968. According to Takatso Mafokeng,

---

43. Walshe, *Church versus State*, 149.

44. Although white liberals have often been criticized for interference or "managing" the black struggle (whatever the truth of such claims may be), it is nevertheless fair to say that a select group of white liberals and white liberal organizations made significant contributions in advancing black consciousness at a crucial time during the liberation struggle.

45. Frostin, *Liberation Theology in Tanzania*, 91.

46. Walshe, *Church versus State*, 149.

47. Walshe, *Church versus State*, 149.

SASO, which developed out of the UCM, became the first organizational expression of Black Consciousness. He posits that "the UCM, a Christian organisation, became the organisational ground on which the idea of Black Consciousness solidified... It is important to note that the SASO and thereby the Black Consciousness philosophical approach was born inside Christian circles."[48] For Basil Moore, the matter is more nuanced. In his words:

> Many of the founding members of SASO, like Steve Biko [also an executive member of the UCM] and Nyameko [Barney] Pityana, were Christians and wanted to maintain their involvement in the UCM. They also recognised that SASO was not and could not become a Christian movement. Thus, SASO became the coordinating agency for black student politics and committed itself to the development of the Black Consciousness ideology and the broader Black Consciousness movement.[49] What Christian members of SASO demanded of the UCM was the development of a theological counterpart to Black Consciousness which would address the issue of Black liberation. These demands became more strident during 1969 and 1970 and black students became increasingly scornful of UCM's engagement in humanistic "Encounter Groups" and the like, which reflected an old [liberal] "reconciliation" mind-set.[50]

SASO further drew together a wide range of groups to form the BPC in 1971.[51] According to Gail Gerhart, the aim was to form an organization that would serve as the central coordinating body of the Black Consciousness

---

48. Mofokeng, *Crucified Among the Crossbearers*, 9.

49. In the SASO policy manifesto of 1971, black consciousness is presented in terms of having a specific focus on cultural liberation in the philosophy of *Ujamaa*: (i) Black Consciousness is an attitude of mind, a way of life; (ii) The basic tenet of Black Consciousness is that the Black man must reject all value systems that seek to make him a foreigner in the country of his birth and reduce his basic human dignity; (iii) The Black man must build up his own value systems, see himself as self-defined and not defined by others. See Regehr, *Perceptions of Apartheid*, 201.

50. Moore, "Black Theology," 24.

51. The BPC was aimed to serve as a national umbrella organization for sympathetic social, cultural, and political organizations. Its inaugural conference was attended by more than 1,400 delegates representing 145 organizations.

movement and fill the political vacuum left by banning the black liberation movements.[52] For Dubow:

> The Black People's Convention further helped to bring together a burgeoning network of grassroots community organisations seeking to give expression to the idea of self-reliance. Here, Julius Nyerere's *Ujamaa* philosophy [socialist system of village cooperatives based on equality of opportunity and self-help, established in the 1960s] in Tanzania was a source of inspiration. A range of health, educational and literacy projects were undertaken under the auspices of the [BCP] . . . The intention was to give practical effect to Black Consciousness and to broaden as well as deepen its support base by locating it in (predominantly) rural communities. Significant funding was made available to the BCP from ecumenical Christian organisations like the Christian Institute and foreign churches.[53]

The BPC went on to play a leading role in the student protests of the 1970s. This reached a watershed with the uprising of Soweto youth in 1976, rapidly spreading throughout the country. Inspired and supported by the Black Consciousness movement, the Soweto student uprising represented the first major black act of resistance and protest since Sharpeville in 1960.[54] This came as a direct response to the government's educational policies requiring the use of Afrikaans (traditionally seen as the language of the apartheid state) as a medium of instruction in schools. For Hermann Giliomee, the reasons for the protest are much broader than this particular issue alone. In his view, "the Soweto uprising that started on 16 June 1976 was rooted in the pass laws, the denial of black political rights, and the lack of any representation in the industrial councils and conciliation boards where wage and other disputes were settled. Black rejection of these structural features of white domination dates back to the earliest days of Union."[55] Whatever the merits, what started as a peaceful protest soon degenerated under the impact

---

52. Gerhart, *Black Power in South Africa*, 292.
53. Dubow, *Apartheid*, 164–165. For an extended discussion on the *Ujamaa* philosophy see Frostin, *Liberation Theology in Tanzania and South Africa*, 29–47.
54. Engdahl, *Theology in Conflict*, 40–41.
55. Giliomee, *The Last Afrikaner*, 108.

of insensitive police action into stone-throwing and police gunfire. After several days of rioting and shooting, 176 people were killed and hundreds injured. John Kane-Berman adds that in the year following the Soweto uprising, the death toll rose dramatically as the army joined the police attempting to crush organized dissent.[56] Among the many deaths, the death of the Black Consciousness leader, Steve Biko, who died in police custody, is particularly significant. According to Dubow:

> Biko was brutally interrogated, chained to a grille, and assaulted. He died, aged 30, of brain injuries . . . on 12 September [1977], after being transported for 1,200 km, comatose and manacled, in the back of a police Land Rover . . . The government soon comprehended the impact of his death and hastened to crack down on all remnants of Black Consciousness. In October [1977], it banned 18 anti-apartheid organisations including SASO, Soweto Students' Representative Council, Black People's Convention, the Christian Institute, and the Black Parents' Association.[57]

Many arrests and banning orders followed as the government tried to contain black demonstrations, strikes and boycotts, which continued to disrupt the country for the remainder of the 1970s and into the 1980s. In this context, the Soweto uprising became an international symbol of blacks rejecting apartheid. What followed did much damage to the reputation of white South Africa, more so than anything else in its history. Following the chain of events, one would have to recognize the role of the Black Consciousness movement as being at the heart of the realization that blacks themselves have to bear responsibility for change in the country. Therefore, the emergence of Black Theology cannot be adequately understood if one neglects the context of Black Consciousness.

4.2.5 The Emergence of a Black Theology of Liberation

The emergence of the Black Consciousness movement indicates that theology and politics interacted in articulating this philosophy. For instance, in his role as leader of this movement, Steve Biko was fully committed to the project of

---

56. Kane-Berman, *South Africa: The Method*, 26–33.
57. Dubow, *Apartheid*, 188.

Black Theology.⁵⁸ The same could be said about Barney Pityana and many others who had close ties with theology and the churches.⁵⁹ During this period, the "liberation" theme became increasingly influential. In theological circles, it became an umbrella term for many theologies reflecting the Christian witness in the struggle for justice in South Africa.⁶⁰ Stimulated partly by Black Theology in the United States and aware of the liberation theology articulated in Latin America, those in the UCM sought an indigenous theology that reflected the South African predicament. As a response, the UCM launched the Black Theology Project in 1971. It was particularly the Black Theology of James Cone (in the United States) that resonated with those in the UCM.⁶¹ Cone's ideas, mainly his focus on Black Theology as a theology of liberation, dominated the Black Theology Project and became a valuable basis for developing a Black Theology arising out of the South African context.⁶² Ironically, it was the UCM Director of Theological Concerns, Basil Moore (a white Methodist minister, considered a Marxist by some conservatives), that Black Theology, as a method of theological reflection, was first imported from the United States.⁶³ In Moore's words:

> He had come to hold that in racist society racism not only structures the experiences of the oppressors and their victims differently, it also makes the 'see' and interpret things differently. As such the nature and meaning of the Gospel is understood radically differently when it is approached from within the experiential context of white oppressors from what it is when black experiences and aspirations inform the interpretation. Thus,

---

58. Biko, "Black Consciousness," 36–47.
59. Howarth, "Black Consciousness," 100.
60. Vosloo, "Christianity and Apartheid," 414.
61. The work of the African American scholar James Cone had particular relevance. See for instance, Cone, *Black Theology & Black Power*; Cone, *Black Theology of Liberation*.
62. Goba, "Black Consciousness," 62; Vellem, "The Symbol of Liberation," 43–46.
63. Chikane, "Foreword," xiv; Also see Mushete, "History of Theology," 31.
  It is ironic that black theology in South Africa was introduced by a white liberal at a time when the black consciousness was at the height of its influence and when its proponents were sceptical about the roles played by white liberals in the black political struggle. Moore was acceptable to those who used black theology as means of self-description because he devoted a lot of energy and effort to encouraging blacks to radicalize themselves on their own terms. In doing so, he was far removed from the many "traditional" paternalistic liberals they were used to. See for instance, Maimela, "Black Consciousness and White," 62.

> Black Theology was about black people interpreting the Gospel in the light of black experience and interpreting black experience in view of the Gospel. Alongside this proposition [he] had come to reject the validity of white theology (a position [he] was later to qualify) on the grounds that Christ was identified with the oppressed both in their suffering and their struggle for liberation. Thus, [he] argued that 'black' referred not simply to all the victims of racism inclusively (i.e. had to include 'Coloureds' and 'Indians'), but specifically to those victims of racism who were engaged personally and directly in the liberation struggle. 'Black', if you like, referred exclusively to black freedom fighters. As a result, [he] argued that Black Theology had to grow out of the liberation, and its subjects were the liberation activists.[64]

In this sense, Moore believes that his exposure to American Black Theology was very influential in helping shape this methodological stance in South Africa.

The first local colloquium on Black Theology was organized by the Director of the Black Theology Project, Sabelo Ntwasa. The immediate result was a series of further colloquia (throughout the country) and the publication of a selection of the essays presented at these meetings. The publication, the first of its kind in South Africa, *Essays in Black Theology*, edited by Mokgethi Motlhabi, was immediately banned.[65] This was followed by a banning order against at least six contributing authors, including Moore and Ntwasa.[66] The essays, supplemented by a few others, were later published by the London

---

64. It is important to note that this stance was not universally accepted in the UCM (as well as SASO). Firstly, there were those in the UCM who came from the PAC and the Africanist tradition. While many agreed with Moore's analysis that racism was the fundamental cause of black oppression, the Africanists argued that his methodology could give no significant place to traditional African culture, especially to traditional African religious culture. According to this view, black theology had to take seriously the theology that was taking shape within the African Independent Churches. Secondly, there were those UCM members who had been nurtured in the socialist traditions of the ANC. In their view, Moore's methodology, including much of what was happening in the black consciousness movement, simply ignored the fundamental issue of capitalism and class. For them, any analysis of the struggle of black people had to include role of capitalism. Racism and capitalism in South Africa were fundamentally tied to each other. In other words, one would have to prioritize both racism and capitalism. The methodology for black theology did not do this. See for instance, Moore, 25–26.

65. Motlhabi, *Essays in Black Theology*.
66. De Gruchy, *Church Struggle*, 149–150.

publisher Christopher Hurst under the title *Black Theology: The South Africa Voice* and was edited by Moore while in exile in Australia.[67]

The immediate challenge facing Black Theology in South Africa was the dominance of what Moore refers to as "liberal ecumenism," where the theme of reconciliation through interpersonal contact was emphasized. This "liberal reconciliation ideology" of opposition to apartheid was attractive to many white English speakers as well as some of the more conservative blacks.[68] This was the case for the UCM (including the Black Theology Project) as well as what was happening in the churches. Following Cottesloe, the churches' opposition was fundamentally more anti-National Party than anti-racist. In this sense, they (especially the English-speaking churches) never seriously addressed the issue of their own racism. Instead, more focus was placed on the need for multi-racialism. In practice, this did very little to alter the white-dominated power structures of these churches. Key positions were still in white hands. This includes especially English-speaking whites still being appointed as bishops, general secretaries, and other office bearers. They were often appointed in positions concerning financial control, publications and theological education (especially that of blacks). Alongside the dominance of whites arose the clamour for multiracial contact. Moore posits that:

> The religious rationale for this 'contact', which also had its secular counterpart, was 'reconciliation'. Against the rising tide of racialism, the Churches or their leaders came to see the crucial need as being for 'reconciliation' between blacks and whites. This need for 'reconciliation' led to an almost pathological 'got-to-get-me-a-black-man-to-find-out-what-he-is-thinking' attitude among many whites.[69]

Over time, however, this particular approach had to contend with the growing mood among blacks against the "phoney" reconciliation implied in the multi-racialism (and liberal ecumenism) of the time. This may be regarded as one of the most significant factors making the emergence of Black Theology in South Africa possible.[70] It further prompted a creative phase in

---

67. Moore, "Black Theology: In the beginning," 19.
68. Moore, 20.
69. Moore, "What is Black Theology?," 3.
70. Moore, "What is Black Theology?," 3.

the development of Black Theology in the 1970s – with several black theologians working towards developing Black Theology in relation to their confessional traditions. Among them were Manas Buthelezi, Desmond Tutu, and Simon Maimela. A younger generation of scholars including Buti Tlhagale, Takatso Mofokeng, Bonganjalo Goba, Allan Boesak, Itumeleng Mosala, and Mokgethi Motlhabi, among others, followed them.[71] However, despite the significant influence of Black Consciousness and Black Theology, the social basis of this new type of intellectual reflection was quite limited. Bonganjalo Goba points to this when he argues:

> So many of us are remote from the everyday experiences of our black people. There is a gap between the black élite and the ordinary black man. We have allowed our acquired intellectualism to separate us from the ordinary people. Today when we speak of the Black Consciousness movement, we immediately think of students in SASO and a few clerics. The rest of the people are not involved. If black solidarity is to achieve anything this gap cannot be allowed to exist.[72]

Per Frostin points that it was only later, with the formation of the Institute for Contextual Theology (1982), that the relationship between grassroots communities and the academic study of Black Theology was given the necessary attention – this also relates to feminist concerns about the role of black women in the discipline.[73] In the meantime, Black Theology was propagated mainly through colloquia and ministers' caucuses. During this period, some of the most significant scholarly contributions on the topic, including some doctoral dissertations, were produced – this continued well into the "Kairos" period during the 1980s.[74]

---

71. Tshaka and Mafokane, "Continued Relevance," 534–535.

72. Goba, "Corporate Personality," 73.

73. Frostin, *Liberation Theology in Tanzania*, 94.

74. Among the first of these dissertations published were Allan Boesak's Farewell to Innocence: A Socio-Ethical Study on Black Theology and Black Power (1976); Bonganjalo Goba's *An Agenda for Black Theology: Hermeneutics for Social Change* (1988); Takatso A. Mofokeng's, *The Crucified Among the Crossbearers: Towards a Black Christology* (1983); Itumuleng Mosala's, *Biblical Hermeneutics and Black Theology in South Africa* (1989); and Cecil Ngcokovane, *Demons of Apartheid* (1989). One notable unpublished doctoral dissertation by a white male theologian is Klippies Kritzinger's, "Black Theology: A challenge to mission" (1988). Among the books published by black theologians include Desmond Tutu's *Hope and Suffering: Sermons and*

4.2.6 Prologue to Kairos

The late 1970s saw the apartheid ideology transforming into something searching for what Deborah Posel refers to as a "new language of legitimation."[75] The apartheid state was in decline, and its leadership had to find new ways to sustain the ideology. At this time, the phrase "adapt or die" became commonplace in some Afrikaner circles.[76] Not only were there significant tensions within the government, but the "apartheid is a heresy debate" (discussed in the previous chapter) also strained relations within the NGK.[77] For many, this signalled the beginning of the end of Afrikaner unity in church and state. This also came in the wake of Prime Minister, Pieter Willem (PW) Botha's attempts to reform apartheid through a power-sharing system (without losing control).[78] This included some movement away from racial discrimination, leading to the amendment of the constitution.[79] Among other things, the new constitution of 1984 gave people from the "coloured" and "Indian" communities limited political representation in the so-called Tricameral Parliament. Black people were not offered representation because they were not considered citizens of South Africa but rather citizens of the Bantustans. The search for this "new language of legitimation" had a polarizing effect on the Afrikaner community. Dubow remarks that "in promoting national survival over Afrikaner ascendancy, hitherto core elements of the *volk* were pushed to the margins: the white working class, large parts of the rural *platteland*, as

---

Speeches (1983) Allan Boesak's, *Black and Reformed: Apartheid Liberation and the Calvinist Tradition* (1984). In 1986 a joint collection of essays entitled, *The Unquestionable Right to Be Free: Black Theology from South Africa* was published – edited by Itumeleng J. Mosala and Buti Tlhagale. A festschrift in honour of Desmond Tutu was published in 1986 – it is entitled, *Hammering Swords into Ploughshares: Essays in Honour of Archbishop Mpilo Desmond Tutu*. Simon Maimela's, *Proclaim Freedom to My People* (1987) is also notable. A collaborative effort between South African and American black theologians came in the form of a collection entitled, *We are One Voice: Black Theology in the USA and South Africa* (1989), edited by Dwight Hopkins and Simon Maimela with contributions from both countries. For the complete list see Motlhabi, *African Theology/Black Theology*, 12; Also see Tshaka and Mafokane, "Continued Relevance of," 534.

75. Posel, "Language of Domination", In: Marks and Trapido, *Politics of Race*, 419.
76. Schrire, *Adapt or Die*, 29–47.
77. De Gruchy, "Grappling with the Colonial," 168.
78. Giliomee, *Last Afrikaner Leaders*, 139–174.
79. In some ways, these reform initiatives were less repressive than before: interracial marriage and miscegenation – both completely banned since the late 1940s – were legalized, and the constitutional prohibition on multiracial political parties was lifted. During this period the Group Areas Act, which barred "non-whites" from living in certain areas, was also relaxed.

well as Verwoerdian true-believers. This shift in the demographic patterns of power eventuated in a right-wing split in 1982 when . . . Andries Treurnicht led a break-away from the National Party to form the Conservative Party."[80]

In the meantime, the United Democratic Front (UDF), a broad coalition of 600 anti-apartheid organizations, was established in 1983.[81] The formation of the UDF came as a direct response to Prime Minister Botha's reform proposals which were seen as an attempt to co-op segments of the black community into an ideology of segregation. Instead, the UDF promoted a non-racial state "undiluted by racial or ethnic considerations" as the only constitutional solution for South Africa – in their terms: "Apartheid had to be dismantled, not reformed."[82] Significantly, the UDF leadership consisted of prominent clergypersons, including Desmond Tutu, Allan Boesak, and Dennis Hurley. According to Pauw, this is a good indication that the church struggle now aligned itself firmly with the liberation struggle as the only way to end apartheid – the result was a shift in church debates away from theological arguments to plans of action against apartheid.[83] Nevertheless, the theological critique of apartheid continued at the recently founded Institute for Contextual Theology (ICT). De Gruchy remarks that it "had been formed in 1982 as a means of fostering the development of progressive or liberating theological responses to the unfolding social and political situation."[84] Its first director, Frank Chikane, was an Apostolic Faith Mission Church minister. Chikane was a product of the Black Consciousness movement and on the forefront of black student politics following the Soweto uprising.[85] Together with other anti-apartheid theologians, most notably the Catholic theologian

---

80. Dubow, *Apartheid*, 203.

81. The lesser-known black consciousness-aligned National Forum was also formed in 1983. This organization emerged directly out of the Azanian People's Organisation (AZAPO), which was formed in 1978 to provide a political home for the Black Consciousness Movement. It should be pointed out, however, that the National Forum's focus on black exclusivism limited its scope of influence. On the other hand, the UDF's focus on "non-racialism" and "multi-racialism" made it more appealing to a wider racially diverse audience. Notwithstanding the ideological issues at play, this may explain why the UDF support base far exceeded that of the National Forum. For an interesting discussion on the National Forum and the UDF. See Dubow, *Apartheid*, 206–207.

82. Balia, *Christian Resistance*, 102.

83. Pauw, "Anti-apartheid Theology," 128; De Gruchy, "Christianity in Twentieth-century," 107.

84. De Gruchy, "Christianity in Twentieth-century," 108.

85. Chikane, *No Life of My Own*.

Albert Nolan, they helped formulate a theological response that grew out of the country's challenges. Most importantly, this included working towards a better understanding of social-political structures and their impact on the conditions of the poor.[86] According to Walshe, the ICT

> became the cutting edge for liberation theology, or what the [ICT] preferred to call 'contextual theology' – in part, to distinguish South African initiatives from those in Latin America. The South African movement, it was argued, needed to take account not only of race and class exploitation as in Latin America, but of the more complex range of Christian denominations, Islam, and the rich heritage of African religion in South Africa.[87]

In 1985, Prime Minister Botha declared a state of emergency. This was prompted by the mounting political dissent, most notably the urban uprisings of 1984–1986. The cause of the uprising was linked to cost increases in essential services, which had a detrimental effect on the already deteriorated living standards of blacks. This was especially the case in the heavily industrialized Vaal Triangle, south of Johannesburg, where the protests started. While this was prompted by the grievances particular to black townships, the overarching factor was the government's reform policies in the shape of the 1984 constitution. Here it is important to note that the Vaal uprising started the same day the new constitution was formally adopted. Robert Price describes the uprising as an insurrection rather than a rebellion. In his view, this insurrection not only sought to destroy whatever legitimacy the state had left, but it was also an attempt to replace that with new structures of popular authority.[88] In this context, the role of the UDF in leading the popular resistance became increasingly important. Dubow remarks that:

> Government allegations that the UDF orchestrated the uprising are difficult to sustain, but there can be no doubt that the UDF played a major role in sustaining the revolt and that the uprising in turn gave the UDF new importance. By the end of 1985 the

---

86. Walshe, *Prophetic Christianity*, 116.
87. Walshe, "Christianity and the Anti-apartheid," 392.
88. Price, *Apartheid State in Crisis*, 191–192.

founding slogan 'UDF unites apartheid divides' was beginning to be replaced with a more specific objective 'people's power'.[89]

This also speaks to the fact that the urban revolt of 1984–1986 was the most sustained and widespread resistance that the country has ever seen. In contrast to the uprisings in 1976–1977, the uprisings of 1984–1986 enjoyed a much broader support base. The latter was backed by trade unions, community organizations, students and even the unemployed. This show of unity was apparent in November 1984 when as many as 800,000 workers and 400,000 students in the Transvaal participated in a two-day stayaway in support of UDF demands.[90]

The decision to declare a state of emergency granted the state greater power to contain and, if necessary, crush political opposition. De Gruchy mentions that this created an environment where detention without trial, torture, the murder of political activists and the incitement of violence in black townships, became the routine business for state security agencies. He further posits that thousands of people, including many Christians, were detained, tortured and even killed under these circumstances.[91] Therefore, the state of emergency of 1985 represents a particularly brutal chapter in the apartheid government's familiar *kragdadige* (strongman) response to the growing popular resistance to apartheid.[92] This, together with the massacre of protestors in the Eastern Cape township of Langa, urged the SACC leadership to issue a "Call to Prayer for End to Unjust Rule in South Africa" on June 16, 1985.[93] Exactly nine years after the Soweto student uprising, the SACC called on the Christian community to pray for the demise of the apartheid government.[94] More than just a simplistic call to prayer, this also symbolized a radical challenge to the churches. In Van de Water's words, churches were challenged "to move away from the position of merely calling for fundamental

---

89. Dubow, *Apartheid*, 211.
90. Dubow, 211.
91. De Gruchy, *Church Struggle*, 196.
92. Van der Water, "Legacy of a Prophetic," 16.
93. An ominous tone was set when, on the 17 March 1985, twenty people were shot dead and twenty-seven injured when police opened fire on a funeral procession in Langa. The tragic incident occurred when police opened fire on a large procession of people on their way to a memorial service for those who lost their lives in the Sharpeville massacre exactly 25 years before.
94. DeYoung, "Christianity: Contemporary Expressions," 70.

reform on the part of a government, to that of aligning themselves with those forces seeking the replacement of the nationalist rulers with a democratically elected government."[95] However, given the history of the churches' inability (or reluctance) to move beyond mere protests and moral appeals, the call to prayer did not receive the necessary support from church leaders. It also failed to attract a significant response from church communities at large. What it did achieve, however, was to highlight the incongruity between church statements and action.[96] In the interim, it was left to ecumenical bodies like the SACC to lead the charge against the state. De Gruchy suggests that the call to prayer was a decisive moment in the church struggle because, for the first time, the SACC declared the state to be "tyrannical" and urged people to pray for its removal.[97] This placed the SACC in direct opposition to the state, placing the church struggle on a different trajectory.

With state repression reaching unprecedented levels, Christian activists became increasingly impatient with the churches and church leaders for their apparent inability or unwillingness to confront the state definitively. At a "crisis meeting" convened by ICT staff, a small group of activist theologians, "comprising of Revd F. Chikane (ICT General Secretary), Fr. A. Nolan, the Revd Dr. B. Goba, Sister B. Ncube, Mr M. Tsele and Fr. C Langefeld met secretly at the Ipelegeng Community Centre in Soweto. This group defined their aim as stating 'the present crisis theologically and to forge appropriate responses that Churches may adopt.'"[98] They emphasized the growing conviction that a process was needed which would be qualitatively different from other church-related pronouncements. Those at the meeting critically observed that:

> From the way Church-leaders responded to the crisis it is clear that they lack political analysis. Their eagerness to talk over the crisis with the State President shows that they do not see the political interests of the government . . . There is a crisis in communication. The leaders do not have contact with grass-roots. Most of them are inaccessible. There is no solidarity even

---

95. Van der Water, *Legacy of a Prophetic*, 13–14.
96. Villa-Vicencio, *Trapped in Apartheid*, 152.
97. De Gruchy, "Christianity in Twentieth-century," 108.
98. Van der Water, *Legacy of a Prophetic*, 21.

between Church-leaders themselves. An example is the split on the June 16 Prayer controversy . . . What impact on the life of the Church as theologians of the periphery can we make? How can we influence the leadership and not discredit and antagonize them? We need to draft a statement that is critical of the Church and self-critical.[99]

Robert McAfee Brown remarks that it was envisaged that the statement reflects a specific focus on "analysing the present situation," not "lofty theological analysis" or the "reiteration of eternal (and abstract) truth." However, there was also an intention not to limit theology to social analysis. Instead, their approach harnessed social analysis as a means to enrich theology. In other words, social analysis was deemed essential to make theology more relevant to the specific situation.[100]

After much consultation with various stakeholders, including meetings with prominent theologians, the ICT released the *Kairos Document* in September 1985.[101] The intention was to broaden the consultation process beyond the first edition's publication. Moreover, the second edition, having had the benefit of further responses, was published in January 1986. However, due to the significant interest around its initial release, the revised second edition was only published in September 1986. Those who contributed to the process represented a broad ideological spectrum. This included representatives from the UDF, the Black Consciousness-aligned National Forum, and they were united in terms of the urgency to redefine their role as Christians, as well as to explore ways in which the Christian community would be challenged to realize the urgent need to participate in the liberation struggle. For some of them who had been part of the Christian Institute, the UCM and the Black Theology Project, their involvement in the formulation of the document represented a catalyst for a critical evaluation of their theological position.

---

99. Minutes of ICT Theological Crisis Meeting, Ipelegeng Community Centre, Soweto, 28 July 1985 (ICT Archives, Kairos Files, Johannesburg) quoted in Van der Water, *The Legacy of a Prophetic*, 22.

100. Brown, *Kairos: Three Prophetic Challenges*, 10–11.

101. Some of the individuals listed to participate in the consultative meetings were: "Fr. B. Thlgale, M. Mothasi, T. Mafokeng, Dr. S. Maimela, the Revd. E. Tema, Fr. S. Mkhatswa, Dr. B. Goba, D. Masoma, S. Masemola, Fr. L. Sebidi, Fr. C. Langefeldt, Bishop D. Tutu, Dr. B. Naude, Dr. W. Kistner, the Revd. F. Chikane, Bishop M. Buthulezi." See Van der Water, 24.

This allowed them to contribute to the ongoing struggle for liberation from a more inclusive premise.

4.3 The *Kairos Document*

4.3.1 An Overview of the *Kairos Document*

The document itself consists of seven chapters. This includes a Preface, five Chapters, and a Conclusion.[102] In the Preface, the authors (hereafter the "*Kairos* theologians") define the document as "a Christian, biblical and theological comment on the political crisis in South Africa today."[103] The message of the *Kairos Document* is directed mainly to the churches and Christians. In this context, the document calls on them to "reflect on the situation and to determine what response by the Church and by all Christians would be most appropriate."[104] However, it is important to note that even though the document was directed to the churches, it was not produced by the churches. In this sense, the document did not represent the views of any particular denominational body, individually or collectively. Instead, it was the contributions of individuals affiliated with the different denominations highlighting their views in their personal capacity. However, the *Kairos* theologians recognized the responsibility of the churches to work towards dismantling apartheid and contributing to the reconstruction of a society based on the principles of justice, democracy, and peace. Thus, the input of the document could be narrowed down firstly to the challenge directed at the churches and, secondly, the urgency of the need to address that challenge. According to the *Kairos* theologians, the situation dictated that the churches could no longer afford to ignore their responsibility.

The opening paragraph of Chapter 1, entitled, "The Moment of Truth," makes a direct reference to the church. It states that:

> The time has come. The moment of truth has arrived. South Africa has been plunged into a crisis that is shaking the foundations, and there is every indication that the crisis has only just begun and that it will deepen and become even more threatening

---

102. The Kairos Theologians, "The Kairos Document."
103. The Kairos Theologians, 45.
104. The Kairos Theologians, 43.

in the months to come. It is the *Kairos* or moment of truth not only for Apartheid but also for the Church and all other faiths and religions.[105]

Here the *Kairos* theologians locate the crisis not only in the socio-political arena but also within the churches themselves. Moreover, the churches addressed in this section are the churches that have a long tradition of opposition to apartheid. Even though no specific church groupings are mentioned in the "challenge," the thrust of the message is aimed at the English-speaking churches and other ecumenical groupings. Here the concern is derived mainly from the many proclamations opposing apartheid that had been made, at least since Cottesloe in 1960. However, despite the many criticisms of apartheid, the responses of the churches and church leaders lacked the necessary urgency and effectiveness. According to the *Kairos* theologians, this ineffectiveness was largely due to existing theological suppositions that informed and governed the churches' responses. More importantly, these theological suppositions lacked any semblance of 'social analyses' and any real sense of 'an adequate understanding of politics and political strategy'. The *Kairos* theologians state:

> Changing the structures of society is fundamentally a matter of politics. It requires a political strategy based on a clear social and political analysis. The Church has to address itself to these strategies and to the analysis upon which they are based. It is into this political situation that the Church has to bring the gospel. Not as an alternative solution to our problems as if the gospel provided us with a non-political solution to political problems. There is no specifically Christian solution. There will be a Christian way of approaching the political solutions, a Christian spirit and motivation and attitude. But there is no way of bypassing politics and political strategies.[106]

The reason for the inadequacies in the churches' response is influenced mainly by the following factors. First, the *Kairos* theologians critically refer to as "State Theology." The "Critique of State Theology" is Chapter 2 of the document.

---

105. The Kairos Theologians, 47.
106. The Kairos Theologians, 61.

According to the *Kairos* theologians, the apartheid state developed its own theology. The document describes this theology as "State Theology." This brand of theology legitimized the politics of repression and violence against black people. It is merely "the theological justification of the status quo with its racism, capitalism and totalitarianism." While "State Theology" claims to be based on Romans 13:1–7, the *Kairos* theologians argue that the experience of the majority of South Africans suggests that the state is not acting as a "servant of God" for the benefit of all people. In quoting Revelation 13, the *Kairos* theologians suggest that within the South African context, the contrary was, in fact, the case. They state that: "If we wish to search the Bible for guidance in a situation where the State that is supposed to be 'the servant of God' betrays that calling and begins to serve Satan instead, then we can study Chapter 13 of the Book of Revelation. Here the Roman State becomes the servant of the dragon (the devil) and takes on the appearance of a horrible beast."[107]

"State Theology" further claims to undergird the principle of "law and order" in South Africa. However, according to the *Kairos* theologians, "this *law* is the unjust and discriminatory laws of apartheid and this order is the organized and institutionalized disorder of oppression. Anyone who wishes to change this law and this order is made to feel that they are lawless and disorderly. In other words they are made to feel guilty of sin."[108] The *Kairos* theologians further argue that the direct association of all those who oppose the apartheid state as being "communists," and, therefore, by implication "atheists" is problematic simply because most South Africans who have been active against apartheid are members of the church and the African religious traditions. The claim in the preamble of the South African constitution, "in humble submission to Almighty God," was therefore denounced as blasphemous. The *Kairos* theologians state that: "This god is an idol. It is as mischievous, sinister and evil as any of the idols that the prophets of Israel had to contend with . . . It is a god of superior weapons who conquered those who were armed within nothing but spears. It is the god of casspirs and hippos, the god of teargas, rubber bullets, sjamboks, prison cells and death sentences . . . the god of the South African State is not merely an idol or false god, it is the

---

107. The Kairos Theologians, 51.
108. The Kairos Theologians, 51.

devil disguised as Almighty God – the antichrist."[109] This section is followed by what the document critically refers to as "Church Theology." The "Critique of Church Theology" is offered in Section 2 of the document.

According to the *Kairos* theologians, "Church Theology" is the "type of faith and spirituality that has dominated church life for centuries." The kind of faith and spirituality that undergirds "Church theology" is described as "other-worldly." The *Kairos* theologians state:

> As we all know, spirituality has tended to be an other-worldly affair that has very little if anything at all to do with affairs of this world. Social and political matters were seen as worldly affairs that have nothing to do with the spiritual concerns of the Church . . . finally the spirituality we inherit tends to rely on God to intervene in God's own good time to put right what is wrong in the world. That leaves very little for human beings to do except to pray for God's intervention.[110]

The *Kairos* theologians further suggest that this "other-worldly" faith and spirituality is at the heart of the inadequate theological formulations perpetuated by the churches. As a result, the churches tend to resort to "stock ideas," such as "reconciliation," "justice" and "non-violence" to respond to the prevailing crisis in South Africa.

The *Kairos* theologians criticize the churches' use of the "reconciliation" concept. They note that many people, including Christians, have affirmed that there can be no reconciliation while socio-political injustice continues unabated. The *Kairos* theologians state that "there can be no doubt that our Christian faith commits us to work for *true* reconciliation and *genuine* peace. But as so many people, including Christians, have pointed out, there can be no true reconciliation and no genuine peace *without justice*. Any form of peace or reconciliation that allows the sin of injustice and oppression to continue is a *false* peace and *counterfeit* reconciliation. This kind of 'reconciliation' has nothing whatsoever to do with the Christian faith."[111] They further suggest that "'Church Theology' is not always clear on this matter, and many

---

109. The Kairos Theologians, 54.
110. The Kairos Theologians, 61.
111. The Kairos Theologians, 70.

Christians have been led to believe that what we need in South Africa is not justice but reconciliation and peace. The argument goes something like this: 'We must be fair. We must listen to both sides of the story. If the two sides can only meet to talk and negotiate, they will sort out their differences and misunderstandings, and the conflict will be resolved.' On the face of it, this may sound very Christian. But is it?"[112] The Kairos theologians argue that the churches were guilty of calling for reconciliation at all costs, making it an "absolute principle that must be applied in all cases of conflict and dissension." Therefore, the insistence upon reconciliation and peace before the present injustices were removed is regarded to being "unchristian." As far as the Kairos theologians are concerned, it would be a total betrayal of the Christian faith to "try and reconcile good and evil, God and the Devil." They further posit that "We are supposed to oppose, confront and reject the devil and not try to sup with the devil."[113] In other words, according to them, "No reconciliation is possible in South Africa *without justice*, without the total dismantling of apartheid."

The *Kairos* theologians also raise serious questions about the meaning when churches call for justice. The document states that "the question we need to ask here, the very serious theological question is: What kind of justice? An examination of Church statements and pronouncements gives the distinct impression that the justice that is envisaged is the justice of reform, that is to say, a justice that is determined by the oppressor, by the white minority and that is offered to the people as a kind of concession."[114] What is clear from this analysis is that the political reforms initiated by the Botha regime were considered irrelevant because these reforms did not constitute fundamental steps towards a just social order. The *Kairos* theologians judged reform initiatives as a mere tactic to maintain political domination and survival. The Kairos theologians argue:

> True justice, God's justice, demands a radical change of structures. This can only come from below, from the oppressed themselves. God will bring about change through the oppressed as he did through the oppressed Hebrew slaves in Egypt. God does not

---

112. The Kairos Theologians, 55.
113. The Kairos Theologians, 56.
114. The Kairos Theologians, 57.

bring his justice through reforms introduced by the Pharaohs of this world.[115]

The *Kairos* theologians conclude that the justice called for by the churches is not the "radical justice that comes from below and is determined by the people of South Africa."

"Non-violence" is the third "stock idea" used by the church, which comes under strong criticism in the document. The escalation of violence was indeed a contentious issue as reflected by many involved in drafting the document. In this respect, they were very conscious that participation in the liberation struggle meant that the issue of violence had to be considered. In this context, the call for non-violent actions was almost always directed at blacks in the townships and not first to the severe violence of the state. The *Kairos* theologians highlight that throughout the Bible the word "violence" is used to describe everything that the wicked oppressor does and never used to outline the activities of Israelite armies in attempting to liberate themselves or to resist aggression.

Having offered a critique of both "State Theology" and "Church Theology," the *Kairos* theologians direct their challenge to the churches to critically examine or re-examine their theological foundations, firstly, about their theological self-understanding as churches, and secondly, the theological suppositions which were used by the state and its supporters to justify, maintain apartheid. This sets the stage for a proposal on a new theological way forward. The section entitled "Toward a Prophetic Theology" suggests that given the serious problems with "State Theology" and "Church Theology," the need exists to formulate new contextual theological paradigms. The *Kairos* theologians suggest that these theological paradigms would have to take seriously, among other things, the role of social and political analysis. They posit that "a prophetic response and a prophetic theology would include a reading of the signs of the times. This is what the great biblical prophets did in their times and this is what Jesus tells us to do. When the Pharisees and Sadducees ask for a sign from heaven, he tells them to 'read the signs of the times' (Matt 16:3) or to 'interpret the Kairos' (Luke 12:56)."[116] According to the *Kairos* theologians, integral to "reading the signs of the times" was the

---

115. The Kairos Theologians, 58.
116. The Kairos Theologians, 63.

task of discerning what the root causes of the conflict are. For instance, the *Kairos* theologians argue that the portrayal of the current conflict merely as a "racial war" is misleading, as this suggests two equal partners standing in opposition to one another. The race component is a central feature of the conflict, but this does not fully explain the situation whereby the opposing groups are defined as the "oppressor" and the other the "oppressed." For the *Kairos* theologians, the starting point for a "Prophetic Theology" is the experience of people subjected to oppression and tyranny. In this context, it is precisely this experience of oppression and tyranny that constitutes the prevailing *Kairos*. Therefore, for the *Kairos* theologians, it is crucial to identify the parties involved as "oppressors and the oppressed" because the situation of tyranny is no accident of history but integral to the social structure of South Africa. The *Kairos* theologians posit that "what we are dealing with here, in the Bible or in South Africa today, is a social structure. The oppressors are the people who knowingly or unknowingly represent a sinful *cause* and unjust *interests*. The oppressed are people who knowingly or unknowingly represent the opposite *cause* and *interests*, the cause of justice and freedom. Structurally in our society these two causes are in conflict."

The *Kairos* theologians further charge that if "Prophetic Theology" identified oppression from a biblical perspective, it also discerned an expectation directed towards God in such oppression. They state that "Throughout the Bible, God appears as the liberator of the oppressed. 'For the plundered poor, for the needy who groan, now I will act', says Yahweh (Ps 12:5) God is not neutral. He does not attempt to reconcile Moses and Pharaoh, to reconcile the Jewish people with any of their later oppressors[117]." So, whenever "Prophetic Theology" identifies the oppressor, guided by the Christian tradition, it cannot avoid confronting them. The implication for churches is evident in this regard. According to the *Kairos* theologians, the churches had no option but to take the side of the poor and oppressed. It is to this kind of theology and praxis and the ambiguity thereof that the *Kairos* theologians challenged the churches. However, they also point out that at the heart of the prophetic faith is rooted in "hope." They state that "Jesus has taught us to speak of this hope as the coming of God's kingdom. We believe that God is at work in our world turning hopeless and evil situations to good so that God's kingdom

---

117. The Kairos Theologians, 70.

may come and God's will may be done on earth as it is in heaven."[118] However, according to *Kairos* theologians, the hope of the people needs affirmation. The *Kairos* theologians' call for "Prophetic Theology" therefore insists that what is required in the prevailing crisis in the country is not theology which merely rehashes or repeats generalized Christian principles. Instead, what is called for is a theology which responds to the particular context in which people live, suffer and die at the hands of an oppressive state. The "Prophetic Theology" through which the churches are challenged therefore does not allow Christians and the churches the luxury of taking a neutral stance. The *Kairos* theologians argue that "the attempt to remain neutral in this kind of conflict is futile. Neutrality enables the status quo of oppression (and therefore violence) to continue. It is a way of giving tacit support to the oppressor."

The final chapter of the document is entitled "Challenge to Action." Here the *Kairos* theologians shift attention to the need for the endemic violence in the country to be ended. Here the message is unambiguous. The *Kairos* theologians argue that it is not enough for Christians and churches to merely condemn apartheid or even the violence that is inherent in the system. It is also not acceptable for churches to try to remain neutral or seek to act as a mediator between opposing groups. The *Kairos* theologians call on Christians and churches to be united in faith and action with oppressed people. One of the tangible ways in which solidarity could be demonstrated was for the churches and Christians to engage in acts of "civil disobedience." The Kairos theologians posit that:

> In the first place the Church *cannot collaborate with tyranny* . . . Secondly, the Church should not only pray for a change in government, it should also mobilise its members in every parish to begin to think and work and plan for a change of government . . . And finally the moral legitimacy of the Apartheid regime means that the Church will have to be involved at times in *civil disobedience*. A Church that takes its responsibilities seriously in these circumstances will sometimes have to confront and to disobey the State in order to obey God.[119]

---

118. The Kairos Theologians, 71.
119. The Kairos Theologians, 75.

In this context, the actions of civil disobedience would represent the outward witness of the churches in their defiance of apartheid. The *Kairos* theologians also called for the transformation of "inward" activities such as services of worship, Eucharist services, baptisms, funerals, etcetera. They call on the church's "specific activities" to be "reshaped to be more fully consistent with a prophetic faith related to the Kairos that God is offering us today." The challenge to the church in this regard is to make a conscious connection between the rituals of the Christian faith and the daily experiences of people subjected to the oppression associated with the state. For instance, the evil forces alluded to in the Christian baptism ceremony should become more explicit.

Moreover, the unity Christians profess in the Eucharist should be demonstrated in acts of solidarity outside the church. The *Kairos* theologians further challenge the churches about the racial divisions within the churches themselves. They posit that: "What the present crisis shows up, although many of us have known it all along, is that the Church is divided. More and more people are now saying that there are, in fact, two Churches in South Africa – a White Church and a Black Church. Even within the same denomination there are in fact two Churches."[120] According to the *Kairos* theologians, the prevailing crisis in the country has exposed the ongoing racial divisions within the churches themselves. The churches, therefore, no less than society, are faced with the challenge of addressing the racial division within their own ranks. The document's message to the churches in this respect is not merely that the churches lack integrity as the Body of Christ but that such division was the consequence of diverse socio-political persuasions and actions among church members, split along racial lines.

4.3.2 The *Kairos Document* in Perspective

The publication of the *Kairos Document* proved to be controversial. Its reception, however, was not uniform – some praised the document for its attempt to energize the vocabulary of political resistance, whereas others judged it to be politically dangerous and theologically suspect.[121] The apartheid government

---

120. The Kairos Theologians, 71.

121. For reactions to the *Kairos Document*, see Borer, *Challenging the State*, 121; Suggit, "Kairos: The Wrong Way," 58, 70–74; Torrance, "South Africa Today," 42–45; Beyerhaus, *Kairos Document: Challenge*.

responded immediately by detaining many who signed the document. They further dismissed supporters of the document, accusing them of being part of the anti-Christian revolutionary "total onslaught," waged against South Africa – apparently, this was part of a government strategy to regain Christian legitimation and support within the English-speaking churches.[122] For their part, the NGK instructed rejection, arguing that the document was the work of communists and heretics. Except for two churches, the document was never officially adopted by any of the churches to which it was primarily addressed.[123]

Rejecting the "liberal rhetoric of reconciliation," the *Kairos Document* called for direct participation in the liberation struggle.[124] This includes participating in acts of civil disobedience against the apartheid state. This was in contrast to the views of many white South Africans and church leaders who believed they could be agents of reconciliation without actively engaging in the liberation struggle. Not only this, according to De Gruchy, "even Churches and church leaders who had rejected apartheid and who were engaged in the struggle to end it, such as Archbishop Tutu, were unhappy about how 'church theology' and reconciliation were, in their terms, caricatured and criticized." Also, "There was sharper criticism of the *Kairos Document* emanating from a circle of black theologians who remained faithful to the more radical concerns of the Black Consciousness movement. For them, the discourse of reconciliation was controlled by the 'ruling class' rather than by those who were alienated from whites, from the land, from the means of production, and thus from power. If reconciliation was to mean anything significant for them it will have to reverse this alienation."[125] Also, the reluctance of some black theologians to give their full support is attributed to document's emphasis on social oppression in general terms, instead of a more specific focus on the racist foundations of apartheid.[126] Itumeleng Mosala, one of the foremost proponents of Black Theology, later remarked that:

---

122. De Gruchy, "Christianity in Twentieth-century", 108.

123. The only two churches that officially adopted the *Kairos Document* were the Evangelical Presbyterian Church of Southern Africa who adopted it in 1985, and the United Congregational Church of Southern Africa, who adopted it in 1986. See Van der Water, 28.

124. De Gruchy, *Reconciliation*, 36.

125. De Gruchy, *Reconciliation*, 36.

126. Goba, "Role of Religion," 18.

The real hope of Black Theology in South Africa/Azania may well lie in the fact that it has never been co-opted by the Establishment. No Church has ever officially affirmed Black Theology as a legitimate and correct way of doing theology in South Africa . . . This did not happen, and the situation was exacerbated by the *Kairos Document's* total neglect of Black and African theologies. In fact, many of us were incensed by the fact that this potentially empowering document was careful not to mention the word 'black' once – despite its Sowetan origins.[127]

Notwithstanding the concerns raised, the Kairos theologians' critique of "reconciliation" as a form of "Church Theology" attracted considerable attention. Most notably, Desmond Tutu did not sign the document, citing that it was not fair to the church or the New Testament's rendering of reconciliation.[128] The main concern was the presupposition of liberation within the context of justice, repentance and forgiveness before reconciliation can be achieved. The *Kairos* theologians argue that "No reconciliation is possible in South Africa without justice. What this means in practice is that no reconciliation, no forgiveness and no negotiations are possible without repentance. The Biblical teaching on reconciliation and forgiveness makes it quite clear that nobody can be forgiven and reconciled with God unless he or she repents of their sins. Nor are we expected to forgive the unrepentant sinner." In their view, good and evil cannot be reconciled because that would amount to a betrayal of the Christian faith. Anders Göranzon suggests this particular approach to reconciliation is "clearly" informed by Black Theology.[129] Here, Per Frostin's contribution on the place of reconciliation in Black Theology is particularly helpful.[130] According to Frostin, the ministry of reconciliation is emphasized by different interest groups (see the previous chapter) in South Africa. This is not only concerning those that opposed apartheid but also those proposing its theological legitimacy (*Ras, Volk en Nasie*).[131] For the proponents

---

127. Mosala, "Spirituality and Struggle," 81.

128. Doxtader, *With Faith in the Works*, 40; Botman, "Church Partitioned," 113.

129. Göranzon refers also to Per Frostin's important contribution on the influence of black theology in the *Kairos Document*. See Göranzon, "The Prophetic Voice," 53.

130. Frostin, *Liberation Theology*, 169–176.

131. As Doxtader puts it, "Held out as a vindicating 'potential' of separate development, reconciliation was defended by the state-aligned Dutch Reformed Church as a condition yet to

of Black Theology, Frostin posits, the validity and value of the ministry of reconciliation are not in question. What is questioned, however, is the strategy on how to go about working towards this ideal.

> Underlying much of the critique of Black Theology seems to be the notion that reconciliation can be brought about *hic et nunc* provided that the conflicting parties have an open attitude. Black theologians, by contrast, argue that reconciliation between the oppressed and the oppressor is impossible as long as the oppressor insists on their privileged position.[132]

In this, Frostin identifies two distinct approaches to reconciliation – one is "synchronic" and the other "diachronic." The synchronic approach to reconciliation suggests that mutuality can be achieved immediately by a change in mentality and attitude. In contrast, the diachronic approach to reconciliation suggests that reconciliation can only be arrived at as a result of the process through which the opposing parties are liberated from their different types of alienation. Thus, in the diachronic approach, the distinction between "authentic" and "cheap" reconciliation will often be made.

> Underlying this distinction is the black analysis of apartheid as a state of oppression and injustice. In the context of oppression, cheap reconciliation denotes a situation where the oppressor and the oppressed recognize and accept each other without questioning the roles each plays in the relationship determined by the structures of oppression. The structural analysis by Black Theology, by contrast, implies that *metanoia* is a necessary condition for authentic reconciliation.[133]

Black theologians insist that the confession of sin is a necessary condition for reconciliation. Here, Frostin refers to the *Kairos Document* when it states, "No reconciliation, no forgiveness and no negotiations are possible without repentance."[134] However, this does not mean that metanoia is not necessary

---

come, a future of 'unity in diversity' that followed from the logic and law of race classification and division." See Doxtader, 41.

132. Frostin, *Liberation Theology*, 170.
133. Frostin, *Liberation Theology*, 170.
134. Frostin, *Liberation Theology*, 170–171.

for blacks, merely that the call for repentance has different implications for blacks and whites. Thus, the reconciliation in Black Theology (and by implication the *Kairos Document*) cannot be adequately understood if isolated from the truth claims of its social analysis. Moreover, the social analysis revealed that apartheid was a form of tyrannical oppression, not merely a race war. For the *Kairos* theologians, the state's espoused promise of legal equality was contradicted by its historical commitment to violence and oppression. This contradiction proved that the apartheid "regime has no moral legitimacy."[135] This was also taken as an explanation of why God was not neutral in the liberation struggle. Tied to the relative merits of revolutionary violence, the *Kairos Document* troubled and redefined the idea of reconciliation.[136] This was in contrast to general calls for reconciliation, which was judged to be "superficial and counter-productive."

Moreover, what distinguished the *Kairos Document* from other church-related statements (see the previous chapter) is how the central argument was constructed and performed. The approach in the *Kairos Document* is counterintuitive, using reconciliation as a mode of opposition, which contrasts with how the concept is traditionally understood. From this vantage point, the promise of reconciliation is radicalized. In Doxtader's words, "as such reconciliation [is] indeed not cheap, especially as its promise for the present depended on its abiding commitment to justice."[137] Accordingly, this commitment to justice contends that "one side is right and the other wrong." Reconciliation, thus, could not mean negotiation or compromise because tolerance beckoned "false peace" and the perpetuation of "evil," resulting in "a total betrayal of all that the Christian faith has ever meant." The *Kairos* theologians contend, as the dominant theological discourse defined reconciliation in terms of personal guilt, it neglected to address injustice effectively, thus bolstering the claim in *Ras Volk en Nasie*, that the present situation of separation expressed the will of God. Accusing the NGK of heresy, the *Kairos* theologians argued that apartheid's distorted words of reconciliation had to be returned to the Word.[138] Unlike "cheap" reconciliation, "authentic" reconcilia-

---

135. The Kairos Theologians, 68.
136. Doxtader, *With faith in the works of words*, 82.
137. Doxtader, 74.
138. Doxtader, 41.

tion takes inspiration from the burden of the cross. For the *Kairos* theologians, it begins with a testimony that remembers an experience of suffering and confesses the offences that each individual had inflicted upon others – this, they charge, "does not separate the individual from the social or one's private life from one's public life."[139] Authentic reconciliation creates relationships between human beings and between humans and God. In other words, as individuals concede their transgressions in the name of forgiveness, they provide an environment for collective action. The *Kairos* theologians state:

> We must begin to plan for the future now but above all we must heed God's call to action to secure God's future for ourselves in South Africa. There is hope. There is hope for all of us. But the road is going to be very hard and very painful. The conflict and the struggle will intensify in the months and the years ahead. That is now inevitable – because of the intransigence of the oppressor. But God is with us. We can only learn to become the instruments of his peace even unto death. We must participate in the cross of Christ if we are to have hope of participating in his resurrection.[140]

The *Kairos Document* reflects a deep commitment to justice (and by implication liberation) in South Africa. However, in so doing, it is accused of giving primacy to justice at the expense of reconciliation. For some, the struggle for justice must not be regarded as an end but as a means to achieve reconciliation. However, based on the political situation in the country, the *Kairos* theologians may have underestimated how difficult this task would be. De Gruchy remarks that "the problem with the *Kairos Document* was that while it distinguished between cheap and costly reconciliation, it did not differentiate between various forms of justice even though it spoke clearly enough about justice in terms of God's reign."[141] That there is no coherent understanding of justice complicates the matter even further. Another concern is what Botman refers to as the document's focus on reconciliation, lacking a vision of how exactly the new nation will be established.[142] In other

---

139. The Kairos Theologians, "The Kairos Document," 21.
140. The Kairos Theologians, 21.
141. De Gruchy, *Reconciliation*, 199–200.
142. Botman, "The Church Partitioned?," 112.

words, the hope and promise articulated in the *Kairos Document* must now be translated into concrete theological programmes for nation-building. This is closely aligned with Charles Villa-Vicencio's proposal for a theology of reconstruction (discussed below), calling for a theology that is more than just oppositional, which the *Kairos Document* appears to be.[143] On the doctrine of reconciliation, Botman charges that the *Kairos Document* lacks the Christological depth found in *The Message* or the *Belhar Confession* for example. In his view, a stronger Christological emphasis would have clarified that God is not revealed anywhere else but in Jesus Christ. He believes this would have aided the document in providing something distinct, particularly regarding reconciliation's potential in the Christian tradition. The document's narrow interest-based notion of theological irreconcilability is thus judged to be less than adequate.[144]

4.4 Closing Reflections

It is essential to highlight that the *Kairos Document* and its associated tradition employ what may be referred to as "inductive" logic.[145] According to this approach, the need for a wider frame of reference follows the argument that any breach in a relationship has broader implications than only for the two parties concerned. If such a breach has almost cosmic ramifications, the final resolution of such conflict must consider the problem's widest possible scope. In this context, reconciliation between two individuals is only possible if the whole of that society is reconciled with itself. Ultimately, reconciliation between two individuals is possible only through reconciliation with God. For apartheid South Africa the situation demanded an immediate remedy where the consequences of the problem were alleviated. Here it may be helpful but not enough to experience solidarity and companionship amidst suffering. In this sense, a victory of some sort is required. Unlike the approach highlighted in the previous chapter, here, the symbol of the cross is not enough. In highlighting the *Christus Victor* or classic view of the atonement, the victory must

---

143. Villa-Vicencio, *Theology of Reconstruction*.
144. Botman, "The Church Partitioned?," 112–113.
145. See my discussion on the deductive logic as an approach to the doctrine of reconciliation in Chapter 1. This approach is borrowed from Conradie, "Reconciliation as One," 17–21.

be more than "moral victory" or a new vision. Apartheid and its associated evils have to be negated. In this context, victory may be ascribed to one's efforts and commitment. Here the category of redemption is often used to capture the thrust of such salvific experiences. Regarding the classic type in the context of the South African struggle, one may speak of liberation from oppression and a victory over forces of death, destruction and evil (the main thrust of Aulén's argument). In this context, the most important Christian symbol which may be used is the resurrection of Christ because it symbolizes the power of God to address any situation and to conquer even death. In other words, it is a triumphal manifestation of God's decisive victory over the forces of evil. In this case, that victory is over evil associated with apartheid.

In turn, this invites reflection on the cosmic scope of God's work of reconciliation. This would include not only human beings and human societies but the whole created order. In other words, everything is included in God's work of reconciliation in Christ. Therefore, reconciliation should be understood in the context of God's work of creation and salvation. What is at stake is the tension between the Creator and the creature that has emerged because of captivity to the principalities and powers of this world (Col 1:18–23). "God's cosmic reconciling activity precedes and provides the framework within which God's reconciliation of humanity occurs."[146] However, the main concern with the "inductive" approach is the danger of self-secularization, of reducing the Christian confession to nothing more than an example of religious affiliation that may be tolerated as long as its particular claims are not foregrounded. As may be the case with the Kairos Document, the apparent danger is being socially relevant without having anything distinct to offer in response to the challenge one may face.

---

146. De Gruchy, *Reconciliation*, 53.

CHAPTER 5

Reconstruction Requires National Reconciliation

5.1 Introduction

The aim of this chapter is to describe and analyse the way in which the symbol of reconciliation has been understood among proponents of a theology of reconstruction and development – by those emphasizing the need for national reconciliation and nation-building, by those recognizing that reconciliation is a necessary requirement for processes of social transformation and moral regeneration in South Africa.

This description and analysis will be done primarily on the basis of literature during the period of the transition to democracy and in ongoing theological discourses on nation-building, development, social transformation, and moral regeneration reflected in the decision to establish the TRC. This chapter will illustrate that the shift in emphasis from liberation to reconstruction during the transitional period (1990–1994) led to a different notion of how the discourse on reconciliation was understood and interpreted.

5.2 Towards the Truth and Reconciliation of South Africa

This section entails a brief survey of selected developments that led to the South African TRC. Of course, this significant development in the discourse of reconciliation cannot be understood apart from the events leading to it, which will be addressed in summary form.

5.2.1 The Transitional Period

In a comprehensive study of the South African crisis during the 1980s, Robert Price maintains that a precondition for the collapse of legislative apartheid, leading to fundamental change, was an extended period of economic decline combined with the political unrest of the 1980s.[1] So, despite the state's efforts to uphold what it described as "law and order," it became apparent that it could no longer maintain the mounting international combined with international pressures. In more detail, Walshe underscores the combination of pressure brought about by the Mass Democratic Movement in conjunction with the threat of further sanctions, a debt-service crisis, and a stagnating economy that made it difficult for the apartheid state to continue with its campaign.[2] The burden of these factors coupled with ill health, eventually led to the forced resignation of Prime Minister Botha in the final months of 1989.[3]

Frederik W. de Klerk, an active member of the Gereformeerde Kerk in Suid-Afrika, and son of a former National Party leader, eventually replaced Botha.[4] According to Dubow, De Klerk was a skilled political operator with a long record of supporting traditional apartheid measures but few deep ideological convictions other than his religious conservatism.[5] On his appointment, many expected a continuation of apartheid policies, but what followed surprised many observers. De Klerk moved decisively to establish his authority and called a general election in September 1989. In this election, the National Party lost considerable support to the Conservative Party and the liberal Democratic Party.

Notwithstanding its majority, this was the ruling party's poorest electoral performance since it came to power in 1948. Through all of this, De Klerk's efforts to stabilize the political situation transformed him from a supporter of apartheid into a progressive reformer. Amid much volatility, De Klerk

---

1. Price, *Apartheid State*, 12.
2. Walshe, *Church Versus State*, 75.
3. Giliomee, *Last Afrikaner*, 277–279.
4. Burger, "Reformed Liturgy," 160; Giliomee, *The last Afrikaner Leaders*, 282–283.
5. Dubow, *Apartheid*, 262.

set a new tone. In Dubow's words, "One of his first acts as president was to prohibit the use of the *sjambok* whip, that potent symbol of rural disciplinary power and police brutality, for purposes of crowd control. Another potent change was De Klerk's decision, under some pressure, to permit a big march of over 20,000 people, led by Archbishop Tutu and other church leaders, to proceed through central Cape Town."[6] In De Klerk's terms, the door to a new South Africa was open and in this environment, it was not necessary to batter it down. He appealed to those involved in the liberation movement to encourage their leaders to come to the negotiating table.[7] De Klerk further concretized this new approach in his now famous speech at the opening of Parliament in February 1990. Dramatically, De Klerk announced the unbanning of anti-apartheid political organizations, including the ANC, the PAC and the South African Communist Party (SACP). Moreover, he announced the release of political prisoners, most importantly Nelson Mandela, who effectively became the symbol of the struggle against apartheid.[8] In this context, De Klerk's actions set in motion a series of events that fundamentally changed the trajectory of South Africa.[9]

In the meantime, secret talks were already underway with leaders to consider the possibility of a peaceful transition through a negotiated settlement. The Groote Schuur talks from 2 to 4 May 1990 marked the beginning of official negotiations between Afrikaner leaders (led by De Klerk) and the

---

6. Dubow, 263.

7. Renwick, *Unconventional Diplomacy*, 138.

8. In a thoughtful assessment of De Klerk's role in the transitional period, Giliomee writes that, "Five hundred years ago Niccolo Machiavelli set out in *The Prince* some of the realities of power. There are, he wrote, two ways of fighting: by law and by force. 'The first way is natural to men and the second to beasts. But as the first way often proves inadequate, one must have recourse to the second. So, a prince must understand how to make nice use of the beast and the man.' Machiavelli went on: 'As a prince is forced to know how to act like a beast, he should learn from the fox and the lion; because the lion is defenceless against traps and a fox is defenceless against wolves. Therefore, one must be a fox in order to recognize traps and a lion to fight off wolves. Those who simply act like lions are stupid.' If PW Botha was a lion, FW De Klerk was a fox and everything depended on whether he would see the traps the ANC would lay for him. He came to power disgusted with the way in which the government and its security forces had acted like lions. As a [lawyer], he believed that laws and the constitution could settle disputes and that judges would weigh up arguments judiciously and fairly before delivering and honest verdict. His entire attempt to bring about a constitutional settlement in South Africa hung on this belief – that a deal could be struck that balanced the interests of minorities with the aspirations of the majority." See Giliomee, *The last Afrikaner Leaders*, 311-312.

9. See S. Johnson for a detailed account of the developments during South Africa's transition. Johnson, *Strange Days Indeed*.

African nationalist movement (led by Mandela).[10] This was followed by the Convention for a Democratic South Africa (CODESA) at the end of 1991. At this stage, it was clear that the political situation dictated that neither side could achieve a decisive victory. In this context, working towards a negotiated settlement appeared to be the sensible way forward. However, after the initial euphoria, the opening of negotiations was followed by a general sense of disillusionment as the talks seemed to drag on inconclusively. This happened amidst rising black-on-black violence in townships across the country.[11] The situation on the East Rand, near Johannesburg, together with what was going on in Natal province, was alarming. Here clashes between supporters of the ANC and the Inkatha Freedom Party (IFP) often resulted in the killing of political opponents. Also, the political assassination of Chris Hani, the SACP leader, in 1993 threatened to destabilize the situation. In Dubow's words, Hani, a popular leader of the resistance movement, "was gunned down outside his house outside Johannesburg. Two right-wingers, one English-speaking, another Polish, were arrested. The assassination raised political tensions to dangerous levels amidst fears that black anger would explode into violence. In an act of consummate statesmanship, Mandela intervened publicly to call for calm. Hani's burial, which was covered in full by South African television, amounted to an unofficial state funeral. The shock of the killing prompted the leading negotiating participants to press harder to resolve the country's future."[12] Discussions on the causes of the violence during

---

10. "De Klerk's entire team consisted of Afrikaner men – nine politicians and six government officials. The latter were Niel Barnard and Mike Louw of the National Intelligence Service, S. J. J. (Basie) Smit of the police, W. H. Willemse of prisons, Fanie van der Merwe of the Department of Constitutional Development and Jannie Roux from the office of the state President. Neither Minister of Defence Magnus Malan nor any other military officer was included. In terms of symbolism, omitting a military figure was a blunder. De Klerk had clearly indicated that he staked everything on a constitutional solution. Always attentive to symbolism, the ANC put together a team of ten black men, one black women (Ruth Mompati), one Afrikaner man (Beyers Naudé), one Jewish man (Joe Slovo), one coloured woman (Cheryl Carolus) and one Indian man (Ahmed Kathrada). Nine of the ANC team gave the Lusaka address, and three (Mandela, Kathrada and Walter Sisulu) had recently been released from prison. It was an early sign that the ANC in exile, together with Mandela, would dominate the movement after the transfer of power, although the UDF and trade unions bore the brunt of the struggle on the ground." See Giliomee, *The last Afrikaner Leaders*, 322–323.

11. For a detailed analysis on the violence at the time see Chidester, *Shots in the Streets*.

12. Dubow, *Apartheid*, 271.

this period continued unabated.[13] However, based on the evidence later presented at the TRC, it came to light that a "third force" (with links to the state) was directly involved in the incitement of township violence.[14] During this period, church leaders, together with Christian activists, continued to play an important role, not only in preventing the violence in the first place but also through intervening and mediating talks between the opposing factions. Church leaders, like the Methodist Bishops, Mmutlanyane Stanley Mogoba, Peter Storey, and the General Secretary of the SACC, Frank Chikane, played a major role through the various national and regional peace structures established to deal with township violence.[15]

5.2.2 Rustenburg: Redefining the Role of the Churches

In the context of unpredictable transitional politics and protracted negotiations, the question concerning the role of the churches had to be addressed. The unbanning of the liberation movements meant that the churches no longer assumed the primary role of political opposition in the country. Some churches responded by scaling down their political activities. Those who remained active found it increasingly difficult to re-orientate themselves to the new situation – Christian leaders struggled to develop appropriate tactics and strategies. For some, the abolition of apartheid presented the opportunity to get back to "normalcy" – to get back to the basics of "being church." In this respect, the 1990s were already thought of as the decade of evangelization, with social justice treated as a separate issue. De Gruchy warns, however, that while this attitude may have been understandable given the many years of struggle against apartheid, this period also reflects the failure of the churches to respond to new challenges. In his view, "being the church" now included working towards justice and reconciliation.[16] At the time, the General Secretary of the SACC, Frank Chikane, echoed similar sentiments on the question of "being the church." In an address entitled, "The Church's Role during a period of Democracy," organized by Diakonia, an ecumenical organization based in Durban, he spelled out his understanding of what

---

13. For an interesting discussion on violence during the transitional period see Adam and Moodley, *The Negotiated Revolution*, 121.
14. Doxtader, *With Faith in the Works of Words*, 173; De Gruchy, *Church Struggle*, 216.
15. De Gruchy, *Theological Odyssey*, 32.
16. De Gruchy, *Church Struggle*, 219.

was now required given the abolition of apartheid.[17] In his view, the Gospel imperative was to be involved on the side of justice and not necessarily on the side of any particular political party. He further underscored the need for the churches to act as mediators between conflicting parties. Moreover, to work towards reconciliation, but always with the demands of justice in mind. Chikane further stressed that restitution must be an integral part of the reconciliation process. Walshe charges that it is within this context that the SACC attempted to chart a dual ministry, with intervention and mediation in the short run, allied to reconstruction in the long term:

> This, it was argued by Villa-Vicencio, Boesak and others, required a revised contextual theology to sustain the endeavour. It also meant tackling the immediate crisis of political transition by setting out to check the spread of violence through monitoring, accurate exposé and persistent mediation. Furthermore, it meant nurturing the fraught process of negotiations with a view to maintaining a dialogue between a broad range of political organisations as possible, the hope being to form a multiparty transitional executive, elect a constituent assembly and then activate a non-racial constitution bolstered by a comprehensive Bill of Rights. Simultaneously, the prophetic church supported, and attempted to refine a set of social and economic policies designed to produce a more egalitarian yet pluralistic society in which the sense of the common good would be nurtured. These pressing issues included, *inter alia*, land redistribution, the restructuring of economic institutions and the reordering of economic priorities so as to meet the basic needs of all citizens; protecting the environment; redesigning the country's collapsing educational and medical systems; supporting the women's movement to eradicate sexism; and critiquing an international economic system that engenders gross inequalities within South

---

17. Diakonia was the vision of the Catholic Archbishop Denis Hurley. It was formed in 1970 and the aim was to create an ecumenical organization to work for justice in the Durban area. At the time the work of the organization was motivated mainly by the injustices caused by apartheid.

Africa, just as it polarises industrialised and developing societies across the world.[18]

With this understanding, the SACC, under the leadership of Chikane, went on to play a crucial role in organizing the famous Rustenburg meeting called the National Conference of Church Leaders in November 1990.[19]

The Rustenburg meeting brought together church leaders from a broad spectrum that went beyond those affiliated with the SACC. This included church leaders from the NGK, African Initiated churches, Pentecostal churches, and independent charismatic churches. It is estimated that the meeting was attended by 230 representatives of 97 denominations and 40 church associations, as well as ecumenical agencies like Diakonia and the ICT.[20] In this sense, the church in the country was comprehensively represented. This included church leaders and denominations with longstanding suspicions of liberation theology and those who supported the apartheid state's attempts to reform apartheid during the 1980s. This also included the NGK, the Baptist Union, the Apostolic Faith Mission Church, the white-dominated Lutheran churches, evangelicals like the Rhema churches and several African Independent Churches who were not members of the SACC.[21] While Rustenburg was characterized by the presence of a broader spectrum of churches, the SACC and its member churches took a leading role. Consequently, the agenda was set by the proponents of contextual theology, especially those in the SACC who was at the forefront in resisting apartheid during the 1980s. Through their combined experiences, they developed a strong sense of their historic responsibility to reconstruct a more just South Africa. The end result of their efforts was the *Rustenburg Declaration* which the participants adopted.[22]

Despite some delegates not agreeing to everything said at the conference, the *Rustenburg Declaration* indicates that all agreed on "the rejection

---

18. Walshe, "Christianity and Democratisation," 76.
19. Chikane, "Church's Role," 1–11, an address given at a breakfast briefing, 12 August 1992, organized by Diakonia's Sociopolitical Development Programme. On the four task forces, see SACC, "Report of the General Secretary to the National Executive Committee Meeting, 26–27 May 1992, 5, and Annex II." See Walshe "Christianity and Democratisation," 78.
20. Walshe, "Christianity and Democratisation in South Africa," 78.
21. Walshe, 78–79.
22. National Conference of Church Leaders in South Africa, "Rustenburg Declaration."

of apartheid as a sin."[23] Participants further underscored the "critical time of transition," which held out the "possibility of a new dispensation and the promise of reconciliation between all South Africans." In this context, Christians were called to be a sign of hope from God and to share a vision of a new country. Delegates further emphasized "repentance and practical restitution" as a prerequisite for God's forgiveness and justice as a preparatory step towards reconciliation. They further described South Africa's challenges within "the context of Western colonialism" and a "weakness common to the worldwide church in dealing with social evil." Those who supported or refused to resist apartheid confessed their "misuse of the Bible," "ignoring apartheid as evil," as well as the "spiritualising of the Gospel by preaching the sufficiency of individual salvation without social transformation." In other cases, some were "bold in condemning apartheid but timid in resisting it." Those who were victims of apartheid acknowledged their "own contribution to the failure of the church." While apartheid damaged self-esteem and "eroded the fibres of *ubuntu*" (humanness), many responded with "timidity and fear, failing to challenge [their] oppression." The meeting also responded to church leadership often "ignoring the sexism of many of the church, social, political, economic and family structures." In the same way, church leaders were called to confess their failure to involve young people in the full life of the church.[24]

The meeting affirmed the need for a just economic order based on "justice, compassion and co-responsibility so that those in need benefit more than those who have more than what they need." In this context, South Africa's white population would have to accept "affirmative acts of restitution in health care, psychological healing, education, housing, employment, economic infrastructure and especially land ownership." The church and state were charged to work towards restoring land "to the dispossessed people." In committing themselves to establish a "just, democratic, non-racial and non-sexist South Africa," the Rustenburg meeting called for a popularly elected constituent assembly. In turn, this should produce a new constitution that would enshrine the "value of human life created in the image of God" and entrench a Bill of Rights "subject to the judiciary alone." All of this should happen within a

---

23. National Conference, "Rustenburg Declaration."
24. National Conference, "Rustenburg Declaration."

multiparty democracy within a unitary state. Concerns were also raised at the rising levels of violence. In their estimation, the rising levels of violence were rooted in the denial of political rights, the emergence of a "third force" with links to the state, rivalry for limited resources and "power struggles between some political parties." Church agencies were encouraged to collect evidence and expose the perpetrators of violence, support victims, and convene a task force to coordinate strategy. Furthermore, churches were called to move from confession and declaration to restitution and action. In practical terms, this meant redistributing church land, opening white-only schools to blacks, and planning a national day of prayer for "forgiveness and reconciliation."[25]

The Rustenburg meeting acknowledged the different understandings of the message of reconciliation.[26] The gathering further acknowledged the need to admit guilt and to ask for forgiveness and acceptance within the church of Christ. The respected NGK theologian, Willie Jonker, underscored that an experience of reconciliation was necessary to enable the church to come to a united witness in promoting reconciliation in anticipation of a new South Africa. Jonker argued that mutual trust could not be restored without acknowledging guilt and asking for forgiveness and acceptance. In addition, the meeting recognized that the churches shared a responsibility to stand with the marginalized. Here the notion of reconciliation was invoked to address the violation of human rights in the country. In addition, the gathering agreed that a confession of guilt and restitution on the basis of reconciliation with all people and all churches was essential.

5.2.3 Rustenburg in Perspective

The main objective of the Rustenburg was to foster reconciliation and redefine the churches' role after the abolition of apartheid. This meant helping the

---

25. National Conference, "Rustenburg Declaration."

26. Firstly, there were those who were deeply moved by the sinful violent situation in the country, thereby proclaiming reconciliation with God and their neighbours. Secondly, there were those who argued that the Christian faith had a very clear political function and message, which called people to liberating political action. These Christians read and interpreted the gospel from the perspective of the marginalized, who are seen as God's redemptive activity. They argued that the South African situation was characterized by totalitarian oppression, which was idolatrous, and completely under the judgment of God. In this context, traditional theology would be naïve in its attempt to present the middle way between opposing forces, thereby asserting the notion of reconciliation was not suitable in the present situation because it could be misused by the oppressors.

churches come to terms with the changing political terrain and enabling them to contribute to developing the new South Africa. Among other things, the conference is known for the spirit of confession, which became a characteristic feature of the gathering. The most significant of these came from Willie Jonker. Jonker, who had been on the more progressive wing of the NGK, expressed deep regret that his church and the Afrikaner people defended apartheid. In his view, he could do little more than acknowledge their guilt and to ask for forgiveness and acceptance:

> I confess before you and before the Lord, not only my own sin and guilt, and my own personal responsibility for the political, social and economic and structural wrongs that have been done to many of you, and the results of which you and our whole country are still suffering from, but vicariously I dare also to do that in the name of the DRC of which I am a member, and for the Afrikaans people as a whole.[27]

Jonker's confession received mixed reactions. Some believed that Jonker had no right to confess on their behalf, while others felt that the NGK was still not doing enough to seek unity within its own ranks (i.e. NG Sendingskerk).[28] Nevertheless, many responded favourably, including Desmond Tutu, who responded with a warm embrace as a sign of accepting the apology. Boesak observes, "In the hall that day when Tutu strode to the podium, spoke into the stunned silence, and said, 'We forgive you,' he made this an unforgettable, historic moment."[29] Frits Gaum, one of the senior NGK figures, remembers the moment's immensity, stating that: "The applause was deafening . . . Tears of gratitude and forgiveness were flowing."[30] Notwithstanding the significance of the moment, Tutu's action also received its fair share of criticism, especially from blacks who felt he had no authority to accept the NGK apology for anyone other than himself; whereas others were inspired to make their own confessions.[31]

---

27. Jonker, "Understanding the Church Situation," 92.
28. Vosloo, "Christianity and Apartheid," 418.
29. Boesak and DeYoung, *Radical Reconciliation*, 133.
30. Gaum and Gaum, *Praat Verby Grense*, 82–83.
31. Phiri, *Proclaiming Political Pluralism*, 124.

According to Boesak, Tutu's reconciliatory gesture also spells the beginning of something that often goes unnoticed. In this context, his response may have been met with resistance by some, but this reconciliatory act also cleared the way for something else to emerge. The words, "we forgive you," as spoken by Tutu, deserve particular attention. In Boesak's view, the language of forgiveness transformed ("redeemed") Tutu in the eyes of many whites. Tutu, a key figure in the church's struggle against apartheid, was a fierce opponent of the NGK's policies on race, and for many of its members, this reconciliatory act came as a surprise. Frits Gaum, a senior NGK official, described the experience as "a moment of liberation." They were convinced that he had "proved in practice" that he meant what he had been saying all along. In essence, Tutu became the redemptive presence in South Africa: "the embodied forgiveness of whites, and simultaneously the embodied example of magnanimity for blacks. His was a piety that might be beyond the reach of most, but he personified the hope that a miracle was not impossible."[32] So while not everyone shared Tutu's sentiments and the consequence of reconciliation at that very moment, there is very little doubt that his action brought him renewed and certainly even new veneration across racial lines.[33]

Critically, the Rustenburg conference was supposed to mark the beginning of a new era of the churches. However, in reality, it seems more plausible to suggest that it signalled the beginning of the end of the influence of the churches. For many, Rustenburg did very little to help facilitate the process of rebuilding. Some even go as far as describing the Rustenburg conference as a disappointment – in many respects lacking new insights.[34] This is attributed to the view that the *Rustenburg Declaration* is a compromise document, with much of the prophetic demands that were called for subdued by the burden of consensus.[35] The influence (or lack thereof) of the Rustenburg conference should also consider the many developments outside of the ecumenical movement. In this context, the voices of the churches now had to compete with the voices of the unbanned political movements that were starting to take

---

32. Boesak and DeYoung, *Radical reconciliation*, 133.
33. Boesak and DeYoung, 133–134.
34. Phiri, *Proclaiming Political Pluralism*, 125.
35. De Gruchy, *Church Struggle*, 214.

shape.³⁶ So, while the SACC and its affiliates did much in trying to invigorate the churches in the post-apartheid environment, denominational responses were largely disappointing. Walshe notes that the dynamic, populist responses generated in the 1980s were now largely absent – appeals from church leaders all too often encountered timid local clergy and uninterested parishes.³⁷ This was also the case with the second ecumenical conference, Cottesloe II, held in Cape Town approximately one year after the Rustenburg meeting. The hope was that Cottesloe II would prompt a renewal of the ecumenical movement through a pastoral programme of nation-building – much as the Rustenburg meeting had anticipated. But here also, the result was disappointing, a sobering reminder that the "fire in the belly was gone."³⁸ Overwhelmed by the complexity of the transition, many churches withdrew and occupied themselves mainly with internal church affairs.³⁹

In December 1992, at the centennial celebration of the Free Ethiopian Church of Southern Africa, Nelson Mandela made a plea in which he underscored the contribution of the "broad ecumenical movement in South Africa and internationally." Mandela emphasized the role of the churches in the anti-apartheid struggle, stating that: "One has just to look at leaders such as Archbishop Desmond Tutu, Dr. Frank Chikane, Dr. Beyers Naudé and many more to measure the role of the church in the struggle." Furthermore, with the abolition of apartheid the churches could "not afford to retreat to the cosiness of the sanctuary." Rather, that it now had to assume the role "as midwife to the birth of our democracy." In Mandela's view, this role suggested a number of responsibilities. Among other things, this included the involvement of the church in "national reconciliation that is underpinned by confession and restitution." Moreover, the church was called "to take an active part in the building of a new nation in South Africa."⁴⁰ Inevitably the responses from the churches remained hesitant. In this context, the churches were again challenged to formulate a revised contextual theology. James Cochrane and Gerald West make this point by stating that given the changes in the political

---

36. Phiri, *Proclaiming Political Pluralism*, 125.
37. Walshe, "Christianity and Democratisation," 81–82.
38. Villa-Vicencio, "South Africa's Churches," 35.
39. Walshe, *Prophetic Christianity*, 144.
40. "Mandela's Challenge to the Church," 20–21.

landscape, the churches needed a prophetic vision that went beyond protest to one which was prepared to be "constructive." In their view, much of what came from the churches before the transitional period was rooted in the need to object and protest against the injustices of apartheid. The situation dictated that more was needed. That protest alone would not suffice. In their view, there was a need to move from "liberation" to "reconstruction."[41] This came in the wake of the views expressed by Charles Villa-Vicencio, who not long after the abolition of apartheid proposed a "theology of reconstruction" to address the new situation.

5.2.4 The Proposal for a Theology of Reconstruction

The proposal for a theology of reconstruction emerged during the 1980s as an approach to African theology. The Kenyan theologian, Jesse Mugambi, was the first among African scholars to propose a departure from liberation to reconstruction.[42] Mugambi began advocating for "reconstruction" as a new theological metaphor, especially when it became apparent that apartheid was coming to an end. He argued that, in post-colonial Africa, theological articulation (be it South African Black Theology, African Women's Theology, Liberation Theology or Cultural Theology) needed a new theological motif to address the emerging challenges.[43] Mugambi argued that this new phase on the continent represents an opportunity for theological articulation to shift from "liberation" to "reconstruction." Comparing Africa to 15th–16th century Europe (and the respective awakenings of the Renaissance and the Reformation), Mugambi declared the 1990s to be the beginning of Africa's Renaissance and Reformation and, therefore, the commencement of a process of reconstruction.[44] This proposal was taken further through the All Africa Conference of Churches (AACC) under its president, Desmond Tutu and General Secretary Jose Chipenda, who also advocated for a paradigm shift. In February 1990, the AACC invited various theologians to participate in discussions on the changing global patterns that followed the end of the Cold War and the relevance of these changes for the African continent. Various

---

41. Cochrane and West, "War, Remembrance and Reconstruction," 25–40.
42. Vellem, "Symbol of Liberation," 130.
43. Gathogo, "Black Theology of South Africa," 328.
44. Mugambi, *From Liberation to Reconstruction*.

papers on the reconstruction of Africa were later presented in March of the same year. Some of these contributions were published in a book entitled *The Church of Africa: Towards a Theology of Reconstruction*, with Mugambi as one of the co-editors.[45] Since then, the concept of reconstruction has been an important component of the discourse on African Christianity, particularly African church history.[46]

In South Africa, the proposal for a theology of reconstruction was put forward by Charles Villa-Vicencio.[47] In his view, much emphasis was placed on the Exodus motif in the articulation of Black Theology of liberation in South Africa – in this context, blacks are likened (metaphorically) to the people of Israel on their way from the land of bondage in Egypt (oppressive regime) to the promised land (anticipated liberation). Here Black Theology of liberation is modelled on the Exodus event (Exod 3), where Moses led the Hebrews to freedom from oppression. With the abolition of apartheid and the subsequent transitional period, Villa-Vicencio identifies a shift, which he likens to the Old Testament post-Exilic period.[48] Accordingly, this new phase in the history of South Africa provides the basis for the "reconstruction" motif in contextual theology. In this context, the post-Exilic metaphor derived from Nehemiah, not that of Moses, represents the lens through which one interprets the mission of the churches to redefine what is needed in the country. For Villa-Vicencio, "liberation," which has largely been associated with the Exodus theme, is no longer adequate to deal with some of the new challenges. In his words: "Hitherto the task of liberation theology has essentially been to say 'No' to all forms of oppression. The prophetic 'No' must, of course, continue to be part of a liberating theology. As the enduring struggle for democracy in some parts of the world begins to manifest itself in differing degrees of success, so the prophetic task of the church must include a thoughtful and creative 'Yes' to options for political and social renewal."[49] In this sense, the abolition of apartheid and the demands of the transitional

---

45. Chipenda, Karamaga, Mugambi, and Omari, *Church of Africa*.
46. Phiri and Gathogo, "Reconstructive Motif," 185–206.
47. Villa-Vicencio, *Theology of Reconstruction*.
48. Villa-Vicencio, 6–8.
49. Villa-Vicencio, 1.

period demanded more than mere resistance; it demanded the reconstruction of South Africa in the 21st century.[50]

The proposal for a "theology of reconstruction" emerged in a climate where reconstruction and development were central themes in discussions on South Africa. It also came at a time when the churches struggled to articulate an effective strategy on a way forward. Thus, for many, reconstruction, as a contextual theology, was not only necessary but also appeared the sensible thing to pursue. This is also the case for those directly involved in political negotiations where discourses on reconstruction became increasingly important. At this stage, the ANC had already begun to discuss the Reconstruction and Development Programme (RDP), a programme central to its bid to become the first democratically elected government. Tinyiko Maluleke observes that the RDP became the ANC's "rallying call." Moreover, that it was during the transitional period where the term reconstruction was popularized through the ANC's labour alliances – "This reality has helped to entrench reconstruction as an important concept in so-called 'progressive circles' including the churches."[51]

In the context of transitional politics, much emphasis was placed on the need for reconstruction in the context of nation-building. Except for the scepticism from some quarters, it appears many favoured this proposed shift.[52] However, on the theological front, those using Black Theology as a self-description were not as enthusiastic. Among other things, they sharply criticized the project of reconstruction on the basis that it takes minimal account of the heritage of liberation theologies in South Africa.[53] Nevertheless, like those using Black Theology as a self-description, the proponents of a theology of reconstruction also appear to be using significant biblical motifs to support their views. Here concepts such as "reconciliation," "repentance," and "forgiveness" are essential building blocks in the formulation of this theology.[54] These components were further explicated through the proceedings of the TRC.

---

50. Villa-Vicencio, 14.

51. Maluleke, "Proposal for a Theology," 245–246.

52. For an interesting discussion on the general reception of the RDP, see Maluleke, "Proposal for a Theology," 245–246.

53. For an in-depth discussion on the theological reception of a reconstruction, see Vellem, "The Symbol of Liberation," 128–236.

54. Maluleke, "Proposal for a Theology," 250.

Here it is important to note that Villa-Vicencio, the leading proponent in the call for a shift, became the Director of Research for the TRC. It is, therefore, not surprising that many of these principles were ever present in the approach and conceptualization of the TRC. Here the notion of reconciliation, although inspired by theological principles, appears to be unrelated to Christian beliefs or practices; it is a process in society. According to Villa-Vicencio, reconciliation, within the context of reconstruction, is a process driven by an energy that stands at the intersection between theology and experience, in which the biblical invitation to reconcile and the experiences of those who have suffered are taken seriously.[55] He argues that reconciliation requires sincere and lasting repentance, which invites theological and ethical reflection.[56]

Villa-Vicencio further identified the following distinctive features of the process of reconciliation. Firstly, that "reconciliation does not necessarily involve forgiveness." For Villa-Vicencio, the perpetrators may be ready to confess and repent their wrongdoing, but this does not necessarily mean the victim will respond by offering forgiveness. Secondly, that "reconciliation interrupts an established pattern of events." Engaging in reconciliation is to step beyond enmity, amidst violence, without any guarantees. To allow for the possibility of reconciliation is to make time for speech. Thirdly, "reconciliation is a process." It is a process that begins with intrigue, curiosity, and perhaps morbid fascination as to what it is that makes the alienated person who he or she is. Fourthly, "reconciliation involves understanding." Understanding does not necessarily lead to reconciliation, but when the perpetrator's story is thoughtfully told, heard and deeply understood by the victim or survivor, it opens the possibility of a new kind of interaction between those alienated from each other. Fifthly, "reconciliation requires acknowledgement." Acknowledging the truth does not necessarily lead to reconciliation; it does not mean forgetting the ghastly deed, and it also does not mean befriending the perpetrator. However, it does mean a break from unconcealed enmity.

---

55. Villa-Vicencio, *Art of Reconciliation*, 13–14.

56. Elsewhere he states that, "Reconciliation with God involves accepting the claim of God on one's life. But this can be little more than homiletical appeal if it is not translated into cultural and structural controls and incentives designed to order our lives. At best, under the continuing challenges of the gospel, these structures can become part of the process of renewing, transforming and redirecting personal and social goals." See Villa-Vicencio, *Theology of Reconstruction*, 162.

This implies the beginning of a different kind of relationship open to new possibilities. And lastly, "reconciliation takes time." For most people, only a first enquiring venture beyond hatred is possible. In this context, reconciling takes time and may only come later. With this in mind, reconciliation as a national project could be considered.

5.3. The Truth and Reconciliation Commission of South Africa

5.3.1 Reconciliation as a National Initiative

South Africa's transition marks when the discourse on reconciliation shifted from an almost exclusive theological endeavour to something that was now seriously considered a national issue. Through various developments on the political front, the discourse on reconciliation evolved from its traditional theological associations into something that now formed part of a guiding vision for the country. Until the Rustenburg meeting, theologians and church leaders used reconciliation in the church struggle, inspired by biblical and theological language and aiming to reconcile the races and later on to reconcile the opposing parties in the context of the then apartheid state and its growing violent polarization. These religious positions informed the public debate on the future of the country. But the discourse on reconciliation grew more important when key political figures started using and contesting the concept. In this context, the discourse on reconciliation moved from being a theological issue into something that now formed part of the general plan of national reconstruction. Notwithstanding its deep theological roots, it became an issue firmly observed through the lens of public morality. This does not mean that theologians did not continue to grapple with this controversial symbol but simply that it became a national rather than strictly theological matter. As Eddy Van der Borght observes, the discourse on reconciliation was now incorporated into various spheres, including the vocabulary of psychology, sociology, philosophy and political science as well as being embraced by politicians, especially during the transitional period.[57]

The beginning of reconciliation and a national initiative is traced to the decisions reached during the multiparty negotiating process. An essential

---

57. Van der Borght, "Reconciliation in the Public," 413.

aspect of the negotiations was the issue of an interim constitution that would replace the old constitution that formed the basis of apartheid legislation. Among other things, one of the more controversial aspects of this interim constitution was the issue of whether the advent of democracy would include the possibility of amnesty.[58] The lack of an amnesty provision in the interim constitution posed a particular problem, especially to those forming part of the military and human rights communities. The issue of amnesty was temporarily "solved" by allocating a place for it in the post-amble of the interim constitution and by framing it within the context of reconciliation on the road to national unity. In Doxtader's words:

> The pursuit of national unity, the well-being of all South African citizens and peace require *reconciliation* between the people of South Africa and the *reconstruction* of society. The adoption of this constitution lays the secure foundation for the people of South Africa to transcend the division and the strife of the past, which generated gross violations of human rights, the transgression of humanitarian principles in violent conflicts and a legacy of hatred, fear, guilt, and revenge. These can now be addressed on the basis that there is need for understanding not for violence, need for reparation but not retaliation, a need for ubuntu not for victimisation.[59]

On this basis, an amnesty provision was announced:

> In order to advance such reconciliation and reconstruction, amnesty shall be granted in all respect of acts, omissions, and offences associated with political objectives and committed in the course of conflicts of the past. To this end, Parliament under this constitution shall adopt a law determining a firm cut-off date . . ., and providing for the mechanisms, criteria, and procedures, including tribunals, if any, through which such amnesty shall be dealt with at any time after the law has been passed.[60]

---

58. For the most complete study on the amnesty provision during the transitional period see Toit, *Amnesty Chronicles*.

59. Doxtader, *With Faith In The Works Of Words*, 213.

60. For the full text and the interpretation of the post-able to the interim constitution, see Doxtader, *With Faith in the Works of Words*, 211–217.

Van der Borght observes that the amnesty provision in the post-amble did not satisfy the various stakeholders. The representatives of the apartheid government understood this as "forgive and forget," and accordingly, they wanted to "close the books on the past." On the other hand, the victims of gross human rights violations opposed the amnesty provision because they were not prepared to consider immunity to prosecution. Moreover, some were convinced that to prevent the explicit risk of forgetting the past, a process was necessary to help facilitate the transition from a violent past to a more sustainable future.[61] The main issue was that the post-amble did not provide the tools for such a procedure. Due to the uniqueness of the situation, it would be fair to suggest that at this stage, such tools had not yet been developed. In the context of the negotiated settlement, Kader Asmal, in his inaugural lecture as Professor of Human Rights Law at the University of the Western Cape in 1992, had already explained why and how the past needed to be opened. Asmal explained that "we must take the past seriously as it holds the key to the future. The issues of structural violence, of unjust and inequitable economic social arrangements, of balanced development in the future cannot be properly dealt with unless there is a conscious understanding of the past."[62] In this context, he was convinced that in order to come to terms with the complex history of South Africa, something more than a Nuremberg-style trial was needed. He argued that such an approach would lack the capacity to deal with the humiliation, brutality, deprivation, and degradation of the past. In his view, South Africa needed a truth commission because the harm done by apartheid exceeded the law's grasp. For this reason, South Africa needed to embrace the mode of reconciliation that carefully considered the past, located accountability and supported the revival of moral conscience. Reconciliation entailed more than the mere creation of new structures and arrangements. For Asmal, reconciliation's potential needed to serve three ends. Firstly, it required a demonstration of apartheid's illegitimacy. The process needed to illuminate the past to better grasp the current predicament. Secondly, reconciliation's potential to enact change largely depended on its capacity to broker disputes and disputation. This would forge consensus and

---

61. Van der Borght, "Reconciliation in the Public Domain," 417.

62. Truth and Reconciliation Commission of South Africa Report Volume One, 49; Doxtader, *With Faith in the Works of Words*, 230.

deter denials about the evils of apartheid. Finally, reconciliation offered the chance for cathartic truth-telling, a process in which South Africans could hear the experiences of fellow citizens, stories that set the stage for the "justice" of acknowledgement, "restitution," and "atonement."[63]

After the adoption of the interim constitution, the organization Justice in Transition, headed by Alex Boraine, organized an international conference in February 1994 to reflect on dealing with the past in the context of a negotiated transition. Through these deliberations and others, it became apparent that amnesty without history and truth-telling would not yield the intended aim of reconciliation. Doxtader explains that "the spirit of transition called for the constitution of individual and collective identity while emphasizing that apartheid's violent identitarian logic was precisely why citizens needed to remember the past in the name of creating the identifications of reconciliation."[64] The end of the political negotiations reached its symbolic climax with the inauguration of Nelson Mandela as the country's first democratically elected President on 11 May 1994.[65] This was followed by the passing of the Promotion of National Unity and Reconciliation Act in mid-1995. This legislation gave birth to the TRC. Chapter 2, section 3:1 (a–d) of the Act, spells out the commission's mandate. Here the commission is tasked with: (a) establishing a picture of the gross violations of human rights in the period between 1 March 1960 and 10 May 1994 through investigations and hearings; (b) facilitating the granting of amnesty to those who made full disclosure of all the relevant facts to acts associated with political objectives; (c) establishing and making known the fate or whereabouts of victims, restoring dignity by allowing victims to relate their own accounts, and recommending reparations, and (d) compiling a comprehensive report with findings and recommendations.[66] De Gruchy observes that through the Promotion of National Unity and Reconciliation Act, reconciliation was crucial in trying to uncover the truth and how the country should deal with the

---

63. For an analysis of Asmal's inaugural lecture, see Doxtader, *With Faith in the Works of Words*, 229–232.

64. Doxtader, *With Faith in the Works of Words*, 239.

65. South Africa first non-racial, democratic elections took place on 27 April 1994.

66. Van der Borght, "Reconciliation in the public domain," 419.

past and define the future. Moreover, reconciliation was now seen as part of defining the national goals of democratic transformation and reconstruction.[67]

5.3.2 The Mandate of the TRC

The seventeen-member commission, headed by Desmond Tutu as the chairperson, was inaugurated in December 1995. The commissioners (including Tutu) were nominated by a representative panel appointed by President Mandela. The commissioners included people from different backgrounds, with Christian leadership well represented. Besides Tutu, they included the deputy chairperson Alex Boraine, a theologian by training and also a former leader of the Methodist Church. Other church leaders included Khoza Mgojo, theologian and former president of the SACC; Charles Villa-Vicencio, theologian; Bongani Finca, church leader and prominent ecumenist; Tom Manthata, a former employee of the Justice and Reconciliation division in the SACC; Rev Xundu, church leader and Piet Meiring, theologian and prominent figure in the NGK.[68]

The idea of the commission is not unique to South Africa. There are other examples, particularly in Latin America, where similar ventures have been undertaken in post-conflict situations.[69] However, these commissions differed in their approaches. Elsewhere they tended to opt for approaches focused on providing "blanket amnesty" or for "Nuremberg-style trials" to deal with past atrocities.[70] In contrast, the South African commission attempted to balance the two approaches. In Tinyiko Maluleke's words:

---

67. De Gruchy, *Reconciliation*, 25, 41.
68. Tshaka, "Black Church as the Womb."
69. For a comparative study of different truth commissions, see Hayner, *Unspeakable truths: Transitional*.
70. Jennifer Harvey posits that: "In the challenge coming out of apartheid and birthing a new civic society, (a) it was not feasible to imagine one could prosecute and punish all the perpetrators for their gross participation in human rights violations; (b) layers of secrecy and lies made getting to the truth of the past virtually impossible without significant cooperation from perpetrators; (c) learning such truth was perceived as one of the most important needs of victims if they were to become full participants in a new civic community; and (d) the possibility of massive social violence (civil war even) threatened at every turn in the transition to a 'new South Africa' such that some type of honest, collective, and public contending with the past had to take place if nationhood was to have any hope of success." See Harvey, *Dear White Christians*, 91.

On the one hand, the plan aims to grant amnesty 'at a price' – the price being the requirement for those applying for amnesty to make 'full disclosure of all the relevant facts' regarding their activities. On the other hand, through its processes of public and private 'hearings,' the TRC hopes to give the victims of 'gross human rights violations' a chance to tell their story, not only to the TRC but also to the nation as a whole, with some prospect of possible reparations.[71]

Moreover, at the heart of the TRC process is the notions of "reconciliation and reconstruction" rather than retribution or justice in a judicial sense. Catherine Cole underscores this "balancing act," stating that "the TRC was neither here nor there, located somewhere between the islands of the past and an imagined future integration – integration for the races, of course, but also integration for South Africa itself within both the continent and the larger world from which it had been severed through years of cultural and economic boycotts."[72] With no template on how to proceed and what to expect, the TRC sprang from "the morality as a people" and reflected a cultural interest in realizing the common humanity (ubuntu) of the people of South Africa.[73] Coupled with what is described as an international "fetishisation," the South African commission became one of the most ambitious projects of its sort ever undertaken.[74]

With much fanfare, scepticism and pointed opposition, the TRC started its work in 1996. The commission was divided into three sub-committees. This included a) the Committee on Human Rights Violations; b) the Committee on Amnesty; and c) the Committee on Reparations and Rehabilitation. The initial plan was that these committees would hold simultaneous hearings around the country during the two years of operation. Due to the public nature of its work, it was the Committee of Human Rights Violations that attracted the most attention when it started its work. This commission was entrusted to hear the stories of victims to determine whether gross human

---

71. Maluleke, "Truth, National Unity", 60. Also see Boraine, Levy and Scheffer, *Dealing with the Past*; Asmal, Asmal and Roberts, *Reconciliation Through Truth*, 11.

72. Cole, *Performing South Africa's*, Preface and Acknowledgments.

73. Moodley, "African Renaissance", 3.

74. Doxtader, *With Faith in the Works of Words*, 5.

rights violations had occurred.[75] It took the testimonies of more than 21,000 victims and witnesses – 2,000 were selected to appear in public hearings. The hearings received extensive media coverage. In the process, the weekly Truth Commission Special Report became South Africa's most-watched news show.[76] This was in line with the TRC's mandate to promote national reconciliation by providing ordinary South Africans (who were neither perpetrators nor victims of gross violations of human rights) with the opportunity to reflect on their past and future through the publicity around the TRC.[77]

The most innovative – yet also the most controversial aspect of the TRC's work – was its power to grant amnesty for gross human rights violations. The Promotion of National Unity and Reconciliation Act made provision for granting amnesty to persons who fully disclosed all the relevant facts. The amnesty provision stated that:

> In order to advance reconciliation and reconstruction, amnesty shall be granted in all respect of acts, omissions and offences associated with political objectives and committed in the course of the conflicts of the past. To this end, Parliament under this constitution shall adopt a law determining a firm cut-off date . . ., and providing for the mechanisms criteria and procedures, including tribunals, if any, through which such amnesty shall be dealt with at any time after the law has been passed.[78]

In his critical assessment of the amnesty provision, Richard Wilson argues that the post-amble's "amnesty provisions were the only indispensable and necessary part of the process of national unity and reconciliation." In his words, "reconciliation was the Trojan horse used to smuggle an unpleasant aspect of the past (that is, impunity) into the present political order, to transform political compromises into transcendental moral principles."[79] It is for

---

75. According to the *Promotion of National Unity and Reconciliation Act*, no. 34 of 1995, a gross human rights violation is defined as the "violation of human rights through the killing, abduction, torture, or severe ill treatment of any person . . . which emanated from conflicts of the past . . . and the commission of which was advised, planned, directed, commanded, or ordered by any person acting with a political motive."

76. Hayner, *Unspeakable Truths*, 28.

77. Hendrikson, *Journey with a Status Confessionis*, 147.

78. Doxtader, *With Faith in the Works of Words*, 215.

79. Wilson, *Politics of Truth*, 99, 97.

this reason that the TRC legalization was often described as weak, in some ways favouring the perpetrators at the expense of victims.[80] After granting amnesty to key political and army figures, the fear of prosecution and condemnation among many perpetrators subsided. Instead of coming forward and disclosing, many decided not to apply for amnesty. Consequently, many of the crimes committed during apartheid were never revealed. There were 7,115 applications for amnesty, 4,500 were rejected, and another 145 were granted partial amnesty.[81]

The Committee on Reparations and Rehabilitation was tasked with determining how each victim should be compensated and making recommendations to the president in an endeavour to restore the human and civil dignity of such victims. Whereas the Committee on Amnesty had the power to grant amnesty, the Committee of Reparations and Rehabilitation, which dealt with reparations for victims, could only make recommendations to either the president or a parliamentary standing committee. In this context, the TRC had the mandate to provide amnesty to perpetrators but was only mandated to make recommendations for the provision of reparations for victims. In Maluleke's view, beyond the complex arguments about whether the TRC ought to have been given more judicial "teeth" to adopt a prosecution-centred approach or a blanket amnesty approach, there is a sense that, as things stood, the scales were tilted slightly in favour of the perpetrators of apartheid atrocities. However, there was the feeling that as things stood, the scales were tilted slightly in favour of the perpetrators of apartheid atrocities. Indeed, the very clause of the interim constitution that gave rise to the TRC referred mainly to amnesty and not reparations.[82]

5.3.3 Religious Symbolism and the TRC

The central aim of the Promotion of National Unity and Reconciliation Act was to promote national unity and reconciliation. While the detail of this mandate remained vague, the legislation charged the TRC to facilitate consultations that would contribute to the public's ability to understand and redress apartheid atrocities and work towards national reconciliation.

---

80. Maluleke, "Truth, National Unity," 59–86, 63
81. Van der Borght, "Reconciliation in the public domain," 420.
82. Maluleke, "Truth, national unity and reconciliation in South Africa," 67.

This was set against notions of "vengeance" or "justice" in a judicial sense. Notwithstanding the religious underpinnings of this approach, the establishment of the TRC, as John Allen observes, had very little to do with religious ideals. Instead "it was rather the providential outcome of realpolitik, which reflected a convergence of pressures from three directions: idealistic human rights activists within the ANC, frightened generals of the old order, and nongovernmental lobby coordinated by the man who was to become Tutu's deputy in the commission."[83] Nevertheless, under Desmond Tutu's leadership, the commission's religious character became a distinctive feature. The prominence of religious, predominantly Christian leaders was not random. Here one would have to come to terms with the role of Christian activists (including the commissioners) in the struggle against apartheid. However, Maluleke explains that the commissioners were not appointed as church representatives, but rather as individuals who proved their worth in the struggle against the injustices of apartheid. In his words, "We must never forget that the TRC is a juridical entity with a political rather than a spiritual or theological agenda . . . It is therefore erroneous to assume that the presence of church people in the commission means that the church is represented in it or that its objectives are spiritual and theological."[84] Notwithstanding Maluleke's observation, the language and conceptualization of the TRC was largely inspired by Christian principles. De Gruchy remarks that TRC's mode of "operation sometimes resembled a pastoral counselling chamber presided over by a father confessor rather than a court of law chaired by a judge."[85] The chairperson, Desmond Tutu, was always dressed in purple clerical robe and clearly acting as a religious figure. Moreover, public hearings sometimes resembled a church service more than a judicial proceeding. Alex Boraine, who served as vice-chairperson of the TRC, remarks that from the beginning, it was clear that there would be both praise and criticism for how Tutu handled public hearings. Tutu's wearing of clerical dress, offering prayers and often using Christian metaphors became a cause for concern for some who

---

83. Allen, *Rabble-Rouser for Peace*, 344.

84. Maluleke, "Truth, national unity and reconciliation in South Africa," 69.

85. De Gruchy, "From Church Struggle," 226; Cole's perceptive book on the TRC provides the reader with a detailed account of the different sensory elements in the process, See Cole, *Performing South Africa's*.

preferred a more forensic approach to public proceedings.[86] Nevertheless, in responding to criticism, Tutu insisted that President Mandela was acutely aware that he (Tutu) was an archbishop when he appointed him chairperson of the commission.[87]

The firm emphasis on the religious (especially Christian) aspects of the TRC should have been expected. In Piet Meiring's words,

> The South African community is by and large a religious community. The vast majority of South Africans belong to one of the Christian denominations or to the Muslim, Hindu, Buddhist, Bahai, Jewish or African traditionalist communities . . . the influence of the churches and other faith communities is still a force to be reckoned with. From the onset, the faith communities were involved in discussing the possibility of a truth commission and eventually in the drafting of the TRC Act. Workshops and conferences to further the aims of the TRC and to identify the churches' and other communities' role in the process were the order of the day. And when the TRC hearings started, the local churches were the staunch co-workers of the Commission, helping to disseminate news, to encourage victims and perpetrators to approach the TRC and to act as facilitators and spiritual guides throughout the life of the Commission.[88]

The development of a TRC "liturgy" that sets the pattern for public hearings is against this background. This included an "order of worship" that consisted of the singing of hymns, prayers (interdenominational and interfaith), scripture readings in many languages, the lighting of candles and the presenting of olive branches. In this context, Archbishop Tutu, understanding the spiritual needs of victims and the audience, made ample use of prayers to open and close meetings and guide the process through sometimes difficult periods.[89]

---

86. Boraine, *Country Unmasked*, 266.
87. Boraine, 101.
88. Meiring, "Pastors or Lawyers?," 332.
89. Meiring, "Pastors or lawyers?," 332–333.

5.3.4 The Framing of Reconciliation at the TRC

In all probability, the notion of the TRC was borrowed from the Roman Catholic model of penance, confession, and absolution. In this context, the notions of "truth" and "reconciliation," underscored in the commission's name, are central elements in the Christian tradition. Fundamental to the work of the commission was to establish the truth about the past. Meiring notes that the Minister of Justice, Dullah Omar, in introducing the Promotion of National Unity and Reconciliation Act to Parliament, highlighted the inextricable link between truth and the search for genuine reconciliation.[90] In this context, Anthea Jeffery raises serious criticisms on the difficulty of establishing the "truth" and the TRC's handling of the "truth."[91] Meiring's interpretation of the "truth" and how it was dealt with at the TRC is quite perceptive. In his view:

> The quest for truth also had a deeper side to it. Searching for the truth, in the tradition of all religions, is a spiritual exercise. Finding the truth goes well beyond establishing historical and legal facts. It has to do with understanding, accepting accountability, justice, restoring and maintaining the fragile relationships between human beings, as well as with the quest to find the Ultimate Truth, God Himself. Leading the nation on this road indeed posed a huge challenge to the faith communities in the country. The search for truth needed to be handled with the greatest sensitivity. Would that not be the case, the nation could bleed to death. But if we succeeded, it would lead to a national catharsis, peace and reconciliation, to the point where the truth in all reality sets one free.[92]

The work of the commission was further complicated by linking truth-seeking with reconciliation. Megan Shore explains that, on their own, these concepts are quite difficult to comprehend. Not only was the relationship between "truth" and "reconciliation" expressed in the name of the commission, but it was also publicized in the commission's slogan, "Truth, the Road to

---

90. Meiring, *Chronicle of the Truth*, 12–14.
91. Jeffery, *Truth about the Truth*, 13.
92. Meiring, "Pastors or Lawyers?," 336.

Reconciliation."[93] Meiring remarks that the somewhat naïve expectation from the onset of TRC's work is "that once we have welcomed truth in at the front door of our house, reconciliation would slip in by the back door."[94] However, there were instances of reconciliation between perpetrators and victims, but for the most part, these cases were not indicative of the broader quest for national reconciliation. Part of the problem was defining what exactly was meant by reconciliation. This was much easier to define on an individual basis, but what this meant on a societal level remained elusive.

The lawyers, jurists and politicians were much more grounded and less starry-eyed in their interpretation of what reconciliation meant within the context of the TRC. People did not kill each other, and for them, that was enough. However, people like Desmond Tutu and other religious leaders favoured a loftier ideal. In Meiring's words:

> When they spoke about reconciliation they clothed it in religious terminology. Referring to Paul's Second Letter to the Corinthians, it was often said that only because God had reconciled us to Him by sacrificing his Son Jesus Christ on the cross, true and lasting reconciliation between humans became possible (2 Cor 5:17–12). Trying to define reconciliation, references were often made to the shalom, the peace that God alone could provide. Psalm 85:10–14 was often quoted. In similar fashion, spokespersons for the other faith communities used deeply religious terminology, referring to the deepest sources of their beliefs, when they joined in the debate.[95]

The different parties agreed on the fragility and costliness of working towards reconciliation. Also, it would be nearly impossible to refer to reconciliation without taking seriously the issue of justice, accountability and restitution. In this context, Tutu emphasizes the need to reach into the "spiritual wells of our different religious traditions" to address the challenge of healing and nation-building. In his view, the Christian tradition has "a special responsibility" because of how Christian theology was used to justify apartheid.[96]

---

93. Shore, *Religion and Conflict Resolution*, 107.
94. Meiring, "Pastors or Lawyers?," 337.
95. Meiring, "Pastors or Lawyers?," 337–338.
96. Tutu, "Foreword," 8.

5.3.5 Narrative and the TRC

The place of narrative is crucial in trying to understand the inner logic of TRC. Here the public hearings of the Committee of Human Rights Violations are particularly important. For Russel Botman and Robin Petersen: "While the importance of narrative has been a central issue in much contemporary theology and ethics, this theory is rarely demonstrated with as much power as it is at the TRC hearings."[97] Victims of apartheid were encouraged to tell their stories. In being encouraged to share their stories of pain and suffering, victims routinely used overtly Christian terminology to describe their situation and how they dealt with their loss. In the context of dealing with violence committed against an individual or dealing with a loss, Lyn Graybill posits that "it is important that victims be allowed to share their stories; survivors often feel misunderstood and ignored, their sacrifice unacknowledged, their pain unrecognised, and their identity destroyed."[98] In addition, narrative also relates to the construction of a shared memory of the past for victims, perpetrators, and bystanders. For Graybill, where shared memory is lacking, where people do not share in the same past, there can be no real community, and where community is to be formed, shared memory must be created. In this context, the TRC provided the victims, perpetrators, and bystanders with the opportunity to participate in each other's humanity in story form.[99] Kader Asmal, Louise Asmal and Suresh Roberts posit that through the stories coming from the TRC, South Africans were confronted with unwelcome truths to "harmonize incommensurable world views" so that conflicts and differences stand "at least within a single universe of comprehensibility."[100] In this context, working towards reconciliation requires general agreement between both sides as to the wrongs committed. In the framework of the TRC, the danger of perpetrators not coming forward threatened that because significant parts of the narrative remained untold.

---

97. Botman and Petersen, "Introduction," 12.
98. Graybill, "South Africa's Truth," 48.
99. Graybill, 49.
100. Asmal, Asmal, and Roberts, *Reconciliation through Truth*, 46.

5.3.6 Forgiveness and Repentance at the TRC

The logic of the TRC confessional process was based on the notion that the perpetrators repent their sins and victims offer forgiveness, leading to reconciliation between individuals and, ultimately, the nation at large. Tutu encouraged this process and implored perpetrators to apologize publically and accept the forgiveness he hoped would be forthcoming. It is important to note that an apology or remorse was not a prerequisite for granting amnesty. In this context, the TRC amnesty process is often described as paradoxical and enigmatic.[101] This leads Graybill to question the TRC's emphasis on forgiveness. With so much emphasis on forgiveness, not forgiving was not given the space it deserved. As she further explains, the reality is that none of the victims could be compelled to forgive any more than perpetrators could be forced to repent. In this sense, Tutu, as a reconciling figure, did much in terms of encouraging forgiveness and repentance, but in reality, this was not a legislative requirement. At the same time, it could not be realistically expected that victims would be ready to forgive even when asked to do so. Tutu emphasized this point more than once.[102] The TRC hearings illustrated that perpetrators often did not always express remorse for the wrongs committed. At the same time, the victims also did not always express forgiveness.[103] Peter Storey does not view the lack of contrition when showing remorse for many amnesty applicants as a particular problem. In his opinion, forced repentance would devalue those moments of apparently genuine repentance that often took place. Thus, whether amnesty applicants were remorseful or not, at the very least, disclosure meant acknowledging the truth of what happened.[104]

5.3.7 The Notion of Guilt at the TRC

The TRC operated from the premise of original sin. This is rooted in the idea that everyone bears some responsibility for what happened – there are varying degrees of guilt that need to be considered. In the South African context, everyone was implicated in the crime of apartheid. Thus, when appearing before the TRC, both sides (in defence or defiance of the system)

---

101. Du Toit, *Amnesty Chronicles*, 15.

102. Harvey, *Dear White Christians*, 92.

103. For a detailed discussion on the aspects of remorse and forgiveness at the TRC see, Gobodo-Madikizela, *Human Being Died*; Kobe, "Relationship between Remorse."

104. Storey, "Different Kind of Justice," 793.

were required to disclose violations of human rights committed. In other words, no moral distinction was made between the violence used to maintain and the violence employed to oppose apartheid. This particular aspect has been severely criticized by some sectors of society, particularly those who committed human rights violations in the name of the liberation movement. Those in the ANC believed that their struggle was a moral one against an unjust system, so they discouraged their members from seeking amnesty. As a response, Tutu threatened to resign from the TRC if the ANC members tried to exempt themselves from the provisions of the legislation requiring all individuals involved to apply for amnesty to avoid prosecution. The ANC later announced that it would no longer discourage its members from applying for amnesty. However, the ANC's insistence on fighting a just war persisted. However, at this point, the TRC leadership had already resolved that the issue did not concern the morality of politically motivated offences, only whether an applicant could be held criminally or civilly liable for their actions. This was affirmed by Boraine, who stated that "No matter how just the cause may be, if there are violations of human rights, the liberation movements must accept responsibility for them."[105]

On the notion of guilt at the TRC, Christian tradition applied, in which each person is responsible for how society conducts itself. In this context, the faithful take upon themselves the guilt of crimes they did not necessarily commit. Although many whites did not directly engage in acts of crimes against black people, they are nonetheless implicated as supporters or beneficiaries of the National Party government. In this sense, the TRC had particular significance for those who maintained that they were unaware of the misdeeds committed in their name. Mahmood Mamdani explains that there may have been few perpetrators but that there are many who benefitted from apartheid.[106] However, Graybill observes that due to the very nature of the commission, ordinary whites were "let off the hook." Because the hearings focused on atrocities, crimes of torture and murder, usually at the hands of the police, it was easy for ordinary whites to simply say, "Well, I never did anything like that, I have nothing to apologize for."[107] On this issue, Maluleke notes that:

---

105. South African Press Association, "TRC Members Not Morally Neutral: Tutu."
106. Mamdani quoted in Krog, "Parable of the Bicycle."
107. Graybill, "South Africa's Truth and Reconciliation Commission," 54.

On the whole, it appeared that while black people are following the proceedings of the TRC with a touch of curiosity, many white people appear to treat TRC proceedings with disdainful apathy. While white amnesty applicants have been steadily appearing before the TRC's Amnesty Committee, white people in general are still conspicuous by their absence and disinterest. Surely, the TRC is not of concern only to the perpetrators of gross human rights violations and their victims. It should be a truly national issue, able to touch the conscience of the entire nation.[108]

To draw the population as a whole, the TRC later in December 1997 established a register of reconciliation that members of the public could sign. This was done to express regret at failing to prevent human rights violations and pledge commitment to a future South Africa in which human rights abuses will not be tolerated.

5.3.8 The Churches and Their Involvement at the TRC

Even with the contribution of Christian theological symbols to guide the proceedings at the TRC, the response of the churches was minimal. Formal responses came early on from the Research Institute on Christianity in South Africa at the University of Cape Town, the Faculty of Theology at the University of the Western Cape and the church leaders from the SACC.[109] The responses from individual denominations were relatively weak. Where and when such specific replies to the TRC happened, they were at the request of individual congregations, individual ministers or by highly specialized groupings, with very little coordination or cooperation. Etienne de Villiers points out that TRC faced a tough challenge in getting NGK involved. He believes the TRC could only function successfully if the NGK and other Afrikaner churches supported the process. In his words: "If the political parties of the Afrikaner, the Afrikaans newspapers, and, in particular, the Afrikaans churches withdraw their support and encourage Afrikaners to refuse any co-operation with the TRC, the TRC will surely not succeed in

---

108. Maluleke, "Truth, national unity and reconciliation in South Africa," 65.
109. Graybill, "South Africa's Truth and Reconciliation Commission," 56.

its objectives."¹¹⁰ Despite this appeal, most white churches, particularly the Afrikaner churches, did not directly participate in the process. Among other churches, the Salvation Army and the Apostolic Faith Mission (AFM) were the first national church bodies to make official submissions to the TRC. Graybill notes that Salvation Army admitted that during apartheid, it had chosen to be silent on the injustices committed. On the other hand, the AFM confessed that it had failed in its duty to question the system and pledged to become a more faithful watchdog to ensure that history does not repeat itself.

In November 1997, more churches responded to the invitation for a special hearing of the faith communities extended by the TRC. With the opening of this special hearing in East London, Tutu warned that no church in South Africa could claim a perfect record regarding opposing apartheid and that all churches would, therefore, need to confess their shortcomings. Over three days, the TRC heard the confessions of various Christian denominations and confessions from the Muslim, Hindu and Jewish communities, who in varying degrees apologized for not doing enough regarding opposing apartheid policies. The most self-critical submission came from the SACC. Notwithstanding the SACC's public opposition to apartheid over many years, for which the state often targeted it, it nevertheless expressed some regrets. Brigalia Bam, the General Secretary of the SACC, confessed that the SACC did not do enough to seek out the victims of apartheid but relied, in the main, on people to come to it for assistance and aid.[111]

What may be described as one of the most significant developments at the special hearings for the faith communities came from the NGK. However, as Graybill observes, the NGK submission was a disappointment because the NGK moderator said very little about the past and how the NGK theology lent credibility to apartheid; instead, the focus was on the present need for reconciliation. "Ironically (though not surprisingly), the denomination that was most explicit in the theological justification for apartheid and support of the National Party's policies was the church body that could find the least for which to apologize."[112] In reflecting on the role of the churches in the TRC process, Maluleke posits that there is nothing to suggest that the churches

---

110. De Villiers, "Challenge to the Afrikaans," 151.
111. Graybill, "South Africa's Truth and Reconciliation Commission," 57.
112. Graybill, "South Africa's Truth and Reconciliation Commission," 57.

were opposed to or highly critical of the commission. Neither was a lack of practical suggestions on what the church should do. However, the lack of an enthusiastic, well-thought-through coordinated response is also evident, equal to the national significance of the TRC itself.[113] For this reason, the churches' role in the TRC process was less than adequate.

5.3.9 The TRC in Perspective

The TRC's framing of the reconciliation discourse emphasized the acknowledgement of history as a means of establishing a shared truth. However, as Audrey Chapman observes:

> What seems appropriate in theory may not be feasible in practice or may be at least very problematic to achieve. Truth commissions, including the TRC, typically function in situations where the legacy of conflict has resulted in deep social divisions and sharply conflicting and contested versions of the past. In such situations, it is difficult for any single body to succeed establishing a widely accepted version of the truth of historical events and the chain of responsibility for them or promoting reconciliation among antagonists or contending groups, let alone both. Moreover, the immediate requirements of these two goals may be in conflict. While truth finding and the formulation of a shared history are prerequisites for long-term nation building, the process may not be conducive for promoting reconciliation, at least in the short term.[114]

Further complicating the commission's work, as Megan Shore observes, is the tension between the different interpretations of reconciliation itself. In Shore's view, the "greatest" contributing factor to this tension is that the TRC had no consensus on the definition of reconciliation. Furthermore, "during the actual functioning of the process, there was no attempt to provide a commission-recognised definition of the term."[115] The Promotion of National Unity and Reconciliation Act states that the commission's overall

---

113. Maluleke, "Truth, National Unity and Reconciliation," 66–67.
114. Chapman, "The TRC's Approach," 45.
115. Shore, *Religion and conflict resolution*, 108.

objective is to promote national unity and reconciliation, but the act fails to define what reconciliation entails. It does not specify a series of activities intended to contribute directly to the reconciliation process. The legislation does not identify the parties that are to be reconciled. Here one needs to consider whether the commission was intended to focus on reconciliation between individuals, races, contending political organizations and other actors. Nor did it offer mechanisms to evaluate the contribution of the TRC to reconciliation.[116] Part of the problem stemmed from the role of the Christian symbols in shaping a particular sense or operational understanding of reconciliation. Kader Asmal observes that the "overly Christian or religious emphasis on the idea of reconciliation," as highlighted in the TRC proceedings, caused much controversy.[117] Whatever the merits of such objections, a Christian understanding of reconciliation was ultimately pursued. This was mainly due to the leadership of Archbishop Tutu and other clergy, all of whom were committed Christians who insisted on an explicitly religious approach to reconciliation.[118] According to the TRC Final Report, this factor created much confusion between what may be considered a religious as opposed to a political understanding of reconciliation. The TRC Final Report refers to "the potentially dangerous confusion between a religious, indeed Christian, understanding of reconciliation, more typically applied to interpersonal relationships, and the more limited, political notion of reconciliation applicable to a democratic society."[119] Consequently, the commissioners and those directly involved in the facilitation of the TRC often pursued very different approaches to reconciliation. Chapman observes that:

> Depending on who was taking the initiative, the public interface and sections of the final report of the commission alternatively conveyed religious and secular perspectives. Some of the commissioners clearly vested reconciliation with religious content. Those with religious backgrounds, particularly . . . Archbishop [Tutu], linked or equated reconciliation with interpersonal

---

116. Chapman, "The TRC's approach to promoting reconciliation in the human rights violations hearings," 46.

117. Asmal, Asmal, and Roberts, "Afterword," *Reconciliation Through Truth*, i.

118. Chapman, "The TRC's approach to promoting reconciliation in the human rights violations hearings," 47.

119. TRC Final Report, 108.

forgiveness. At other times the TRC put forward a more political and judicial concept of reconciliation. Neither statements at public hearings nor in the media or the text of the TRC report makes an effort to integrate or harmonise the very different conceptions of reconciliation. The dominant role of Archbishop Tutu meant that the commission frequently communicated a message that linked reconciliation with healing and forgiveness.[120]

These different interpretations of reconciliation were already observed as early as 1994. At the conference entitled, 'The South African Conference on Truth and Reconciliation', organized by Alex Boraine. Richard Goldstone, in his address to the conference noted that, "on the one hand there is the vital legal underpinning of the Truth and Reconciliation Commission without which such a commission could not succeed and would not exist. On the other hand, there are philosophical, religious and moral aspects without which the commission would be an empty legal vessel, which would do a great deal of harm and achieve nothing."[121] In Goldstone's view, both "streams" to reconciliation were necessary for the success of the commission. He was optimistic that the commission's mandate concerning reconciliation would become more apparent as the commission progressed and that they would merge in the end. This did not happen. Instead, the lack of conceptual clarity meant that the commissioners were left to provide a particular (often religious) interpretation of reconciliation.[122] This is not to say that all non-religious, especially legal scholars, opposed the idea. Like Goldstone, Dullah Omar, a lawyer and Minister of Justice at the time, also supported bringing a religious understanding of reconciliation into the equation. At the same time, people like Jakes Gerwel, the Director-General of the Office of the State President, warned not to misrepresent the TRC as a search for the holy grail of spiritual reconciliation but instead to appreciate it first and foremost as a secular pact, a political agreement, that confirmed the latent national unity that has been present since the Union of South Africa in 1910.[123]

---

120. Chapman, "The TRC's approach to promoting reconciliation in the human rights violations hearings," 47.

121. Goldstone, "To Remember and Acknowledge," 120.

122. Shore, *Religion and conflict resolution*, 121.

123. Gerwel, "National Reconciliation: Holy Grail," in: Villa-Vicencio and Verwoerd, *Looking Back, Reaching Forward*, 277–286.

The discourse on reconciliation and how the concept is understood in the context of the TRC is a discussion on whether the commission was a religious or a political instrument. Dirkie Smit highlights that the TRC was intended to be a political, legal, and not necessarily religious or spiritual undertaking.[124] Smit remarks that the commission's mandate reflects the view of a juridical undertaking rather than a spiritual or Christian one. The commission should thus be seen in the light of the negotiated settlement and not necessarily from the perspective of the religious pursuit of reconciliation. In doing so, Smit may be correct in cautioning against misrepresenting the TRC as something other than a juridical and public instrument. As Piet Meiring observes, given the people who were charged to lead the TRC process, it was only a natural consequence that reconciliation would be interpreted from a religious perspective.[125] Thus, by having religious leaders lead the process and making reconciliation a focal point, it was only natural for the TRC to take on a religious character.[126] De Gruchy posits that "the TRC vision arose out of religious and specifically Christian conviction and was shaped by the Christian doctrine of reconciliation. The debate about reconciliation within the TRC and the wider South African public would undoubtedly have been different if the Commission had been chaired by a judge rather than an archbishop, by a politician rather than a pastor and father confessor."[127] For the most part, the concepts of forgiveness, confession, and reconciliation were far more at home in the religious sphere than in political discourse. In this context, those responsible for appointing the TRC leadership had to be aware that the process would take on a religious character. This may be problematic for various reasons, but simultaneously, it created a space for South Africans to express themselves in ways that were quite familiar.

Systematic reflection on the theological, moral and religious questions on the TRC seems to be lacking. On this point, Maluleke warns that the TRC presents an opportunity to assess what exactly is meant when concepts such as "reconciliation," "truth," and "forgiveness" are invoked. In most cases, South Africans were urged to support the TRC process in various ways. Some

---

124. Smit, "Truth and Reconciliation," 14.

125. Meiring, "Reconciliation: Dream," 242.

126. Tutu, *No Future without Forgiveness*, 71–77; Boraine, *A Country Unmasked*, 360–361; De Gruchy, *Reconciliation*, 41–3.

127. De Gruchy, *Reconciliation*, 41.

theologians, he suggests, go "overboard" in singing the praises of both the TRC and the government. In his words: "It is one thing to acknowledge the need for national healing – even reconciliation or national unity – but not to probe whether the processes, strategies, discourses, gesticulations, and pseudo-theologies [reconstruction] currently in circulation are conducive to genuine national healing, and genuine reconciliation is another." Thus, if national healing, unity, and reconciliation are indeed crucial for the people of South Africa, then sharp, thorough, deep and honest theological reflection is needed. For Maluleke, as the TRC process unfolded, it became clear that the victims of apartheid were once again in a disadvantaged position. In light of this reality, the calls to embrace reconstruction and transformation may not be in the best interest of those most in need.[128] Dirkie Smit's assessment is quite illuminating. He argues that:

> In reading many of the religious, theological and spiritual reactions already available . . . It seems that most of them reflect these ideas. Remembrance is essential; the truth must be told; guilt must be confessed; the perspective of the victim is important; reconciliation must be sought; the church is also guilty; the truth is complex. Yet, I also find it somewhat troubling to read some of these reactions, particularly in the way they give their almost unqualified blessing to every single detail . . . Even if the Christian church and theology support the broad process and the idea of the Commission itself, it looks rather too much like a (new) religious sanctioning of the state's entirely political and judicial proposals in a way that is not going to assist the state.[129]

In this context, the church needs to realize that its pastoral task will continue long after the political and juridical process has been completed.

5.4 Closing Reflections

This chapter underscores the steady movement of reconciliation as a theological concept used by Christian churches and theologians into a critical

---

128. Maluleke, "Dealing Lightly," 341–342.
129. Smit, "The Truth and Reconciliation Commission," 15.

notion in the political discourse in the transition towards a democratic state structure – from a theological to a multi-disciplinary symbol. This approach only became evident after the negotiated settlement was reached between 1990 and 1994 in South Africa. This prompted the recognition of the need for a reconstruction of society and social development. However, this required coming to terms with the apartheid past (including amnesty) for national reconciliation and nation-building. This was expressed (and legitimized) theologically in diverse ways, including the emergence of a theology of reconstruction, but primarily through engagements with the proceedings of the TRC. Drawing on Abelard's moral influence theory rhetorically, this approach is aimed at calling for social responsibility and against the privatization of religion after the advent of democracy. Here one needs to acknowledge the multi-layered nature of the reconciliation symbol and what it means for a democratic South Africa. A diversity of role-players have attributed to the reconciliation symbol, bringing with them a variety of meanings, including proposals to strip reconciliation from its theological fetters. This variety of meanings makes it challenging to bring together, harmonize and reconcile.

Nevertheless, what ties these varying perspectives together is the recognition that reconciliation is a necessary requirement for processes of social transformation and moral regeneration of South Africa. However, the concern with the moral influence theory is that it reduces the work of Christ on the cross to a private affair, a subjective matter, thereby undermining the objective reality of divine reconciliation. In doing this, it seems incapable of appreciating the theological richness of previous approaches, thus failing to grasp the existence of evil and the significance of Christ's work on reconciliation in conquering such evil.

CHAPTER 6

Conclusion

6.1 Recapitulation

The strategy proposed for this study is that there are at least three distinct approaches in response to the question: *How has the symbol of reconciliation been understood in Christian theological literature emanating from the South African context between 1968 and 2010?* As a background to these approaches, in Chapter 2, "The symbol of reconciliation in Christian theology," I provided a brief survey of reconciliation (or atonement) as a central tenet of the Christian faith. This is particularly important because, essentially, the Christian Gospel is about overcoming alienation and estrangement between God and humanity. In this context, the Christian tradition portrays Jesus Christ as the mediator of the broken covenant between God and humanity. Christian reflection on the work of Christ is traditionally discussed within the context of a theology of reconciliation. I mentioned that unlike the "person of Christ," in which the ecumenical councils formally stated their position, the question regarding Christ's work on atonement does not have a singular ecumenical reference point. This makes it particularly difficult to highlight any particular position as the traditional (Nicene) Orthodox reference point. The consequence is that Christ's work on reconciliation (or atonement) has been understood differently. To delineate the discussion, I used Gustaf Aulén's Christus Victor typology to offer a history of the interpretation of atonement, at least until 1930, when this book was published. In doing so, I underscore what Aulén refers to as the three main "types" of Christ's work on atonement.

These three main "types" provide the background to three approaches to the discourse on reconciliation in South Africa.

The term "reconciliation" was at the heart of the church struggle against apartheid. For this reason, it came under close scrutiny in Christian theological reflection, at least since 1968. Such theological controversies concerned the search for appropriate theological models and root metaphors. Reconciliation offered one such concept, but "ecclesial unity," "liberation," "justice," "nation-building," "human dignity," and "reconstruction" offered alternatives. How, for example, is reconciliation related to liberation theologically and methodologically? Should justice and liberation follow upon reconciliation or vice versa? How is reconciliation between different social groups related to the reconciliation in Jesus Christ? What connotations are attached to the symbol of "reconciliation?" I argued that while there may well be a consensus in theological publications on what reconciliation entails, the controversies over the symbol of reconciliation suggest that at least three additional layers of meaning may be identified in the Christian discourse on reconciliation. In this context, it was argued that reconciliation lacks a fixed or singular meaning, lending credence to the idea that it is best conceived as an essentially contested concept. From this vantage point, I provided an overview of the three approaches to the discourse on reconciliation and the context from which it emerged.

a) Justice through Reconciliation in Jesus Christ

Chapter 3 discussed the approach identified as "Justice through reconciliation in Jesus Christ" (drawing especially on the Anselmian or penal substitutionary theory). In this approach, it is assumed that the reconciliation of humanity with God in Jesus Christ implies a ministry of reconciliation in a country divided by race, class, and culture, thus necessitating a concern for social justice. This particular approach employs what I referred to as "deductive logic," moving from reconciliation with God to the church's ministry of reconciliation in society. Here, the fruits of reconciliation in South Africa are contingent upon reconciliation with God – it is assumed that the message of reconciliation has been entrusted to the church as the Body of Christ. For example, in this respect, the *Belhar Confession* suggests that the church is to embody reconciliation among its members. It further asserts that reconciliation must be understood as a gracious gift from God through the blood of

Christ. Also, it calls the church to understand its reconciliation and place in God through the Body of Christ. It further asserts that the church is called to take up the ministry of reconciliation to the point where it is believed to be the church's responsibility. Thus, the church needs to act as a reconciled community reflecting love and peace among people and establishing visible signs of God's kingdom within the context of the divisions in society. However, the church's focus on the ministry of reconciliation transcends the noble idea of merely helping people to "get along." Here the assumption is that no lasting solution to social conflict can be found without addressing the deep roots of such conflict. This social conflict is traced directly to humanity's alienation from God and can only be overcome through God's gracious forgiveness of sins through Christ. In other words, the church must focus on reconciliation with God. Otherwise, too much emphasis on reconciliation in society without reconciliation with God will continue to be inauthentic, shallow, and misplaced, allowing space for renewed conflict. In this sense, this approach goes beyond the requirements for social cohesion and remains firmly rooted in reconciliation with God through God. In other words, God's reconciliation in Jesus Christ becomes the basis for Christians to reject any social system that assumes the fundamental irreconcilability of people. It was argued, however, that through "deductive logic," one runs the risk of using abstract theological language that only focuses on the church more than social needs.

b) *Justice and Reconciliation after Liberation*

Chapter 4 discussed the approach identified as "Justice and reconciliation after liberation" (drawing especially on the Christus Victor theory). Here I described how reconciliation was understood in the context of liberation theology, especially in the *Kairos Document* and in comments on reconciliation in the context of Black Theology. This approach is associated with churches or theologians who see the need to address situations of conflict in society. Here the need for political, economic and cultural liberation was emphasized. Those involved assumed that social justice could only follow upon the liberation from apartheid and that reconciliation is only possible on the basis of (following) justice. They employ what I refer to as an "inductive logic" where conflict situations are rooted in human alienation from God and where social conflict forms the starting point for the ministry of reconciliation. This view suggests that reconciliation has to be understood in the context of both God's work of creation and salvation, given that what is at stake is the tension between Creator and creature, which has emerged because of captivity to the principalities and powers of this world (Col 1:18–23). The "inductive logic" further suggests that not only human beings or human society but the whole of creation are included in God's work of reconciliation in Christ – the need for a broader frame of reference follows the argument that any breach in a relationship has broader implications than only the two parties concerned. If such a breach has almost cosmic ramifications, the final resolution of such conflict must consider the problem's most comprehensive possible scope. In this context, reconciliation between two individuals is only possible if the whole of that society is reconciled with itself. In other words, everything is included in God's work of reconciliation in Christ. God's cosmic reconciling activity precedes and provides the framework within which God's reconciliation of humanity occurs. It is suggested that this approach is significant because through it, the Christian message of reconciliation in Christ is rediscovered through engaging with social problems such as social and economic inequality and the need for restitution, especially in the context where there is a history of social injustices. However, I argue that those using the "inductive logic" as an approach to the discourse on reconciliation are confronted with the danger of self-secularization, of reducing the Christian confession to nothing more than an example of religious affiliation that may be tolerated as long as its particular claims are not foregrounded. The obvious danger, as may be the case with the *Kairos Document*, is being socially relevant without having anything distinct to offer.

c) Reconstruction Requires National Reconciliation

In Chapter 5, the approach identified as "Reconstruction requires national reconciliation" (drawing especially on Abelard's moral influence theory) was discussed. Here I described the steady movement of reconciliation as a theological concept used by Christian churches and theologians into a critical notion in the political discourse in the transition towards a democratic state structure. In other words, the movement of reconciliation as a theological to a multi-disciplinary symbol was discussed. This approach only became evident after the negotiated settlement reached from 1990 to 1994 in South Africa. This prompted the recognition of the need to reconstruct society and social development. However, this required coming to terms with the apartheid past (including amnesty) for national reconciliation and nation-building. This was expressed (and legitimized) theologically in diverse ways, including the emergence of a theology of reconstruction, but primarily through engagements with the proceedings of the TRC of South Africa. Rhetorically, this approach is aimed at calling for social responsibility and against the privatization of religion after the advent of democracy. However, in this approach, the biblical message of reconciliation is taken out of context and reduced to matters directly related to the social transformation and the moral regeneration of South Africa.

6.2 Reconciliation in Christian Soteriology

One may suggest that the three approaches to the discourse on reconciliation are concerned with the search for appropriate theological models and root metaphors within the framework of Christian soteriology. In this context, the use of metaphor is an essential element in interpreting Christ's atoning work – this includes His life, ministry, death and resurrection. In the biblical roots and the subsequent history of Christianity, God's work often invites a diversity of metaphors that describe experiences of what may be called "salvation" or a sense of "comprehensive well-being." Here it is important to appreciate the richness of metaphors and their roots within a particular *Sitz-im-Leben*. These metaphors often relate to specific predicaments in which humans longed for "salvation" or "comprehensive well-being." The Christian discourse on salvation emerges in cases where suffering and anxieties over potential suffering are not only severe, but where there seems to be no other way of addressing such suffering. Here the way in which human beings have collectively been trapped in violent societal structures is typically interpreted in terms of the category of (original) sin, that is, in terms of the alienation that emerged between God and humanity.[1] The sources of suffering often cannot be disentangled from one another. It should be made clear, however, that many of the challenges we currently face are linked to the inefficiencies deeply embedded in the social structures of South Africa. In the biblical roots and the subsequent history of Christianity, we find numerous examples where "salvation" from experiences of suffering are documented. Such salvific

---

1. Conradie, "Towards an Ecological Reformulation," 4–22.

experiences may be expressed in a rich array of metaphors leading to various soteriological concepts that follow from reflection on such metaphors. By utilizing a soteriological map developed by Ernst Conradie, the point is to highlight the core insights of all three types of atonement that Aulén analysed to highlight its significance for the contemporary discourse on reconciliation.[2]

a) Salvation as God's Victory Over the Forces of Evil, Death and Destruction

There are numerous situations where one may be faced with a predicament in which there seems to be no light escape. In this context, many bear evidence that they were rescued from this predicament and that the forces of evil have been conquered. The Bible has many examples of the "victory" ascribed to God's involvement. For example, a military threat is averted through political diplomacy or a victory on the battlefield; a drought or famine is averted through an alternative food supply; after a period of political oppression, a day of liberation dawns where the power of the unjust ruler is ended. The predicament is intolerable and has to be overcome in all these situations. These consequences may follow directly or indirectly from particular actions. It may be the result of one's action, someone else's, or both – the result of societal structures. It could also be the product of pain and suffering embedded in nature and exacerbated through human action. Here the situation demands an immediate remedy. In this case, it may be helpful but insufficient to experience solidarity and companionship amidst suffering. Here, a victory of some sort is required. In this context, the symbol of the cross is considered significant but not enough. The victory must be more than a moral victory or a new vision. Here the consequences of evil that cause the suffering have to be negated. Conradie mentions that:

> When being rescued is experienced in such a situation, it may be ascribed to one's own efforts, to commitment and dedication, to human wisdom, ingenuity or technology, to fortune, to spiritual forces or whatever. It may also be ascribed, at a more ultimate level, to God's presence and involvement in history. The categories of 'redemption' or 'salvation' are often used to

---

2. Conradie, "Salvation of the Earth," 114.

capture the thrust of such salvific experiences. One may also speak of being rescued from danger, liberation from oppression and a victory that has been achieved over the forces of death, destruction and evil.[3]

Strictly speaking, this is the main thrust of Aulén's retrieval of the *Christus Victor* tradition. The resurrection of Christ is a significant symbol because it symbolizes the power of God to address any situation, including conquering death. Conradie states that "the emphasis on a victory over evil brings Oscar Cullman's well-known image from World War II to mind. With the resurrection of Christ, the decisive battle ('D-Day') in the war against sin and evil has been achieved. Although the war is still continuing, the final victory ('V-Day') is assured."[4]

There are several contemporary theological movements in which the significance of such an array of soteriological concepts is emphasized. Here the *Kairos Document* and the subsequent Kairos movements are of particular importance. In more general terms, "liberation" theologies (and Black Theology in particular) have called for liberation from political, racial and economic oppression. Feminist theologies have called for liberation from patriarchy. African theologies also are attracted to the idea of victory over the evil forces that threaten overall well-being.[5] Whether liberation is the most appropriate metaphor to be employed in this regard cannot be taken for granted. As Villa-Vicencio and others proposed, there may be a need to move from "liberation" to a new vision. Again, whether that vision is necessarily "reconstruction" is also not to be taken for granted.[6] Nevertheless, whenever an immediate threat has been averted, there are still dangers that threaten the well-being of communities. The challenges of post-apartheid South Africa underscore this point. There is, thus, a need to address the very roots of such evil and establish measures that would limit the recurrence of such problems. Conradie observes that it is unclear whether such experiences of redemption can be ascribed to the work of the Holy Spirit. He asks: "How does God's work here relate to our work, or is a reference to God's involvement merely

---

3. Conradie, "Healing in Soteriological Perspective," 9.
4. Conradie, "Salvation of the Earth," 120–121.
5. Kärkkäinen, *Christ and Reconciliation*, 380.
6. Villa-Vicencio, *Theology of Reconstruction*.

a metaphoric way of referring to human emancipatory praxis?" In this sense, it may be important whether such notions of redemption could be understood as Christian. In other words, how are they related to the core Christian symbols of incarnation, cross and resurrection of Jesus Christ?[7] Indeed, the *Kairos Document* and other initiatives using an "inductive logic" are confronted with the danger of self-secularization, of reducing the Christian confession to nothing more than an example of religious affiliation that may be tolerated as long as its particular claims are not foregrounded. This results in initiatives that may be socially relevant without having anything distinct to offer.

b) Salvation as Reconciliation between God and Humanity and on That Basis within the Body of Christ and between Humans

In some cases, it is vital to address the consequences and establish the root causes of the problem. Here one may consider the numerous examples in the Bible, in the subsequent history of Christianity and from everyday life where a predicament has to be addressed at its very roots. One may consider criminal and civil court proceedings where the truth has to be established before justice can be served. There are also situations in which conflict between people has emerged. There may be various reasons why the conflict is there in the first place, and in many cases, the parties concerned share in the guilt, albeit not equally. The obvious solution would be to terminate the relationship, but this is not always possible. Here it would be helpful if those involved acknowledged (through regret, signs of remorse and confessing their guilt) their role in damaging the relationship and offered compensation without making further accusations. This may encourage the other party to reciprocate. Conradie mentions that the only lasting solution, in this case, would be a word of unconditional forgiveness, which is a crucial way of addressing evil at its very roots. In his words, "unlike condoning someone, forgiveness is an action in which one indicates to someone else that the continuation of this relationship is more important to the one who forgives that the real damage done by the one who is forgiven . . . Forgiveness is the only way in which a vicious spiral of violence may be broken."[8] Hanna Arendt comments that forgiveness "is the only reaction that does not merely react but

---

7. Conradie, "The salvation of the earth from anthropogenic destruction," 123.
8. Conradie, "The salvation of the earth from anthropogenic destruction," 124.

acts anew and unexpectedly, unconditioned by the action which preceded it and therefore freeing from its consequences both the one who forgives and the one who is forgiven."[9]

There are somewhat similar situations of conflict where whole groups of people may be involved, for example, imminent threats of war between countries, rebellion and ethnic violence. In some cases, the situation may have deteriorated significantly, and an act of forgiveness may not suffice, given the existing mistrust. In this context, a mediator is required to help start a reconciliation process. This mediator should have the trust of the parties involved and be able to identify the root causes of the problem. In addition, the mediator should help uncover the injustices and help find an amicable solution to the conflict. At a more ultimate level, the problem may be understood in terms of our alienation from God – enmity between God and humanity, characterized by a broken relationship. If the problem is not addressed, if the relationship is not restored, there will be no lasting solution to other predicaments that are experienced. In other words, our alienation from God is the root cause of irreconciliation. In response to this predicament, Conradie remarks:

> The most important symbol here is the cross of Jesus Christ. It continues to shock us, to bring us to our senses, to help us to see where religious zeal may lead to. The innocent one has been brutally executed. It brings a lasting moment of catharsis. The guilty may be pardoned. The debt has been paid. Forgiveness is possible. Reconciliation has been achieved. The mediator has sacrificed his life for the sake of peace. Healing becomes possible through the wounded healer. A new day has dawned.[10]

Because forgiveness does not by itself lead to reconciliation, it has to be embedded in a complex and reciprocal interaction between human beings and God. Here sin is not merely condoned (which would be to condone injustice), but the long-term impact of human sin is addressed so that reconciliation, healing and peace become possible. Conradie mentions that: "Christians typically find the clue to such reconciliation in the cross and not so much the

---

9. Arendt, *Human Condition: A Study*, 124.
10. Conradie, "Healing in Soteriological Perspective," 12.

resurrection of Jesus Christ."[11] This emphasis on the cross is significant when observing the approach of the *Belhar Confession*. This contrasts the *Kairos Document*, which emphasizes the resurrection, symbolizing the victory over evil forces. In the context of the cross, the Anselmian or penal substitutionary theory comes to mind. Conradie remarks that various metaphors may have been used to explain how such forgiveness and reconciliation are possible based on what Christ has done. This includes the use of the cultic image, suggesting Jesus Christ has brought a "sacrifice" on behalf of humanity to God – a sacrifice commensurate with the severity of humanity's rebellion against God. Some may use legal images to suggest that Jesus Christ has taken himself (as a substitute) for the appropriate punishment that the judge directed in his sentence on humanity. In other words, Jesus died in our place.

It should be noted that serious theological problems are associated with using these images. Some of them are raised in Aulén's critique of the legal order of the Anselmian theory.[12] Conradie highlights that the cluster of metaphors of salvation is often confused and conflated to the extent that their metaphorical roots are no longer evident. This is particularly the case of attempts to explain the significance of the cross "for us and our salvation" through categories such as "forgiveness," "reconciliation," "sacrifice," "satisfaction," and penal substitution. The mixing of metaphors is particularly evident concerning the notion of "forgiveness," – which may be understood as amnesty or legal pardon, an interpersonal word of forgiveness or the cancellation of monetary debt ("guilt"). The difficult task of unravelling the significance of such metaphors is addressed in the context of theories of atonement. In Protestant theologies, atonement is typically understood in a juridical context, while forgiveness for sinners is subsequently understood forensically. This tends to portray God as a God of law before being a God of love and fails to do justice to the more personal and relational aspects of forgiveness and wrongdoing.[13]

The significance of the juridical emphasis on the forgiveness of sinners is its emphasis on diagnosing the root causes of our estrangement from God and responding to sin at its roots through the good news of the justification

---

11. Conradie, "Salvation of the Earth," 125.
12. Aulén, *Christus Victor*, 143–159.
13. Conradie, "The salvation of the earth from anthropogenic destruction," 127–128.

of sinners through God's grace. This is the lasting significance of the positions of Anselm and Luther and many evangelical theologies of atonement. However, more is needed. Conradie warns that the emphasis on the roots of sin should not be reduced to personalist categories. A more comprehensive notion of God's justice is required to emphasize God's concern to re-establish just rule in a world corrupted by human sin.[14] Colin Gunton seems to agree. He offers a creative reinterpretation of a juridical view of atonement based on "the justice of God."[15] Within the context of the Anselmian theory, Gunton remarks that it was the ruler's duty to maintain order in society, without which society would collapse.[16] In this sense, God does not so much demand satisfaction for sin because God was personally offended but because of the disruptive consequences of sin in society.[17] God acts as a judge not as much to punish sinners but from the vantage point of unwillingness to allow creatures to destroy themselves.[18] What is needed is to create a new dispensation, the way of the cross, which would satisfy the ruler as being appropriate to re-establish order in society. God does not desire punishment, but the justice of God calls for the eschatological transformation of the whole created order. This is what Gunton refers to as God's loyalty to creation.[19] Here there is a fundamental asymmetry between divine and human action, an unbridgeable gulf between the work of Christ through which God reconciled the world to Godself (2 Cor 5:19) and the Spirit's ministry of reconciliation through us. Thus, the notion of the justice of God goes beyond the narrow personalist concept of righteousness through legalistic pardoning of sin and succeeds in integrating all three models of atonement quite neatly.

c) Salvation as Moral Transformation

I have highlighted the need to confront the consequences of evil. It may also be necessary to address the root causes of evil to eradicate it. Eradicating evil may indeed be evasive, if not impossible. The persistence of racism in

---

14. Conradie, "The Salvation of the Earth," 128.
15. Gunton, *Actuality of Atonement*, 87.
16. Gunton, 89.
17. Gunton, 95.
18. Gunton, 92.
19. Gunton, 103.

South Africa may serve as a good example here. It thus becomes necessary to tolerate the presence of evil.

In most cases, any attempt to eradicate evil only creates more evil through the instruments used. It then becomes a question of how evil may be limited to prevent the situation from deteriorating in future. In this sense, Conradie may be correct in stressing that a new beginning (for instance, democratic South Africa) does not guarantee that evil will not emerge again.[20] In reality, the country's state, over twenty years into democracy, leaves much to be desired. The persistence of racism, and rampant corruption in the public and private sectors, to name but a few, confirms this assertion. It is, therefore, necessary to reflect on appropriate guidelines to safeguard society against future evil.

There is, of course, no guarantee that evil will ever be brought under control. History has many examples indicating that the more radically this is done, the more dramatically evil may manifest itself in other forms, including in what is supposed to be good and in the apparatus set up to repress evil. It is, therefore, wise to reckon with a much wider compass of latent evil. Evil is more evasive, widespread and less fathomable than one may wish to admit.[21] In the biblical roots and the subsequent history of Christianity, there are numerous examples where the importance of minimizing injustice, conflict, and violence is recognized. The examples of prophets, judges, kings, priests, saints, martyrs, etcetera serve as an apt example. Moreover, the Christian symbol of the incarnation, life, and ministry of Jesus Christ is deemed the most important in this regard. His followers celebrate and glorify the example set by Jesus of Nazareth. What is at stake here is his vision for a new social order, labelled the coming reign of God, based on solidarity with the marginalized and care for the victims of society. The inspiring example of love, even to the point of death, as demonstrated in the life of Jesus, evokes a similar response from humanity. In Conradie's words:

> His imaginative example of the first concrete steps which may be necessary to actualise something of this coming reign now already is significant here. This emerged from his ministry to the sick, the helpless, lepers, prostitutes, sinners, tax collectors and soldiers. However, there is also a sense in which suffering in

---

20. Conradie, "Healing in Soteriological Perspective," 14.
21. Conradie, 15.

this world cannot always be avoided. Here notions of solidarity in suffering (the suffering servant), kenosis, lament and consolation are crucial. In the biblical texts, this is expressed both Christologically and pneumatologically (the groaning of the Spirit in Romans 8). In addition, one may consider the apostolic admonitions and guidelines for Christian living.[22]

This emphasis on inspiring examples for Christian living is typical of many modern theologies, possibly because it eschews philosophical questions regarding the resurrection and cultural resistance against the bloodiness of the cross. Here Abelard's moral influence theory of the subjective appropriation of Christ's atonement is often emphasized. Furthermore, Friedrich Schleiermacher's view that redemption consists in the transmission of the God-consciousness of Jesus to later believers to Albert Ritschl's understanding of the ethical significance of the proclamation of God's reign is emphasized. There is a tendency in such accounts of salvation to focus on subjective feelings of guilt and underplay the objective disruption of the social order through human evil – sometimes liberation from oppression and victory over evil is required first to re-establish a just social order.[23] In South Africa, the emergence of a theology of reconstruction after the fall of apartheid may serve as such a notion of salvation. Here the focus is on reigning in the latent forms of evil to express an appropriate vision for building a free, democratic dispensation in the company of people from other faiths and worldviews, calling for a sense of solidarity for those experiencing victimization.

6.3 Integrating the Three Approaches to Reconciliation?

The approaches discussed have particular strengths and weaknesses, thus highlighting the need for a more integrated approach. Generally, the range of soteriological concepts present in the discourse on reconciliation allows people to use whatever concepts they deem appropriate to address particular concerns. Firstly, in the *Belhar Confession* (drawing especially on the Anselmian or penal substitutionary theory), the focus is on addressing the

---

22. Conradie, "Salvation of the Earth," 131.
23. Conradie, 132.

root cause of social conflict. Here social conflict is traced back directly to our alienation from God. This, in turn, can only be overcome through God's gracious forgiveness of sins through Christ. Reconciliation in society without reconciliation with God is deemed inauthentic, shallow and misplaced, allowing space for renewed conflict. In other words, God's reconciliation in Jesus Christ becomes the basis for Christians rejecting any social system that assumes the irreconcilability of people. In this approach, one risks using abstract theological language that focuses only on the church more than social needs. Secondly, the Kairos Document (drawing especially on the Christus Victor theory) emphasizes the need for political, economic and cultural liberation. In this approach, social conflict forms the starting point for the ministry of reconciliation. Reconciliation is understood in the context of God's work of creation and salvation, given that what is at stake is the tension between Creator and creature, which has emerged because of captivity to the principalities and powers of this world (Col 1:18–23). God's cosmic reconciling activity precedes and provides the framework within which God's reconciliation of humanity occurs. In other words, the Christian message of reconciliation in Christ is rediscovered through engaging with social problems such as social and economic inequality and the need for restitution, especially in the context where there is a history of social injustice. In this approach, one runs the risk of self-secularization, of reducing the Christian confession to nothing more than an example of religious affiliation that may be tolerated as long as its particular claims are not foregrounded. Thirdly, during the transitional period (drawing especially on Abelard's moral influence theory), the need for reconstructing society and social development was emphasized. This included coming to terms with the apartheid past, including working towards the realization of national reconciliation and nation-building. Rhetorically, this approach is aimed at calling for social responsibility and against the privatization of religion. The main concern with this approach is that the biblical message of reconciliation is taken out of context and reduced to matters directly related to social transformation and moral regeneration issues.

Following Aulén's analysis, this study suggests that the three approaches address the evil consequences of human sin (God's victory over evil, based on the message of resurrection), the roots of such evil in human sin (sinners are forgiven by God through grace, manifested in the cross of Jesus Christ) and a way of life for the present in order to map a better future (following Christ's moral example, redemption is depicted as an achievement that human beings can reach themselves). Here one would have to consider whether integrating these soteriological concepts would be appropriate for the discourse on reconciliation. After all, the history of the Christian tradition indicates that the symbols of the life, cross, and resurrection of Jesus Christ were integrated in order to present a narrative whole.[24] In this sense, it would be problematic to emphasize a single approach at the expense of other existing approaches. Also, no one-size-fits-all approach can ever capture the theological breadth of Christ's atoning work. Respectively, we have used soteriological concepts such as forgiveness, justice, liberation, reconstruction, and reconciliation to better recognize and appreciate the message of salvation. However, in emphasizing Aulén's analysis and applying these models to the South African context, one would need to come to terms with the fact that a focus on the forgiveness of sins in Christ (Anselmian or penal substitutionary theory) has not yet brought an end to injustice.

In the same way, liberation (drawing especially on the *Christus Victor* theory) from social oppression also does not necessarily translate into the end of injustice. Those proposing theologies which are more liberal in their orientation (drawing especially on Abelard's moral influence theory) also need to be reminded that knowledge and moral appeals alone are not sufficient in addressing the deep-rootedness of suffering. In this sense, the social roots of evil must be recognized. The realization of the good relies on more than just a mere focus on the ideal moral example. In this context, it is clear that in order to make progress on the challenge of reconciliation in South Africa, one would have to go beyond the neat compartmentalization of the various approaches. In other words, one would need an integration of the three approaches to reconciliation. This may very well lead to the distorting of soteriological metaphors and their implied *Sitz-im-Leben*. At the same time, it may broaden what may otherwise be considered contrasting soteriological positions. This is often the case in South Africa, where, for example, reconciliation and justice are often used in oppositional terms.[25] The same could be said about liberation and reconstruction.[26] Instead, I am proposing

---

24. Conradie, 133.
25. Volf, "Forgiveness, Reconciliation and Justice," 869–872.
26. Maluleke, "Proposal for a Theology," 252–256.

a broadening of our local understanding of these soteriological metaphors, thereby highlighting their theological relatedness beyond the false dichotomies that are often emphasized. However, one would need to be cautious not to blur the distinct character of the three approaches.

6.4 The Quest for Reconciliation Deferred?

More than 20 years after the TRC had started its work, reconciliation remains a contested concept, and the progress in the reconstruction of society has fallen short in many areas.[27] Along with the legacy of apartheid, the democratic dispensation has brought an array of new challenges.[28] Among other things, rampant corruption in the public and private sectors has undermined much of the progress made in the short democratic history of the country.[29] In this context, the ruling ANC's performance as the champion of the aspirations of most South Africans has been more than disappointing. Without strong ethical leadership, the ANC has progressively become the fiefdom of crude political entrepreneurs, the corrupt and the cynically ambitious. As the ruling political party, the longer the ANC continues on the trajectory of patronage politics and the abuse of incumbency, the more harm will be done – thus relegating the ideals and aspirations on which the democratic dispensation was founded. Though the ANC still dominate the political landscape, the challenges to its electoral power are already starting to take shape.

Nevertheless, today it would be fair to say that the quest for reconciliation still forms part of the public discourse in South Africa, albeit in a way more hidden from public attention. Moreover, the concept has lost its premier status as a guiding vision for social transformation in South Africa. Along with this, the legacy of Nelson Mandela and his vision is being contested more than ever. Notwithstanding his status as the father of the nation and chief reconciler, it is now not uncommon for black people to talk about Mandela as the one who "sold out." Such views are prompted by the notion that under his leadership, the (over)emphasis on reconciliation and forgiveness did very

---

27. Kollapen, "Reconciliation: Engaging with," 23.

28. See for instance, Mangcu, *State of Democracy*; Mckaiser, *Run Racist Run*.

29. See Pieter-Louis Myburgh's recent exposé on the level of corruption between government officials and those in the private sector. Myburgh, *Republic of Gupta*.

little to disrupt the socio-economic vestiges of apartheid. Here forgiveness and reconciliation, without addressing the root causes of injustice, are often cited as a concern.

In the meantime, many young South Africans have become disillusioned, even cynical, about the state of the nation. This scepticism is best expressed in the tension between the work of the TRC and the reality that South Africa remains one of the world's most (if not the most) unequal countries in the world.[30] This is hardly surprising given the social divisions, marked especially by race and class, that continue to characterize the country. Such divisions are monitored through the annual publications produced by the Institute for Justice and Reconciliation (SA Barometer Survey). From this it is evident that South Africans continue to associate strongly with identity groups based on language, ethnicity and race. More recently, the Diagnostic Report released by the government's National Planning Commission acknowledged that the country remains a "deeply divided society." These divisions were ascribed to economic underperformance and deeply entrenched historical privilege and deprivation patterns. This is further aggravated by high unemployment, low quality of education for blacks, inadequate infrastructure, significant spatial development challenges, a resource-intensive and unsustainable growth path, an ailing public health system unable to cope with the national disease burden, and uneven public health sector performance and corruption. In response to such divisions, the government's National Development Plan for 2030 recognizes the need to prioritize reconciliation, social cohesion and nation-building to strengthen the country's social fabric.[31] In the meantime, the lack of expectation and cynicism has often turned to anger and violence. The recent spate of student and public service protests in the country are good examples. These protests often accompany views expressing disenchantment with democracy in the country. In this context, many understand democracy primarily in instrumental terms as a political form through which inequality is curtailed and essential services, such as housing, water and food, are to be made available. This understanding of democracy and the disparity between, what many believe is and what ought to be, leaves South Africa's

---

30. Conradie, *Reconciliation*, 65; Kollapen, "Reconciliation," 24.
31. Institute for Justice and Reconciliation, Barometer.

democracy vulnerable should socioeconomic inequalities continue.[32] This is why the quest for reconciliation gets less attention than some believe it deserves. Some question whether reconciliation should be prioritized at all?[33] Hence the question, does reconciliation matter? In this context, one would have to once again (re)consider, as Dirkie Smit did in the 1980s, whether the reconciliation symbol has the potential to transform society.[34] Since the term needs constant clarification, it often loses its power as a symbol. A symbol is precisely something that is self-evident and needs no explanation – it grips the imagination. It is precisely for this reason that some often find it necessary to talk about "true," "genuine," or authentic reconciliation, thereby implying that they reject a notion of reconciliation considered "cheap" or "inauthentic". If anything, the question of whether reconciliation has a role to play in addressing some of the most difficult challenges facing us would have to be addressed. The assumption that it lacks the incentive to do this could very well be contingent on a secular (political) as opposed to a theological understanding of reconciliation's potential.

6.5 The Quest for Reconciliation as a Shared Dispute

Fanie du Toit and Erik Doxtader underscore the persistent nature of reconciliation as a shared dispute and the challenges it brings. In their words:

> There is a good chance that reconciliation was a necessary condition for the negotiated revolution that ended apartheid *and*, that at the same time, it directed us away from, if not distracted us from, some of South Africa's most pressing problems. It is possible that the TRC taught us a great deal about reconciliation's value *and*, at the same time, did not teach us a great deal about how to carry on the process ourselves. Today we have likely grown tired listening to the debates over reconciliation's promise *and yet*, at the same time, we still hear the commission's profound claim that reconciliation is fundamental for the

---

32. Butler, *Contemporary South Africa*, 216.
33. Harvey, *Dear White Christians*, 5.
34. Smit, "The Symbol of Reconciliation," 88.

development of a just society. These ambiguities make it difficult to agree on what reconciliation means, how it works and why it is important. Sometimes we think of it as our most prized idea, the next moment as cheap deception.[35]

For this reason, some speak of reconciliation as a secular, political process instead of the spiritual, religious process, as the event of the TRC seems to have been.[36] Others dismiss the "spiritualisation" of reconciliation because, in their estimation, the Christian notion of reconciliation simply sets the bar too high. They simply refer to a more modest notion of reconciliation. Villa-Vicencio remarks that this involves

> pardon, mercy, understanding and a willingness to seek ways to live with adversaries, despite past scars that refuse to go away. It involves political common sense rather than religious magnanimity; clear-headedness rather than heroism; responsible living rather than monk-like self-denial. It involves treating others in the kind of way we would like them to treat us. We do not necessarily have to forgive one another in order to live together in peaceful-coexistence. We do not have to respect one another and establish certain economic, social and political ground rules that enable this to happen. This level of political realism may be the only realistic political option we have.[37]

In some respect, Villa-Vicencio echoed what Jakes Gerwel raised a few years earlier when he warned that a "spiritual" or theological understanding of reconciliation creates a utopian dream that contradicts what human beings are able to achieve. In his view, the spiritualization of reconciliation poses the risk of "pathologizing" a nation in relatively good health by insisting on the perpetual quest for the "Holy Grail" of reconciliation. Gerwel further maintained that the framing of reconciliation in the context of "love" and "forgiveness" takes us back to "primitive" notions not suitable for modern societies. Moreover, that "mechanisms of solidarity" of contemporary South Africa are

---

35. Du Toit and Doxtader, *In the Balance*, ix.
36. Villa-Vicencio, *Walk with Us*.
37. Villa-Vicencio, "Reconciliation in Bloemfontein," 1.

no longer "love for neighbour" but rather "commitment to consensus-seeking, cultivation of conventions of civility and respect for contracts."[38]

Others, like Boesak and DeYoung, insist on a more "radical" notion of reconciliation.[39] For them, the discourse on reconciliation can only be sustained if shallow or cheap forms of reconciliation are contrasted with what they describe as "radical reconciliation." Here the tension between cheap and radical reconciliation is related to a tension embedded in the very nature of the discourse, which, Boesak and DeYoung believe should be returned to its biblical (theological) roots – biblical reconciliation is radical reconciliation.[40] In their estimation, the reconciliation promoted through social cohesion polarizes the notions of justice and peace, whereas justice and peace are inextricably linked in biblical reconciliation. In their words, biblical reconciliation consists of the following: Firstly, "The God of justice calls for a love that transforms relationships, societies, indeed the world, so that justice and peace can embrace (Ps 85:11). *Reconciliation without social justice, equity, and dignity is not reconciliation at all*. Reconciliation and social justice are two sides of the same biblical coin."[41] In this context, reconciliation is more than just political accommodation that accommodates some at the expense of others. For Boesak and DeYoung the mechanisms of solidarity promoted by those who propagate political reconciliation have failed – this, they maintain, is simply not enough.

In contrast, "radical reconciliation questions the assumption that justice can be served, social contracts honoured, and solidarity enacted through politics and policies grounded in a neoliberal capitalism whose very survival depends on the exclusion of the powerless, the exploitation of the poor, and the nurturing of inequality the scale of which is devastatingly clear in South Africa." Secondly, in their view, forgiveness entails more than just forgetting or moving on. "Forgiving is not forgetting, but holding the memory as Holy before God, so that the victim is honoured and the atrocity is never repeated again. *Reconciliation is holding the memory holy before God as a means of responding to God's demands for justice for the vulnerable and the*

---

38. Gerwel, "National Reconciliation: Holy Grail," 283–286.

39. Boesak and DeYoung, *Radical Reconciliation*; Boesak maintains this position in a recently published book. See, Boesak, *Pharaohs on Both Sides*, 159–161.

40. Boesak and DeYoung, *Radical Reconciliation*, 154.

41. Boesak and DeYoung, 154.

powerless, the neglected, and the excluded. There is nothing sentimental about it." Thirdly, Christian reconciliation is radical, costly reconciliation that can only take place between equals. This calls for addressing systemic injustices and the reordering of social structures. Importantly, this also calls for the transformation of the heart and mind. In their view, this does not oppose the call for justice. Instead, through this, reconciliation is sustained. The essential point for both personal and societal reconciliation is the restoration of justice, equity, and dignity. They point that *"radical reconciliation means that the deeply personal does not cancel out the thoroughly systemic."* Fourthly, there is a need to oppose unreal or idealistic notions of biblical reconciliation. In this, they oppose the more modest approach posited by Villa-Vicencio in his search for political reconciliation.[42] In their words, *"reconciliation makes it incumbent on us to change this situation by liberating the global poor, and radically so."*[43] Finally, they posit that *"reconciliation emerges from the margins and not from the centers of political or religious power."*[44] In this context the voices from the margins invigorate the discourse on reconciliation, calling those in authority to join the process meant to "re-humanise" all the children of God.[45] Ultimately, for them, there is a place for secular (political) reconciliation. As the "litmus test of a successful political transition and peace endeavour," as Villa-Vicencio observes, there is undoubtedly a place for it.[46] Given the fragility of the country's transition, one could even argue its necessity. However, Boesak and DeYoung contend that a Christian understanding of reconciliation demands more. In their words:

> We are saying that Christians are called as agents of reconciliation, that that reconciliation is radical, and that the demands of that radical reconciliation should be made applicable to the political, social, and political realities within which they live and work. As such, Christians are suspicious of reconciliation as pure political accommodation, which secures only the world of the powerful, distrustful of a minimalist process that does

---

42. Villa-Vicencio, *Walk with Us and Listen*, 2.
43. Boesak and DeYoung, *Radical Reconciliation*, 155.
44. Boesak and DeYoung, 155.
45. Boesak and DeYoung, 154–155.
46. Villa-Vicencio, *Walk with Us and Listen*, 2.

not make compassionate justice and transformation the heart of the endeavour.[47]

Equating the reconciliation concept with the political settlement strips the word of its deeper theological meaning, thus prompting the need to reaffirm the theological roots of the discussion. Notwithstanding its shortcomings, Dirkie Smit reminds us: "The Christian church has naturally been in the business of truth and reconciliation, guilt and forgiveness from its beginnings. This is our job, the industry we work in. This is the reason for our existence."[48] This makes reconciliation and the quest for conceptual clarity more important in the future.

6.6 Navigating the Discourse on Reconciliation in South Africa

Navigating the discourse on reconciliation, one would have to ask whether indeed the Christian Gospel offers hope in a country such as ours. Gregory Jones reminds us that "the restoration of our communion with God requires something beyond my repentance, my initiative or any human initiative, but not beyond God the Father's gracious will for communion with Creation."[49] In this context, one would have to come to terms with the distinction between the church's ministry of reconciliation and what Christ has done outside (*extra nos*) and on behalf (*pro nobis*) of us, and not only in us and through us (*in nobis*), once and for all (the *ephapax* of Rom 6:10).[50] At this point, we need to recognize that what holds the ecclesial community together is not a common moral activity but the fundamental asymmetry between divine and human action underscored by the work of Christ through which God reconciled the world to himself (2 Cor 5:19) and our ministry of reconciliation. John Webster posits that:

---

47. Boesak and DeYoung, *Radical Reconciliation*, 156; Elsewhere, Boesak posits that, "Reconciliation is not just secular political settlements. It is about 'healing'. It is not the Christian understanding of reconciliation that confuses the issue." See Boesak, *Tenderness of Conscience*, 178.

48. Smit, "The Truth and Reconciliation Commission," 3.

49. Jones, *Embodying Forgiveness: A Theological*, 18; Also quoted in Conradie, "Reconciliation as a Guiding Vision," 77.

50. Conradie, "Reconciliation as a Guiding Vision," 77.

> The church, therefore, lives in that sphere of reality in which it is proper to acknowledge and testify to reconciliation because we have been reconciled; in which it is fitting to make peace because peace was already made; in which it is truthful to speak to and welcome strangers because ourselves have been spoken to and welcomed by God, and so have become no longer strangers but fellow-citizens.[51]

In this context, Volf's cautionary remark reminds us, however, that final reconciliation is not the work of human beings but is attributed to the new beginning offered by the Triune God.[52] Emphasizing Christ's atoning work in its proper Trinitarian perspective helps widen the multifaceted meaning of reconciliation. In the South African context, this has particular relevance for healing and bringing together broken relationships. In the context of all the soteriological metaphors discussed above, reconciliation has the potential to be the most inclusive and comprehensive. Ross Langmead remarks that the comprehensive potential of reconciliation includes "cosmic reconciliation, the Hebrew notion of *shalom*, the meaning of the cross, the psychological effects of conversion, the work of the Holy Spirit, the overcoming of barriers between Christians, the work of the church in the world, peace-making, movements towards ethnic reconciliation and the renewal of ecological balances between humanity and its natural environment."[53] In all of these examples, an essential facet of reconciliation is undoubtedly the motif of restoring broken relationships.

Wolfhart Pannenberg underscores the goal of reconciliation as the restoration of the sin-broken fellowship of humanity with God, the source of life. This does not mean human relationships are relegated from this equation. In fact, filial human relationships are positively affirmed by God. However, through the affirmation of human relationships independent from God, human beings run the risk of being separated from God. In Pannenberg's words:

> In the process the creaturely independence of humans had to be, not set aside, but renewed. It had been eliminated by the

---

51. Webster, "Ethics of Reconciliation," 77.
52. Volf, *Exclusion and Embrace*, 110.
53. Langmead, "Transformed Relationships," 5–20, 6.

bondage of sin and by death, though sin had deceived us by picturing an autonomy in full possession of life that it would make it possible for us to attain. If, however, our reconciliation to God is to renew us in independent existence, to free us for the first time for true independence, this cannot come solely from the Father, nor can it be achieved solely by the sending of the Son into this world. It must happen on our side as well.[54]

In other words, "this taking up is not merely in the sense of something that happens to them from outside but as a liberation to their own identity, though not in their own power. This takes place through the Spirit. Through the Spirit reconciliation with God no longer comes upon us solely from outside. We ourselves enter into it."[55] On this point, Christoph Schwöbel's formulation is to the point. In his view, "the gift of the Spirit places the life of believers in a twofold horizon: it bridges the gulf between the past death and resurrection of Christ and the present life of believers and makes the eschatological horizon of the ultimate future already present for believers as a transforming power which includes them and the universe in relationship to the love of God in Christ."[56] So, whatever else Christ's atoning work may be about, its central focus is the restoration of broken relationships. This is not just a past event but an ongoing process through the work of the Holy Spirit. Here Paul Fiddes uses the example "forgiveness," not just as the "cancelling of debt" but as the restoration of a broken relationship leading to a new covenant-based relationship of mutual love and commitment.[57] In this context, one may suggest that the theological perspectives provide not only inspiration but also underscore the accountability of Christians to continue engaging in the ministry of reconciliation in church and society. God has reconciled the world to himself in Jesus Christ through the Holy Spirit; this means that South Africans (and Christians in particular) should continue working towards reconciliation, irrespective of the social markers that continue to divide us. The cross and the resurrection of Jesus Christ provide hope that injustices and enmity, even death and destruction, do not have the final

---

54. Pannenberg, *Systematic Theology*, 449–450.
55. Pannenberg, 449–450.
56. Schwöbel, "Reconciliation: From Biblical," 20.
57. Fiddes, *Past Event and Present Salvation*, 15.

word. Desmond Tutu cogently reminds us that God's forgiveness yields the imperative to forgive one another and that the grace bestowed on those who receive it has to be shared with others.[58]

In the most profound theological sense of the word, reconciliation is best conceived as an elusive mystery, a dream that cannot be fathomed or achieved. It is what may sometimes be referred to as an eschatological reality. However, this should not allow anyone to domesticate the vision of reconciliation. In Conradie's words:

> It is precisely this vision, juxtaposed with current realities, that provides the source of hope, inspiration and dedication to engage in the ongoing process of reconciliation, precisely in the midst of enmity, faction fighting and structural violence. If this eschatological vision of reconciliation is retrojected into the distant past, one can indeed do justice to the 're-' in reconciliation: to be together *again* – even where no such togetherness existed in the past.[59]

Taking Aulén's typology into consideration, the *Belhar Confession* as one of the theological texts discussed in this study, represents the most complete account of Christ's atoning work and its implications for the church. Article 3 of the confession states that:

> We believe that God has entrusted the church with the message of reconciliation in and through Jesus Christ, that the church is called to be the salt of the earth and the light of the world, that the church is called blessed because it is a peacemaker, that the church is witness both by word and by deed to the new heaven and the new earth in which righteousness dwells (2 Cor 5:17–21; Matt 5:13–16; Matt 5:9; 2 Pet 3:13; Rev 21–22).
>
> [We believe] that God's life-giving Word and Spirit has conquered the powers of sin and death, and therefore also of irreconciliation and hatred, bitterness and enmity, that God's life-giving Word and Spirit will enable the church to live in a new obedience which can open new possibilities of life for society

---

58. Tutu, *No Future without Forgiveness*, 218–220.
59. Conradie, "Reconciliation as a Guiding Vision," 78.

and the world (Eph 4:17–6:23, Rom 6; Col 1:9–14; Col 2:13–19; Col 3:1–4:6);

[We believe] that the credibility of this message is seriously affected and its beneficial work obstructed when it is proclaimed in a land which professes to be Christian, but in which the enforced separation of people on a racial basis promotes and perpetuates alienation, hatred and enmity; that any teaching which attempts to legitimate such forced separation by appeal to the gospel, and is not prepared to venture on the road of obedience and reconciliation, but rather, out of prejudice, fear, selfishness and unbelief, denies in advance the reconciling power of the gospel, must be considered ideology and false doctrine.

Therefore, we reject any doctrine which, in such a situation, sanctions in the name of the gospel or of the will of God the forced separation of people on the grounds of race and colour and thereby in advance obstructs and weakens the ministry and experience of reconciliation in Christ.

6.7 Towards an Agenda for Further Theological Reflection on Reconciliation

The discourse on reconciliation continues to provoke an array of responses. It tantalizes and annoys, refusing to be quantified, adequately explained or named. It is elusive and, for now at least, beyond conceptual grasp. Moreover, as a theological discourse, it refuses to go away. For this reason, we need to ask what specific contribution Christian theology can make given the new challenges that have emerged. Here I identify at least three areas where theological engagement will be crucial.

Firstly, there is no shortage of calls for justice within the South African context. Such calls seek to address several concerns that are widely recognized. In this context, the title of John de Gruchy's significant contribution, *Reconciliation: Restoring Justice,* is illuminating. The advantage of this, as Van der Borght observes, is that there is broad consensus that reconciliation will only succeed if it includes the notion of restoring justice. As a concept, restorative justice has deep biblical roots that could help articulate an alternative to neoliberal capitalist approaches to life and reconciliation in South Africa.[60] Despite an almost overwhelming emphasis on justice in the South African context, there is a curious lack of theoretical reflection among scholars on the notion of justice, at least in the fields of philosophy, ethics, religion, and theology. The word appears very often, of course, but typically as something self-evident, given the urgency of the issues addressed. It is almost as if there is some hesitation to theorize on justice in case this may create the impression of a distancing, objectivizing, cold, all too rational approach, removed from the heat of the contestation.[61]

Secondly, Van der Borght refers to "the embodiment of reconciled diversity of people in faith communities."[62] Here the issue relates to how the diversity of peoples, cultures, ethnicities, and national identities is celebrated, and at the same time, the unity of the faith as expressed in common Scriptures, common confessions and common rituals can be lived out?[63] In other words, how can this be realized in the now and not as explained in *Ras Volk en Nasie* as an eschatological reality? Van der Borght reminds us that "Sunday morning is the most segregated hour," prompting the need to address the issue of confessional differences and the matter of socio-cultural identities. In this context, faith communities that provide examples of embodied reconciliation may have enormous potential for contributing to reconciliation in divided societies – where societies like South Africa tend to be split along the lines of race, ethnicity and class.[64]

Thirdly, if reconciliation is to be taken seriously by blacks, the need for a "reparations" paradigm would have to be addressed. Given the actual situation in which we find ourselves – with our history of inequality, unaddressed violence, oppression, and subjugation for which whites who have benefitted have yet to apologize, never mind make meaningful repair. On this basis, to presume that interracial relationships are even desirable for blacks is highly

---

60. Van der Borght, "Reconciliation in the Public," 426.

61. This particular issue is already being explored in one of the post-graduate modules convened by Ernst Conradie and myself at the University of the Western Cape. The lack of conceptual clarity is explored in the Course Outline of the Ethics 735 module offered in the second semester of 2017.

62. Van der Borght, "Reconciliation in the public domain," 426.

63. For an interesting discussion on faith communities in the post-TRC context see Thesnaar and Hansen, *Unfinished Business?*

64. Van der Borght, 426.

problematic. A focus on a "reparations" paradigm requires us to ask the question that seems unthinkable to many whites: without repentance and more visible efforts to make meaningful repair, why would whites even assume reconciliation to be desirable or beneficial to blacks? In my estimation, blacks have more pressing concerns than merely focusing on their proximity to whites. These are but some of the issues that need to be addressed if reconciliation is to once again occupy the position as a guiding vision for South Africa.

Bibliography

Adam, H. and Moodley K. *The Negotiated Revolution: Society and the Politics in Post-Apartheid South Africa*. Johannesburg: Jonathan Ball, 1993.

Alberts, L. and Chikane, F., eds. *The Road to Rustenburg: The Church Looking Forward to a New South Africa*. Cape Town: Struik Christian Books, 1991.

Allen, J. *Rabble-rouser for Peace: The Authorised Biography of Desmond Tutu*. Johannesburg: Rider Books, 2006.

Anselm, *Cur Deus Homo*, trans. A Clergyman. Oxford and London: John Henry and James Parker, 1958.

Arendt, H. *The Human Condition: A Study of the Central Dilemmas Facing Man*. Garden City: Doubleday, 1959.

Asmal, K., Asmal, L. and Roberts, R. *Reconciliation Through Truth: A Reckoning of Apartheid's Criminal Governance*. Cape Town: David Philip, 1996.

Augustine. *Contra Faustum* 14.4, trans. Richard Stothert, The Fathers of the Church Database, Online: http://www.newadvent.org/fathers/140614.htm.

Aulén, G. Christus Victor: *An Historical Study of the Three Main Types of the Idea of the Atonement*. London: SPCK, 1931.

Balcomb, A. *Third Way Theology: Reconciliation, Revolution and the Reform in the South African Church during the 1980s*. Pietermaritzburg: Cluster Publications, 1993.

Balia, D. M. *Christian Resistance to Apartheid: Ecumenism in South Africa 1960–1987*. Johannesburg: Skotaville, 1989.

Barth, K. *The Doctrine of Reconciliation*, trans. G.W. Bromiley, 2nd ed. London: Continuum Books, 2004.

Beyerhaus, P. *The Kairos Document: Challenge or Danger to the Church?* Cape Town: Gospel Defence League, 1987.

Biko, S. "Black Consciousness and the Quest for a True Humanity." In B. Moore (ed.). *Black Theology: The South African Voice*, edited by B. Moore. London: C. Hurst, 1973.

———. *I Write What I Like: A Selection of His Writings*. London: Bowerdean, 1978.

Boesak A. A. and DeYoung C. P. *Radical Reconciliation: Beyond Political Pietism and Christian Quietism*. Maryknoll: Orbis Books 2012.

Boesak, A. A. *Black and Reformed: Apartheid Liberation and the Calvinist Tradition*. Johannesburg: Skotaville, 1984.

———. *Farewell to Innocence: A Socio-ethical Study on Black Theology and Black Power*. Johannesburg: Raven, 1977.

———. *Pharaohs on Both Sides of the Blood-red Waters, Prophetic Critique on Empire: Resistance, Justice, and the Power of the Hopeful Sizwe – A Transatlantic Conversation*. Oregon: Cascade Books, 2017.

———. *Running with Horses: Reflections of an Accidental Politician*. Cape Town: Joho Publishers, 2009.

———. *The Tenderness of Conscience: African Renaissance and the Spirituality of Politics*. Stellenbosch: Sun Media, 2005.

Boff, L. *Passion of Christ, Passion of the World: The Facts, Their Interpretation, and Their Meaning Yesterday and Today*. Maryknoll: Orbis Books, 1987.

Boraine, A. A. *Country Unmasked: Inside South Africa's Truth and Reconciliation Commission*. Oxford: Oxford University Press, 2000.

Boraine, A., Levy, J. and Scheffer, R., eds. *Dealing with the Past: Truth and Reconciliation in South Africa*. Cape Town: Idasa, 1993.

Borer, T. *Challenging the State: Churches as Political Actors in South Africa, 1980–1994*. Notre Dame: Notre Dame University Press, 1998.

Bosch, D. J. "The Church as an Alternative Community," *Journal of Theology for Southern Africa* 13 (1975), 3–11.

Botha, C. J. "Belhar: A Century-old Protest." In *A Moment of Truth: The Confession of the Dutch Reformed Mission Church*, edited by G. D. Cloete and D. J. Smit. Grand Rapids: Eerdmans, 1984.

Botha, J. and Naudé, P. *Good News to Confess: The Belhar Confession and the Road to Acceptance*. Wellington: Bible Media, 2011.

Botman, H. R. and Petersen, R. M., eds. *To Remember and to Heal: Theological and Psychological Reflections on Truth and Reconciliation*. Cape Town: Human & Rousseau, 1997.

Botman, H. R. "The Church Partitioned or the Church Reconciled? South Africa's Theological and Historical Dilemma." In *Race and Reconciliation in South Africa: A Multicultural Dialogue in Comparative Perspective*, edited by W. E. Van Vught and G. D. Cloete. Maryland: Lexington Books, 2000.

Boyd, G. A. "Christus Victor View." In *The Nature of the Atonement*, edited by J. Beilby and P. R. Eddy. Illinois: IVP Academic, 2006.

Brown, M. R. *Kairos: Three Prophetic Challenges to the Church*. Grand Rapids: Eerdmans, 1990.

Brümmer, V. *Atonement, Christology and the Trinity: Making Sense of Christian Doctrine*. Aldershot: Ashgate, 2005.

Burger, C. "Reformed Liturgy in the South African Context." In *Christian Worship in Reformed Churches Past and Present*, edited by L. Vischer. Grand Rapids: Eerdmans, 2003.

Butler, A. *Contemporary South Africa*. Hampshire: Pelgrave Macmillan, 2009.

Challenge Magazine 20: Mandela's Challenge to the Church. Speech at the Centenary Celebration of the Free Ethiopian Church of Southern Africa, December 14, 1992.

Chapman, A. R. "The TRC's Approach to Promoting Reconciliation in the Human Rights Violations Hearings." In *Truth and Reconciliation in South Africa. Did the TRC Deliver?*, edited by A. R. Chapman and H. Van der Merwe. Philadelphia: University of Pennsylvania Press, 2008.

Chidester, D. *Religions of South Africa*. New York: Routledge, 1992.

―――. *Shots in the Streets: Violence and Religion in South Africa*. Cape Town: Oxford University Press, 1992.

Chikane, F. "Foreword." In *The Unquestionable Right to be Free: Black Theology from South Africa*, edited by I. J. Mosala and B. Tlhagale. New York: Orbis, 1986.

Chikane, F. *No Life of My Own: An Autobiography*. Johannesburg: Skotaville, 1988.

Chipenda, J. B., Karamaga, A., Mugambi, J. N. K. and Omari, C. K., eds. *The Church of Africa: Towards a Theology of Reconstruction*. Nairobi: AACC, 1991.

Christian Institute of South Africa, *Director's Report for the Period August 1, 1973 to July 31, 1974*. Johannesburg: Christian Institute of South Africa.

Cochrane J. R. and West G. "War, Remembrance and Reconstruction." *Journal of Theology for Southern Africa* 84, no. 9 (1993), 25–40.

Cole, C. M. *Performing South Africa's Truth Commission: Stages of Transition*. Indianapolis: Indiana University Press, 2010.

Cone, J. H. *A Black Theology of Liberation*. Philadelphia: Lippincott, 2010.

―――. *Black Theology & Black Power*. New York: Seabury Press, 1969.

Conradie, E. M. "Healing in Soteriological Perspective," *Religion and Theology* 13, no. 1 (2006), 3–22.

Conradie, E. M. "Reconciliation as One Guiding Vision for South Africa? Conceptual Analysis and Theological Reflection." In *Reconciliation, a Guiding Vision for South Africa?*, edited by E. M. Conradie. Stellenbosch: Sun Press, 2013.

―――. "The Salvation of the Earth from Anthropogenic Destruction: In search of appropriate soteriological concepts in an age of ecological destruction." *Religion and Theology: A Journal of Contemporary Religious Discourse* 13, no. 1 (2006), 111–140.

―――. "Towards an Ecological Reformulation of the Christian Doctrine," *Journal of Theology for Southern Africa*, 122 (2005), 4–22.

Cyprian of Carthage. *Treatises*, 8.5, trans. R. E. Wallis, The Fathers of the Church Database. Online: http://www.newadvent.org/fathers/050708.htm.

De Gruchy, J. W and De Villiers, W. B., eds. *The Message in Perspective: A Book about "A Message to the People of South Africa."* Johannesburg: SACC, 1969.

De Gruchy, J. W. and Villa-Vicencio, C., eds. *Apartheid is a Heresy*. Cape Town. David Philip, 1983.

De Gruchy, J. W. "Christianity in Twentieth-century South Africa." In *Living Faiths in South Africa*, edited by M. Prozesky and J. W. De Gruchy. London: C. Hurst, 1995.

———. "From Cottesloe to the Road to Damascus: Confessing Landmarks in the Struggle Against Apartheid." Paper presented at the Annual meeting of the Theological Society of Southern Africa held at the University of Port Elizabeth, 29–31 August 1990. In *Listening to South African Voices: Critical Reflection on Contemporary Theological Documents*, edited by G. Loots. Theological Society of Southern Africa: Woordkor, 1990.

———. "Grappling with the Colonial Heritage: The English Speaking Churches Under Imperialism and Apartheid." In *Christianity in South Africa. A Political, Social, and Cultural History*, edited by R. Elphick and R. Davenport. Cape Town: David Philip, 1997.

———. "Political Landmarks and the Response of Churches in South Africa, 1936–1994." *Journal of Theology for Southern Africa* 118 (2004), 3–26.

———. "The Church and the Struggle for South Africa." In *Hammering Swords into Ploughshares: Essays in Honour of Archbishop Desmond Tutu*, edited by B. Tlhagale and I. J. Mosala. Johannesburg: Skotaville, 1986.

———. "The Contest for Reformed Identity in South Africa During the Struggle Against Apartheid." In *In Reformed Churches in South Africa and the Struggle for Justice: Remembering 1960–1990*, edited by M-A. Plaatjies-Van Huffel and R. Vosloo. Stellenbosch: Sun Press, 2013.

———. *A Theological Odyssey: My Life in Writing*. Stellenbosch: Sun Media, 2014.

———. *Liberating Reformed Theology: A South African Contribution to an Ecumenical Debate*. Cape Town: David Philip, 1991.

———. *Reconciliation: Restoring Justice*. London: SCM Press, 2002.

———. *The Church Struggle in South Africa*, London: SCM Press, 2004.

De Gruchy, S. "From Church Struggle to Church Struggles." In *The Church Struggle in South Africa*, J. W. de Gruchy with S. de Gruchy. London: SCM Press, 2004.

De Villiers, E. "The Challenge to the Afrikaans Churches." In *To Remember and to Heal: Theological and Psychological Reflections on Truth and Reconciliation*, edited by H. R. Botman and R. M. Pietersen. Cape Town: Human Rousseau, 1996.

DeYoung, C. P. "Christianity: Contemporary Expressions." In *The Wiley-Blackwell Companion to Religion and Social Justice*, edited by M. D. Palmer and S. M. Burgess. Massachusetts: Wiley-Blackwell, 2012.

DeYoung, C. P. "Reconciliation in the Empire: Real, Radical, Revolutionary." In *Radical Reconciliation: Beyond Political Pietism and Christian Quietism*, edited by A. A. Boesak and C. P. DeYoung. Maryknoll: Orbis Books, 2012.

Dillistone F. W. *The Christian Understanding of Atonement*. London: James Nisbet, 1967.

Doxtader, E. "Reconciliation in a State of Emergency: The Middle Voice of 2 Corinthians." *Journal of the Study of Religion* 14, no. 1 (2001), 51–59.

———. *With Faith in the Works of Words: The Beginnings of Reconciliation in South Africa, 1985–1995*. Cape Town: David Philip, 2009.

Du Toit, A. *Amnesty Chronicles: The Inner History of the Amnesty Negotiations During the South African Transition, and the Origins of the TRC's Amnesty Process*, Stellenbosch: Beyers Naudé Centre for Public Theology, Stellenbosch University, 2002.

Du Toit, F. and Doxtader, E., eds. *In the Balance: South Africans Debate Reconciliation* Johannesburg: Jacana Media, 2010.

Dubow, S. *Apartheid: 1948–1994*. New York: Oxford University Press, 2014.

Durand, J. J. F. "Crisis in the Dutch Reformed Church." In *A Moment of Truth: The Confession of the Dutch Reformed Mission*, edited by G. D. Cloete and D. J. Smit. Grand Rapids: Eerdmans, 1984.

Engdahl, H. S. A. *Theology in Conflict: Readings in Afrikaner Theology*. Frankfurt: Peter Lang, 2006.

Fairweather, E. R., ed. and trans. *A Scholastic Miscellany: Anselm to Ochom*. Philadelphia: Westminster Press, 1956.

Fiddes, P. *Past Event and Present Salvation: The Christian Idea of Atonement*. Louisville: Westminster John Knox, 1989.

Fortein, E. "Allan Boesak and the Dutch Reformed Mission Church between 1976–1990." In *Reformed Churches in South Africa and the Struggle for Justice: Remembering 1960–1990*, edited by M-A. Plaatjies-Van Huffel and R. Vosloo. Stellenbosch: Sun Press, 2013.

Frostin, Per. *Liberation Theology in Tanzania and South Africa: A First World Interpretation*. Lund: Lund University Press, 1988.

Gathogo, J. "Black Theology of South Africa: Is this the Hour of Paradigm Shift?" *Black Theology: An International Journal* 5, no. 3 (2007).

Gaum, L. and Gaum, F. *Praat Verby Grense*. Cape Town: Umuzi, 2010.

Gerhart, G. M. *Black Power in South Africa: The Evolution of an Ideology*. Berkley: University of California Press, 1978.

Gerwel, J. "National Reconciliation: Holy Grail or Secular Pact?" In *Looking Back, Reaching Forward: Reflections on the Truth and Reconciliation Commission of*

South Africa, edited by C. Villa-Vicencio and W. Verwoerd. Cape Town: Cape Town University Press, 2000.

Giliomee, H. *The Last Afrikaner leaders: A Supreme Test of Power*. Cape Town: Tafelberg, 2012.

Goba, B. "Corporate Personality: Ancient Israel and Africa." In *Black Theology: The South African Voice*, edited by B. Moore. London: C. Hurst, 1973.

———. "The Black Consciousness Movement: Its Impact on Black Theology." In *The Unquestionable Right to be Free: Black Theology from South Africa*, edited by J. Mosala and B. Tlhagale. New York: Orbis, 1990.

———. "The Role of Religion in Promoting Democratic Values in the Post-apartheid Era: A Personal Reflection." *Journal of Constructive Theology* 1, no. 1 (1995).

———. *An Agenda for Black Theology: Hermeneutics for Social Change*. Braamfontein: Skotaville, 1988.

Gobodo-Madikizela, P. A. *Human Being Died That Night: A Story of Forgiveness*. Cape Town: David Philip, 2003.

Goldstone, R. "To Remember and Acknowledge: The Way Ahead." In *The Healing of a Nation?*, edited by A. Boraine and J. Levy. Cape Town: Justice in Transition, 1995.

Göranzon, A. B. O. "The Prophetic Voice of the SACC after 1990 – Searching for a Renewed Kairos." Unpublished PhD. diss. University of the Free State, 2010.

Graybill, L. S. "South Africa's Truth and Reconciliation Commission: Ethical and Theological Perspectives." *Ethics & International Affairs* 12, no. 3 (1998), 43–62.

Green, J. B. and Baker, M. D. *Recovering the Scandal of the Cross: Atonement in New Testament and Contemporary Contexts*. Cumbria: Paternoster Press, 2000.

Gunton, C. E. *The Actuality of Atonement: A Study of Metaphor, Rationality and the Christian Tradition*. Edinburgh: T & T. Clark, 1988.

Harvey, J. *Dear White Christians: For Those Still Longing for Racial Reconciliation*. Grand Rapids: Eerdmans, 2014.

Hayner, P. *Unspeakable Truths: Transitional Justice and the Challenge of Truth Commissions*. New York: Routledge, 2001.

———. "Same Species Different Animal: How South Africa Compares to Truth Commissions Worldwide." In *Looking Back Reaching Forward. Reflections on the Truth and Reconciliation Commission of South Africa*, edited by C. Villa-Vicencio and W. Verwoerd. London: Zed Books, 2000.

Helm, P. *Calvin: A Guide for the Perplexed*. London: T&T Clark, 2008.

Hendriksson, L. *A Journey with a Status Confessionis: Analysis of an Apartheid Related Conflict Between the Dutch Reformed Church in South Africa and the*

World Alliance of Reformed Churches, 1982–1998. Uppsala: Swedish Institute of Missionary Research, 2010.

Hofmeyer, J. W., Millard J. A. and Froneman C. J. J. *History of the Church in South Africa: A Document and Source Book*. Pretoria: Unisa, 1991.

Hopkins, J. *Companion to the Study of St. Anselm*. Minneapolis: University of Minnesota Press, 1971.

Howarth, D. R. "Black Consciousness in South Africa: Resistance and Identity Formation Under Apartheid Domination." Unpublished PhD. diss. University of Essex, 1994.

Institute for Justice and Reconciliation. "Confronting Exclusion. Time for Radical Reconciliation." SA Reconciliation Barometer Survey: 2013 Report. Cape Town, South Africa, 2013.

International Commission of Jurists, eds. *The Trial of Beyers Naudé: Christian Witness and the Rule of Law*. London: Search Press, 1975.

Irenaeus. *Against Heresies*, Book II, 14.7, trans. Alexander Roberts and William Rambaut, The Fathers of the Church Database, Online: http://www.newadvent.org/fathers/0103214.htm.

Jeffery, A. *The Truth about the Truth Commission*. Johannesburg: South African Institute for Race Relations, 1999.

Johnson, S. *Strange Days Indeed: South Africa from Insurrection to Post-election*. London: Bantam Books, 1994.

Jonker, W. "Understanding the Church Situation and Obstacles to Christian Witness in South Africa." In *The Road to Rustenburg: The Church Looking Forward to a New South Africa*, edited by L. Alberts and F. Chikane, 87–98. Cape Town: Struik, 1991.

Kane-Berman, J. *South Africa: The Method in the Madness*. London: Pluto Press, 1978.

Kärkkäinen, V-M. *Christ and Reconciliation: A Constructive Christian Theology for the Pluralistic World*. Grand Rapids: Eerdmans, 2013.

Kelly, J. N. D. *Early Christian Doctrines*. London: A & C Black, 1968.

Kinghorn, J. "Modernization and Apartheid: The Afrikaner Churches." In *Christianity in South Africa: A Political, Social & Cultural History*, edited by R. Elphick and R. Davenport. Los Angeles: University of California Press, 1997.

———. "On the Theology of Church and Society in the DRC", *Journal of Theology for Southern Africa* 70 (1990), 21–36.

Kollapen, J. "Reconciliation: Engaging with our Fears and Expectations." In *In the Balance: South Africans Debate Reconciliation*, edited by F. Du Toit and E. Doxtader. Johannesburg: Jacana, 2010.

Kritzinger, J. N. J. "Black Theology: A Challenge to Mission." Unpublished PhD diss., University of South Africa, 1988.

Krog, A. "The Parable of the Bicycle." *Mail & Guardian*. 7 February 1997, https://mg.co.za/article/1997-02-07-the-parable-of-the-bicycle.

Landman, W. A. *A Plea for Understanding: A Reply to the Reformed Church in America*. Cape Town: NG Kerk-Uitgewers, 1968.

Langmead, R. "Transformed Relationships: Reconciliation as the Central Model for Mission," *Mission Studies* 25, 2008: 5–20.

Leonard, G. S. D. ed. *The Moment of Truth: The Kairos Documents*. Pietermaritzburg: Ujamaa Centre for Biblical and Theological Community Development and Research, University of Kwazulu Natal, 2010.

Lochman J. M. *Reconciliation and Liberation*. Belfast: Christian Journals Limited, 1980.

Loubser, J. A. *The Apartheid Bible: A Critical Review of Racial Theology in South Africa*. Cape Town: Maskew Miller Longman, 1987.

Lückhoff, A. H. *Cottesloe*. Cape Town: Tafelberg, 1978.

Maimela, M. R. "Black Consciousness and White Liberals in South Africa." Unpublished PhD. diss., University of South Africa, 1999.

Maimela, S. and Hopkins, D. *We Are One Voice: Black Theology in the U.S.A. and South Africa*. Johannesburg: Skotaville, 1989.

Maimela, S. *Proclaim Freedom to my People*. Johannesburg: Skotaville, 1987.

Maluleke, T. S. "Dealing Lightly with the Wounds of my People: The TRC Process in Theological Perspective." *Missionalia* 25, no. 3 (1997), 324–343.

———. "The Proposal for a Theology of Reconstruction: A Critical Appraisal", *Missionalia* 22, no. 2 (1994), 254–258.

———. "Truth, National Unity and Reconciliation in South Africa: Aspects of the Emerging Theological Agenda." *Missionalia* 25, no. 1 (1997), 59–86.

Mamdani, M. "A Diminished Truth." In *After the TRC: Reflections on Truth and Reconciliation in South Africa*, edited by W. James and L. van de Vijver. Cape Town: David Philip, 2000.

———. "Reconciliation without Justice." *Southern African Review of Books* 46 (1996).

Mangcu, X. *The State of Democracy in South Africa*. Scottsville: University of Kwazulu-Natal Press, 2008.

Martin, R. M. "Center of Paul's theology." In *Dictionary of Paul and his Letters*, edited by G. F. Hawthrone, R. M. Martin and D. G. Reid. Illinois: Intervarsity Press, 1993.

———. *Reconciliation: A Study of Paul's Theology*. Atlanta: John Knox Press.

McCarthy, C. "A Response [to Bible and Reconciliation]." In *Reconciliation in Religion and Society: Proceedings of a Conference Organised by the School of Ecumenics and University of Ulster*, edited by M. Hurley. Belfast: Institute for Irish Studies, 1994.

McGrath, A. E. *Christian Theology: An Introduction*. Oxford: Basil Blackwell, 1994.

McKaiser, E. *Run Racist Run: Journeys into the Heart of Racism.* Johannesburg: Bookstorm, 2015.

Meiring, P. "Pastors or Lawyers? The Role of Religion in the South African Truth and Reconciliation Commission process." *HTS Theological Studies* 58 (2002), 1.

Meiring, P. "Reconciliation: Dream or Reality." *Missionalia* 27, no. 2 (1999), 328–339.

———. *Chronicle of the Truth Commission.* Vanderbijlpark: Carpe Diem, 1998.

Migliore, D. L. *Faith Seeking Understanding: An Introduction to Christian Theology.* Grand Rapids: Eerdmans, 1991.

Mofokeng, T. A. *The Crucified Among the Crossbearers: Towards a Black Christology.* Kampen: J. H. Kok, 1983.

Mokgoebo, Z. E. "Broederkring. From 1974 to. . . .? In *Unity and Justice: The Witness of the Belydende Kring*, edited by S. P. Govender. Braamfontein: Die Belydende Kring, 1984.

Moodley, K. "African Renaissance and Language Policies in Comparative Perspective." *Politikon* 271 (2000), 103–115.

Moore, B. (ed.) *Black Theology: The South African Voice.* London: C. Hurst, 1973.

———. "What is Black Theology?" In *Black Theology: The South African Voice*, edited by B. Moore. London: C. Hurst.

———. "Black Theology: In the beginning," *Journal for the Study of Religion* 4, no. 2 (1991).

Mosala, I. J. *Biblical Hermeneutics and Black Theology in South Africa.* Grand Rapids: Eerdmans, 1989.

———. "Spirituality and Struggle: African and Black Theologies." In *Many Cultures, One Nation: Festschrift for Beyers Naude*, edited by C. Villa-Vicencio and C. Niehaus. Cape Town: Human & Rousseau, 1995.

Motlhabi, M., ed. *Essays in Black Theology in South Africa.* Johannesburg: University Christian Movement, 1972.

———. *African Theology/Black Theology in South Africa. Looking Back, Moving On.* Pretoria: Unisa Press, 2008.

Mozley, J. K. *The Doctrine of the Atonement.* London: Gerald Duckworth, 1953.

Mugambi, J. N. K. *From Liberation to Reconstruction: African Christian Theology After the Cold War.* Nairobi: East Africa Educational, 1995.

Mushete, N. "The History of Theology in Africa: From Polemics to Critical Irenics." In *African Theology En Route*, edited by K. Appiah and S. Torres. New York: Orbis, 1979.

Myburgh, P-L. *The Republic of Gupta: A Story of State Capture.* Cape Town: Penguin Random House, 2017.

Naidoo, I. *Island in Chains: Ten Years on Robben Island.* Harmondsworth: Penguin Books, 1982.

National Conference of Church Leaders in South Africa, "Rustenburg Declaration," 1990.

Naudé, P. J. *Neither Calendar nor Clock: Perspective on the Belhar Confession*. Grand Rapids: Eerdmans, 2010.

Ngcokovane, C. *Demons of Apartheid*. Johannesburg: Skotaville, 1989.

Niebuhr, H. R. *The Kingdom of God in America*. Connecticut: Wesleyan University Press, 1959.

Nürnberger, K. and Tooke, J., eds. *The Cost of Reconciliation in South Africa: National Initiative for Reconciliation Reader 1*. Cape Town: Methodist Publishing House, 1988.

Pannenberg, W. *Systematic Theology*, Translated by G.W. Bromiley, Vol. 2. New York: T & T Clark, 2004.

Pauw, J. J. C. "Anti-apartheid Theology in Dutch Reformed Family of Churches: A Depth-hermeneutical Analysis." Unpublished PhD. diss., Vrije Universiteit Amsterdam, 2007.

Peter Abelard. *Ethics: Book I*, trans. P.V. Spade. Indianapolis: Hackett Publishing, 1995.

Phiri, I. and Gathogo, J. "A Reconstructive Motif in South African Black Theology in the Twenty-first Century." *Studia Historiae Ecclesiasticae* 36 (2010), 2.

Phiri, I. *Proclaiming Political Pluralism: Churches and Political Transition in Africa*. London: Praeger, 2001.

Plaatjies-Van Huffel, M-A. "The Belhar Confession: Born in the Struggle Against Apartheid in Southern Africa." *Studia Historicae Ecclesiasticae* 39, no. 1 (2013), 185–206.

———. "Reading the Belhar Confession as a Historical Text." In *The Reformed Churches in South Africa and the Struggle for Justice*, edited by M. A. Plaatjies Van Huffel and R. Vosloo. Stellenbosch: Sun Press, 2013.

Posel, D. "The Language of Domination, 1978–1983." In *The Politics of Race, Class and Nationalism in Twentieth Century South Africa*, edited by S. Marks and S. Trapido. New York: Longman, 1987.

Price, R. M. *The Apartheid State in Crisis: Political Transformation in South Africa, 1975–1990*. New York: Oxford University Press, 1991.

Prozesky, M. "Can Christians Overcome Apartheid: An Evaluation of the "Statement of Affirmation of the National Initiative for Reconciliation." *Journal of Theology for Southern Africa* 54 (1986).

Rand, B., ed. *The Classic Moralists: Selections Illustrating Ethics from Socrates to Martineau*. Boston: Houghton Mifflin, 1909.

Randall, P., ed. *Apartheid and the Church. Report of the Spro-cas Church Commission*. Johannesburg, Study Project on Christianity in Apartheid Society, 1972.

———, ed. *A Taste of Power. The Final Co-ordinated Spro-cas Report.* Johannesburg: Study Project on Christianity in Apartheid Society, 1973.

Regehr, E. *Perceptions of Apartheid: The Churches and Political Change in South Africa.* Pennsylvania: Herald Press, 1979.

Renwick, R. *Unconventional Diplomacy in Southern Africa.* London: Macmillan, 1997.

Robinson, L. E. "The Influence of Social Context on a Theology of Reconciliation: Case Studies in Northern Ireland." Unpublished PhD. diss., University of Edinburgh, 2011.

Ryan, C. *Beyers Naudé: Pilgrimage of Faith.* Cape Town: David Philip, 1990.

Schleiermacher, F. *The Christian Faith*, trans. J. Y. Campbell, ed. H. R. Mackintosh and J. S. Stewart, English translation of the 2nd ed. (1821; repr.). Edinburgh: T&T Clark, 1928.

Schrire, R. A. *Adapt or Die: The End of White Politics in South Africa.* London: Hurst and Company, 1991.

Schwöbel, C. "Reconciliation: From Biblical Observations to Dogmatic Reconstruction." In *The Theology of Reconciliation*, edited by C. E. Gunton. London: T & T Clark, 2003.

Scott, W.B. *What about the Cross? Exploring Models of the Atonement.* New York: iUniverse, 2007.

Serfontein, J. H. P. *Apartheid Change and the NG Kerk.* Emmarentia: Taurus Publishers, 1982.

Shore, M. *Religion and Conflict Resolution: Christianity and South Africa's Truth and Reconciliation Commission.* Farnham: Ashgate, 2009.

Sjollema, B. A *First Answer to Comments Received After the Decision by the WCC Executive to Support Organizations Combatting Racism.* Geneva: WCC, 1970.

Smit, D. J. "Reformed Confession and Ecumenical Reception?: On the Confession of Belhar and Reconciliation." In *Essays on Being Reformed: Collected Essays 3*, edited by R. Vosloo. Stellenbosch: Sun Media, 2009.

———. "The Symbol of Reconciliation and Ideological Conflict." In *Reconciliation and Construction*, edited by W. S. Vorster. Pretoria: Unisa, 1986.

———. "The Truth and Reconciliation Commission: Tentative Religious and Theological Perspectives." *Journal of Theology for Southern Africa* 90 (1995), 3–15.

Smit, N. O'Brien, F. E and Meiring, P. G. J. *Stormkompas.* Cape Town: Tafelberg, 1981.

Sölle, D. *Christ the Representative.* London: SCM Press, 1967.

South African Press Association, "TRC Members Not Morally Neutral: Tutu." March 1997.

Soyinka, W. *The Burden of Memory, The Muse of Forgiveness.* New York: Oxford University Press, 1999.

Stadler, A. "Anxious Radicals: SPRO-CAS and the Apartheid Society." *Journal of Southern African Studies* 2, no. 1 (1975), 102–108.

Storey, P. "A Different Kind of Justice: Truth and Reconciliation in South Africa." *The Christian Century* 114, no. 9 (1997).

Strassberger, E. *Ecumenism in South Africa 1936–1960*. Johannesburg: SACC, 1974.

Suggit, J. "Kairos: The Wrong Way on the Right Road." *Journal of Theology in Southern Africa* 58 (1987), 70–74.

Tertullian, *Concerning the Resurrection of the Flesh*, trans. A. Souter. London: SPCK, 1922.

The Institute for Justice and Reconciliation Barometer. http://reconciliationbarometer.org/wp-content/uploads/2011/12/2011-SA-Reconciliation-Barometer.pdf.

Thesnaar, C. H. and Hansen, L. D., eds. *Unfinished Business: Faith Communities and Reconciliation in Post-TRC Context*. Stellenbosch: African Sun Media, 2020.

Thomas, D. G. *Councils in the Ecumenical Movement in South Africa, 1904–1975*. Johannesburg: SACC, 1979.

Tlhagele, B. and Mosala, I., eds. *Hammering Swords into Ploughshares: Essays in Honour of Archbishop Mpilo Desmond Tutu*. Johannesburg: Skotaville, 1986.

Torrance, J. B. "South Africa Today: The Kairos Debate: Listening to its Challenge." *Journal of Theology of Southern Africa* 55 (1986), 42–45.

Truth and Reconciliation Commission of South Africa Report Vol. 1, 1998. Cape Town: Juta Press.

Tshaka, R. S. "The Black Church as the Womb of Black Liberation Theology?: Why the Uniting Reformed Church in Southern Africa (URCSA) is not a Genuine Black Church?" *HTS Teologiese Studies/Theological Studies*, 71 (2015). http://www.hts.org.za/index.php/HTS/article/view/2800.

Tshaka, R. S. and Mafokate, K. M. "The Continued Relevance of Black Liberation Theology for South Africa Today." *Scriptura* 105 (2010), 532–546.

Tutu, D. M. "Foreword." In *To Remember and to Heal: Theological and Psychological Reflections on Truth and Reconciliation*, edited by H. R. Botman and R. M. Pietersen. Cape Town: Human Rousseau, 1996.

———. *No Future without Forgiveness*. London: Random House, 1999.

———. *Hope and Suffering: Sermons and Speeches*. London: Collins, 1983.

Van der Bent, A. J. (ed) *World Council of Churches' Statements and Actions on Racism 1948–1979*. Geneva: WCC, 1980.

Van der Borght, E. A. J. G. "Reconciliation in the Public Domain: The South African Case," *International Journal of Public Theology* 9(4), 2015, 412–427.

———. "Unity that Sanctifies Diversity: Cottesloe Revisited," *Acta Theologica* 31, no. 2 (2011), 315–328.

Van der Merwe, J. "The Dutch Reformed Church from *Ras, Volk en Nasie* to *Kerk en Samelewing*: The Struggle Goes On." In *Reformed Churches in South Africa and the Struggle for Justice: Remembering 1960–1990*, edited by M-A. Plaatjies-Van Huffel and R. Vosloo. Stellenbosch: Sun Press, 2013.

Van der Water, D. P. "The Legacy of a Prophetic Moment: A socio-theological study of the reception and response to the Kairos Document amongst churches, faith-communities and individuals in South Africa and within the international ecumenical community, focussing on the English-speaking churches in South Africa with special reference to the United Congregational Church of Southern Africa." Unpublished PhD diss., University of Natal, 1998.

Vellem, V. S. "The Symbol of Liberation in South African Public Life: A Black Theological Perspective." Unpublished PhD. diss., University of Pretoria, 2007.

Villa-Vicencio, C. *The Art of Reconciliation*. Östervåla: Life & Peace Institute, 2002.

———. "Reconciliation in Bloemfontein." Unpublished paper, University of the Free State, February 2011

———. "South Africa's Churches: After Resistance . . . ?" *Christianity and Crisis* 52, no. 2 (1992), 35.

———. *A Theology of Reconstruction: Nation Building and Human Rights*. Cambridge: Cambridge University Press, 1992.

———. *Walk With Us and Listen: Political Reconciliation in Africa*. Washington DC: Georgetown University Press, 2009.

———. *Trapped in Apartheid: A Socio-theological History of the English-speaking Churches*. New York: Orbis, 1988.

Volf, M. *Exclusion and Embrace: A Theological Exploration of Identity, Otherness, and Reconciliation*. Nashville: Abingdon Press, 1996.

———. "Forgiveness, Reconciliation, and Justice: A Theological Contribution to a More Peaceful Social Environment." *Journal of International Studies* 29, no. 3 (2000), 861–877.

Vosloo, R. "Christianity and Apartheid in South Africa." In *The Routledge Companion to Christianity in Africa*, edited by E. K. Bongmba. New York: Routledge, 2016.

Walshe, P. "Christianity and the Anti-apartheid Struggle: The Prophetic Voice Within Divided Churches." In *Christianity in South Africa. A Political, Social, and Cultural History*, edited by R. Elphick and R. Davenport. Cape Town: David Philip, 1997.

———. "Christianity and Democratisation in South Africa: The Prophetic Voice Within Phlegmatic Churches." In *The Christian Churches and the Democratisation of Africa*, edited by P. Gifford. Leiden: Brill, 1995.

———. "Church Versus State in South Africa: The Christian Institute and the Resurgence of African Nationalism." *Journal of Church and State* 19, no. 3 (1977), 457–479.

———. *Church Versus State in South Africa: The Case of the Christian Institute.* New York: Orbis, 1983.
———. *Prophetic Christianity and the Liberation Movement in South Africa.* Pietermaritzburg: Cluster Publications, 1995.
Weaver, J. D. *The Non-violent Atonement.* Grand Rapids: Eerdmans, 2001.
Weber, O. *Foundations of Dogmatics, vol. 2.* Grand Rapids: Eerdmans, 1983.
Webster, J. "The Ethics of Reconciliation." In *The Theology of Reconciliation*, edited by C. Guton. London: T & T Clark, 2003.
Wilson, R. A. *The Politics of Truth and Reconciliation in South Africa.* Cambridge: Cambridge University Press, 2001.
Wright, D. F. "The Atonement in Reformation Theology." *European Journal of Theology*, 8, no. 1 (199).

Langham Literature, with its publishing work, is a ministry of Langham Partnership.

Langham Partnership is a global fellowship working in pursuit of the vision God entrusted to its founder John Stott –

> ***to facilitate the growth of the church in maturity and Christ-likeness through raising the standards of biblical preaching and teaching.***

Our vision is to see churches in the Majority World equipped for mission and growing to maturity in Christ through the ministry of pastors and leaders who believe, teach and live by the word of God.

Our mission is to strengthen the ministry of the word of God through:
- nurturing national movements for biblical preaching
- fostering the creation and distribution of evangelical literature
- enhancing evangelical theological education

especially in countries where churches are under-resourced.

Our ministry

Langham Preaching partners with national leaders to nurture indigenous biblical preaching movements for pastors and lay preachers all around the world. With the support of a team of trainers from many countries, a multi-level programme of seminars provides practical training, and is followed by a programme for training local facilitators. Local preachers' groups and national and regional networks ensure continuity and ongoing development, seeking to build vigorous movements committed to Bible exposition.

Langham Literature provides Majority World preachers, scholars and seminary libraries with evangelical books and electronic resources through publishing and distribution, grants and discounts. The programme also fosters the creation of indigenous evangelical books in many languages, through writer's grants, strengthening local evangelical publishing houses, and investment in major regional literature projects, such as one volume Bible commentaries like the Africa Bible Commentary and the South Asia Bible Commentary.

Langham Scholars provides financial support for evangelical doctoral students from the Majority World so that, when they return home, they may train pastors and other Christian leaders with sound, biblical and theological teaching. This programme equips those who equip others. Langham Scholars also works in partnership with Majority World seminaries in strengthening evangelical theological education. A growing number of Langham Scholars study in high quality doctoral programmes in the Majority World itself. As well as teaching the next generation of pastors, graduated Langham Scholars exercise significant influence through their writing and leadership.

To learn more about Langham Partnership and the work we do visit langham.org

www.ingramcontent.com/pod-product-compliance
Lightning Source LLC
Chambersburg PA
CBHW051540230426
43669CB00015B/2666